THE RISK OF INVESTMENT PRODUCTS

From Product Innovation
to Risk Compliance

THE RISK OF INVESTMENT PRODUCTS

From Product Innovation to Risk Compliance

editor

Michael CS Wong

City University of Hong Kong, Hong Kong

World Scientific

NEW JERSEY · LONDON · SINGAPORE · BEIJING · SHANGHAI · HONG KONG · TAIPEI · CHENNAI

Published by

World Scientific Publishing Co. Pte. Ltd.

5 Toh Tuck Link, Singapore 596224

USA office: 27 Warren Street, Suite 401-402, Hackensack, NJ 07601

UK office: 57 Shelton Street, Covent Garden, London WC2H 9HE

British Library Cataloguing-in-Publication Data
A catalogue record for this book is available from the British Library.

ISBN-13 978-981-4354-98-1
ISBN-10 981-4354-98-8

Typeset by Stallion Press
Email: enquiries@stallionpress.com

Printed in Singapore.

FOREWORD

Michael C.S. Wong

1. INTRODUCTION

The global financial crisis in 2008 was a tragedy of the banking and financial sector. Both individual and institutional investors suffered huge losses. Banks compensated their clients and encountered legal actions. Credit rating agencies were scrutinized by governments. Bank employees were laid off. Politicians rushed to enact new rules to protect investors. In the 18 months after the crisis, the world totally lost confidence in financial engineering, hedge funds and structured financial products. Investors had all gone back to the basics, buying government bonds and blue-chip stocks.

Through this crisis, financial institutions learnt a major lesson about the risk of investment products. In the past, chief risk officers (CROs) of financial institutions did not pay much attention to the risk of investment products sold to their clients. The role of CROs was to manage and monitor the risk of their institutions. Managing the risk of clients' portfolios was never their scope of work. Financial institutions might have had a due diligence process in sourcing investment products but their concern was focused primarily on the risk of their financial institutions or the turnovers from relevant deals. Senior bank executives mostly believed that product risk should be transferred to clients. Financial institutions could enjoy high profits from wealth management services with no capital charge on the credit risk and market risk. Now, their scope of risk management may have changed. The clients' risk could be the risk of the banks. When clients lose seriously, financial institutions may need to compensate them 100%.

2. PRODUCT RISK AS THE RISK OF BANKS

After the crisis, financial institutions suffered serious losses in their own investments and in compensating their clients. Financial institutions thus became aware of the complexity of the products they sold to their clients. The following are typical cases:

- *Banks agreed to pay victims US$15.5 billion for loss from Madoff's products*: In May 2010, around 720,000 investors outside the US who lost money in Bernard Madoff's fraud successfully obtained a compensation agreement of US$15.5 billion from those banks that distributed Madoff-linked products. However, it may not be the end of the story because many lawyers claimed that their clients were not put on the compensation list. After the Madoff scandal, many European banks were sued in France, Ireland and Luxembourg because of the Madoff-linked products. For instance, UBS and HSBC were accused of negligence as custodians of the funds. Banco Santander, the largest bank in Spain, compensated its clients US$1.7 billion in 2009 by issuing them preference shares paying 2% interest per year.
- *Banks in Hong Kong agreed to compensate investors US$774 million for Lehman products*: In July 2009, a group of Hong Kong banks agreed to refund more than US$774 million to investors who bought Lehman Brothers minibonds, a retail structured product. Eligible investors could get 60% of the invested amount refunded, while those investors aged 65 or move could get a refund of 70%.
- *Singapore punished financial institutions for selling lehman investment product*: In July 2009, Singapore's central bank banned 10 financial institutions from selling structured notes because these banks sold Lehman Brothers investment products without adequately advising their clients about their risks. The institutions told the clients that the products were safe and they turned out to be risky. Structured notes to be banned include debt instruments with options linked. The central bank said some of the financial institutions did not train their marketing people with accurate and complete information about the notes. Some did not have proper procedures to ensure that their staff was well trained in selling the Lehman products.

3. MISREPRESENTATION OF INVESTMENT PRODUCTS

Many financial institutions compensated their clients without admitting their negligence. After the Lehman collapse, I had the chance to conduct an independent review of banks selling Lehman products to Hong Kong investors and to appear in court to testify on the risk and pricing of complex investment products. This experience provided me with new perspectives on the operational risk of investment services.

When an investor loses in an investment product, his/her lawyer may pay for efforts to find evidence to void the sale and purchase agreement between the investor and the agent who distributed the product. One simple strategy is to find evidence showing the agent's misrepresentation of the product. Did the banks misrepresent Lehman products? There are many issues relating to this question:

(i) Did the banks have procedures to assess the risk of the products?
(ii) Did the banks train frontline people on the risk of the products and how to communicate with clients about their risk?
(iii) Did the banks have any mechanism to monitor the sales practices of the frontline people?

If the answer is "no" to any of the above questions, it would be unfavourable for the banks in court hearings. On 27 March 2010, newspapers in Hong Kong reported a case of misrepresentation:

> Two bank employees were arrested over the lender's sales of securities linked to the failed Lehman Brothers... They were believed to have separately misled and induced eight customers on various occasions to purchase structured products between 2005 and 2008... The arrests may revive questions about whether banks properly supervised staff involved in selling the minibonds... (*South China Morning Post*, 27 March 2010).

If the charge of this case is confirmed, the bank that hired the employees will no doubt have to compensate the customers. This is not only an operational risk event but also a reputation risk incidence. News about this case, including the name of the bank, appeared in newspapers frequently, jeopardizing the bank's business in the long run.

4. THE ISSUE OF DUTY OF CARE

Lawyers may also be eager to find evidence of insufficient duty of care or negligence on the part of the agent in order to revoke the sale and purchase agreement. Duty of care is usually expected from professionals who are qualified via examination or other methods. In many cases, there may be no standard on what degree of care is sufficient. However, laws, regulatory guidelines, codes of conduct of professional associations can be the minimum references. In offering investment advisory services, qualified professionals are usually required to evaluate their clients' investment needs, get familiar with the risk of investment products to be distributed, and ensure suitability between products and clients.

In practice, many financial institutions did not have the appropriate procedures and process to ensure sufficient duty of care. The following cases can illustrate this argument:

- Many financial institutions do not seriously measure the risk profile of their clients. They may purchase or copy some questions from some unknown source and then use them as their investor risk tolerance questionnaires. They never ask why these questions work, or why the total score can measure risk, and/or why each question has equal weight. These financial institutions may not have any detailed documentation on what they are using in their everyday business.
- Financial institutions are generally sales-oriented in wealth management services. They source products from investment banks or fund houses at 9 am and aggressively distribute them to clients. In less than one hour, all the products may be sold. They do not have time to assess the details of the products sold.
- Some financial institutions may have detailed processes to assess the risk of a product when it is first launched. Then, there is no further update even though the market environment has changed substantially. Frontline people keep selling the products using outdated information about the products.

In case of any legal dispute between the financial institutions and their clients, the banks may find it hard to justify the adequacy of their duty of care.

5. COMPLEXITY OF INVESTMENT PRODUCTS

Textbooks on investment may classify risk by product type or volatility. However, the risk of investment products can be more complicated than thought. Traditional perspectives on investment risk may not reflect their true risk nature. Take the following product as an example: the five-year euro-denominated Iceland Government bond. This product may be classified to be "very low risk" because it is a government bond from an advanced economy. In fact, this product has many risk dimensions, such as

- *Interest rate risk*: When the interest rate increases by 1%, the product may depreciate by 3–5%.
- *Currency risk*: The euro may depreciate seriously in 1–2 months.
- *Credit migration risk*: If Iceland were downgraded by ratings agencies, its market price would drop seriously (say 20%).
- *Default risk*: The issuer may default on payment of coupons or other cash flows.
- *Liquidity risk*: When the product is not held to maturity, liquidity will be a serious issue.

When all these risk dimensions are integrated, can we still conclude that it is "very low risk"?

This product is in fact a very simple product. In private banking, there is a wide range of complex investment products including hedge funds, accumulators, range accruals, principal-protected products, etc. Do financial institutions have a robust process or system to classify their risk?

6. STRESS RISK

Risk is not a static concept. In good economic conditions, the risk of AAA-rated bonds and BBB-rated bonds may be close. In stressed conditions, because of flight to quality, AAA-bonds can remain stable but the value of BBB-rated bonds can drop drastically. Also, nobody wants to have BBB-rated bonds in stressed conditions. This is a liquidity risk issue. In addition, in such stressed conditions, issuers or guarantors may go bankrupt. This is the issue of counterparty risk. Obviously our textbooks on investment have not taken these issues into account.

CONTRIBUTORS TO THE BOOK

The risk of investment products has suddenly become a new concept after the crisis. Many financial institutions have explored new methods to measure investment product risk. Lawmakers have developed new rules to protect investors in better ways. In fact these measures eventually mitigate the risk of financial institutions that distribute investment products to their clients. The nine chapters of this book contain different views on investment product risk. Some are related to the complexity of investment products and some are related to the legal issues regarding investment products.

The contributors to the book are as follows:

- **Clark Abrahams** is Chief Financial Architect at SAS, where his global responsibilities span product development and marketing in governance, risk, and compliance. Inventor, author, and former bank executive, he testified before Congress about the need for a better consumer lending approach prior to the financial crisis. A San Francisco native, Abrahams graduated from UC Berkeley and holds an MS from Stanford University. He serves on the Board of Directors of Social Compact and is a member of the CFA Institute, National Association of Corporate Directors, NC Society of Financial Analysts, PRMIA, RMA and the OCEG Technology Council.
- **Maria Beitz** received her diploma degree in mathematics from the Technische Universität Berlin in 2010. She works as a quantitative risk analyst for the Investitionsbank Berlin (IBB), Germany.
- **Tomasz Berent** is Assistant Professor of the Capital Markets Department at the Warsaw School of Economics in Poland. He obtained his PhD in Finance from the University of Wales in the UK. He is an expert/advisor to the Polish Financial Supervision Authority. Berent received teaching excellence awards at prestigious executive and graduate international programmes, e.g. MIM (CEMS) and WEMBA (WSE and University of Minnesota), and Top 10 WSE Faculty Member Awards every year since the launch of the ranking in 2006. He also lectured in the UK at the University of Wales (1992–1995), Bangor University (2009), and the University of Sussex (2010). In 1995–2001, Berent worked in investment banking as Head of Research, Emerging Markets Equity Strategist and Country Analyst in IB Austria (Warsaw), Paribas and BNP (London) respectively. He has published over 100 equity research notes.
- **Hasan Candan** has 20 years' banking experience in audit and risk management functions. He currently works for Türkiye İş Bankasi, the leading private bank in Turkey. He played a key role in establishing the risk management function in the Turkish banking sector after the domestic financial crisis in 2001, and the risk management department at the Bank. Candan holds an MSc from Nottingham Business School

and he is the co-editor of *Risk Management at Banks and Basel II*. He has lectured on risk management at several national and international conferences.

- **Jike Chong** is Founder and Chief Software Architect of Parasians LLC (Parallel Computing Artisans), which specializes in helping clients in compute-intensive industries achieve revolutionary performance on applications directly affecting revenue/cost with highly parallel computing platforms. He is a PhD researcher at the University of California, Berkeley, working on application frameworks in speech recognition and computational finance to help domain experts efficiently utilize highly parallel computation platforms. Chong's prior work in parallel computing led to several patents at Sun Microsystems, Inc., and Intel Corporation. Jike earned his BS and MS in Electrical and Computer Engineering at Carnegie Mellon University, and holds a Management of Technology (MOT) Certificate from the Haas School of Business at the University of California, Berkeley. He was a Mayfield Fellow (2009), and is a member of Eta Kappa Nu, Tau Beta Pi, and the IEEE.

- **Rituparna Das** is Associate Professor in the Faculty of Management at National Law University, Jodhpur, India (NLU), and Additional Director of the Centre for Studies in Banking and Finance which was set up with an initial corpus funded by the Reserve Bank of India. His PhD in econometrics is preceded by a dual Masters in economics and management. He is an author on econometric modelling and risk modelling. He offers executive courses on fixed income and market risk, and postgraduate courses on financial markets and regulatory systems, project finance, risk management and derivatives.

- **Matthew Dixon** is a Krener Assistant Professor in the mathematics department at UC Davis. He received his PhD in applied mathematics from Imperial College (UK) in 2007 and has since held postdoctoral appointments with the Institute for Computational and Mathematical Engineering at Stanford University and the Department of Computer Science at UC Davis. He has also worked as a quantitative risk analyst for a number of leading investment banks and consulted for the Bank for International Settlements.

- **Matthias Ehrhardt** is Full Professor in the Department of Applied Mathematics and Numerical Analysis at the University of Wuppertal. He teaches and researches in the area of computational finance in the Master's Programme in Financial Mathematics at Halmstad University, Sweden, and is available for PhD supervision in this area.

Ehrhardt received his PhD from the internationally renowned Technische Universität Berlin, Germany. He has published over 35 journal articles and book chapters and edited four books. He serves on the editorial boards of four international journals of applied mathematics.

- **Kurt Keutzer** received his BS in mathematics from Maharishi International University in 1978 and his MS and PhD in computer science from Indiana University in 1981 and 1984, respectively. He joined AT&T Bell Laboratories in 1984, and Synopsys, Inc., in 1991, where he became Chief Technical Officer and Senior Vice-President of Research. He became a professor of electrical engineering and computer science at the University of California, Berkeley, in 1998, and served as the associate director of the Gigascale Silicon Research Center. He co-founded the Universal Parallel Computing Research Center at Berkeley in 2007. He is a Fellow of the IEEE.

- **Shwn Meei Lee** is Assistant Professor of Finance at Hsiuping Institute of Technology in Taiwan. She received her MBA from Metropolitan State University in Minnesota and her DBA from Northwestern Polytechnic University in California. Her research interests focus on behavioral management, behavioral finance, and international finance. She has received a number of teaching awards and the Excellent Academic Staff Award from the institute she serves.

- **Paul Latimer** is Associate Professor in the Department of Business Law and Taxation in the Monash University Faculty of Business and Economics in Melbourne, Australia. He teaches and researches in the area of financial services regulation on undergraduate and master's courses, and is available for PhD supervision in this area. He has been on secondment to the Attorney-General's Department in Canberra and to ASIC, and has been a visitor at several overseas universities including Columbia University, the University of Cambridge and the University of Montreal. His annually published textbook *Australian Business Law* of about 1,300 pages, now in its 29th annual edition, is widely prescribed in business law courses at Australian universities.

- **Alper Özün** is the Head of Asset Liability Management of HSBC Turkey (HBTR). He holds an MSc from Brunel University, and an MPhil from Bradford Business School. He is also an associate professor, lecturing on financial management at Koç University, Graduate Business School. He is an external researcher at Bradford Business School, and is working on worst-case scenario analysis in risk management. He is an editorial member of *Finance and Banking Letters, the International Journal of*

Data Analysis Techniques and Strategies, and *the International Journal of Computer Science*.

- **Will Wei Shen** is Assistant Professor at the School of Law at City University of Hong Kong. He obtained his PhD from the London School of Economics and Political Science, LLM from the University of Cambridge, LLM from the University of Michigan, and LLB and LLM from East China University of Political Science and Law. He is qualified as an attorney-at-law in New York. Dr. Shen practised in Shanghai, Sydney, Chicago and Hong Kong for around nine years before joining City University of Hong Kong. He has published widely on commercial law subjects such as company law, financial regulations and commercial arbitration.

- **P.M. Vasudev** is currently Senior Lecturer in Commercial Law at the University of Auckland. He holds an LLM from Western Ontario and is near completion of his PhD at the Osgoode Hall Law School, York University, Toronto. Earlier, Vasudev practised as a corporate lawyer in Bangalore, India, for several years. He is an active researcher and has presented at academic conferences in the US, Canada, Australia and New Zealand. Vasudev's writings have appeared/been accepted in leading journals including the *Journal of Business Law, McGill Law Journal, Banking & Finance Law Review, Journal of Corporation Law* and *American Journal of Legal History*.

- **Michael C. S. Wong** is Associate Professor at City University of Hong Kong and the founder of CTRISKS, a Hong Kong-based rating agency. He was a founding member of the FRM Committee of the Global Association of Risk Professionals in 1998–2002. He architected the first Basel-standard internal ratings-based system successfully validated by the Hong Kong Monetary Authority (HKMA) and advised several banks on credit risk model development and validation. After the Lehman collapse, he advised many banks on risk process re-engineering and developed the first product VaR model successfully validated by the HKMA. Wong received his PhD from the Chinese University of Hong Kong and his MPhil from the University of Cambridge. He has published over 50 journal articles and book chapters and authored four books. He is included in Risk Who's Who.

- **Mingyuan Zhang** is Principal Consultant with the SAS Risk Practice. Over the last 10 years he has successfully developed and implemented many credit and market risk management solutions and economic forecasting models for the financial services industry. He has published research papers in economic journals, co-authored two credit risk management books, and is the inventor for six risk and compliance patents. Zhang received a PhD in financial economics, an MBA, and is a member of the American Statistical Association. Prior to joining SAS in 1997, he served as a financial economist for a leading economic consulting firm.

Finally I would like to express my gratitude to the contributors for their valuable insights. Investment product risk is a never-ending discussion. Regulation always lags behind product innovation. In the coming years, we shall find many new products that we have never encountered. I hope the book will provide scholars, lawyers, regulators, risk specialists, and bank executives with new insights on investment product risk.

CONTENTS

Chapter 1

BANK RISK MANAGEMENT IN EMERGING
MARKETS AFTER THE ENHANCED BASEL RULES

Hasan Candan and Alper Özün

1. INTRODUCTION

The arbitrage opportunity between financial markets is important for
decision making in international investments. It is a general observation
that unsatisfying gains in advanced markets lead to emerging market investments by undertaking higher risks. Historical data shows that the decrease
in interest rates in the advanced markets and stability in the international
FX markets have led emerging capital markets to receive international
portfolio investments and become bullish markets. The level of US interest
rates creates an important impact on bond spreads in emerging markets
(Ferrucci *et al.*, 2004).

As the current global economic crisis originated in the form of
counterparty risk and developed as liquidity and market risk which started
by mid-2007, the Basel II rules have been enhanced with stress-based
VaR models, liquidity stress tests and economic capital rules including
structural interest rate risk, counterparty risk, and legal or regulatory
risk. In this chapter, we discuss how the enhanced Basel rules can affect
bank risk management in emerging markets and consequently investments.
We underline the importance of new risk management rules in terms of
international portfolio investments in emerging markets.

The implementation of the Basel II rules in a banking sector requires
a total change in risk management perspective from modeling risk in
products to regulatory compliance for market participants, investors and

bank risk managers. We also highlight the implications of the banking crisis in emerging markets as perceived by bank risk managers in this chapter.

Previous financial crises, such as the crisis in Mexico in 1994 and the crisis in Russia in 1997, originated in developing countries and had further impacts on global financial markets due to the deterioration in global risk appetite. The current financial and economic crisis, however, have first appeared in the US and EU. Surprisingly, its effects in emerging markets have become limited and mostly restricted to economic activities rather than financial markets except during a short period which coincided with the first months of the crisis. It is definite that despite having been regulated and supervised by the most advanced risk and capital management rules, the US and European banking sectors faced a crisis which emerged as a result of mismanagement of credit, market, and counterparty risks in their markets. Ironically, most of the regulatory authorities in emerging markets have not adopted the Basel II rules yet; the banking sector in those economies have experienced limited financial effects of the financial crisis. The Turkish banking sector is a good example of that experience. For example, the capital adequacy ratio in the Turkish banking sector increased from 17.99% in 4Q 2008 to 19.95% in 1Q 2010. This example is ironic itself also: One cannot form a view on the ratios alone without studying the risk calculations and assessment techniques applied. For instance, since market risk is measured in accordance with the standard method of the Basel I amendment in the Turkish banking sector, price volatility during the crisis has had limited effects on market risk numbers. Another example can be given from emerging markets on the credit risk side: Although the counterparty risk and collateral management triggered liquidity risk in advanced markets, since many banks in emerging markets did not adopt the credit support annex of the ISDA, their liquidity positions arising from the price volatility of their portfolio were affected to a limited extent. Hence, risk measurement and assessment rules and compliance with them in practice are of great significance in a case of crisis, and different risk assessment rules create different investment environments. At this point, we should stress the importance of "model uncertainty" which has philosophical roots dating back to ancient Greek philosopher Xenophanes who wrote

> The gods did not reveal, from the beginning,
>
> All things to us; but in the course of time,
>
> Through seeking, men find that which is the better.

But as for certain truth, no man has known it,

Nor will he know it; neither of the gods,

Nor yet of all the things of which I speak.

And even if by chance he were to utter

The final truth, he would himself not know it:

For all is but a woven web of guesses (Bailey, 2006, p. 328).

The methodological background of model risk, on the other hand, stems from the control theory in electrical engineering. For those who want to examine model risk in the modern world in detail can start with Chandrasekharan (1996) who defines the control of model uncertainty as "the control of unknown plants with unknown dynamics subject to unknown disturbances".

2. IMPLICATIONS OF THE CURRENT BANKING CRISIS FOR THE EMERGING MARKET BANKING SECTOR

Financial Crises and Risk Management

It is impossible to avoid financial crises, and the current financial crisis will not be the last one. There were 139 recorded and documented financial crises in various parts of the world between 1973 and 1997 (Eichengreen and Bordo, 2002). The current crisis provided many lessons for various parties; however, to the risk professionals it has become certain that even the most complex risk models will never be perfect and relying entirely on models will put financial institutions in danger without even being aware of it.

Practice reveals that setting the most advanced risk policies, internal measures, internal risk limits and implementing the most complex risk models will be inadequate for conducting a safe and sound banking system unless they are understood, adopted and used on a bank-wide scale. The crisis we have been experiencing also revealed a number of primary weaknesses of existing bank capital regulations. The model-based risk-weighted capital requirements make sense and should be maintained; however, they are not perfect and it is very likely that they will never be. Risk professionals have had to learn that the modeling of risk involves substantial risk taking.

An important lesson came from an area where the existing regulations and capital requirements did not touch upon effectively: Liquidity risk and its interconnectedness with other risk categories and the bank's activities as a whole. The liquidity holdings of banks turned out to be insufficient in a stressed banking environment. The problem with liquidity was not only with the quantity but also with the quality of liquidity. Secured funding was perceived as the most stable source of refinancing; however, we all witnessed that it was much less stable than what banks and regulators had taken for granted.

Was Basel II Inadequate?

It has been argued that the Basel II framework cannot be an answer to a crisis environment considering that risk models were not able to capture most of the larger risks that put banks in trouble. However, we still have a restricted understanding of how Basel II works in practice. The Basel II framework was finally published in June 2004 and scheduled for implementation by the end of 2006. However, owing to technical and political reasons for a great number of banking sectors it required long transition periods for the implementation. It had not yet been fully implemented by most banking sectors when the subprime crisis emerged in mid-2007. As for the emerging markets the implementation process is still in its infancy. Consequently, it would be an early conclusion that Basel II fell short in providing a sound banking environment in the event of crises.

The major failings revealed by the financial crisis lie in the scope of uncontrolled credit risk transfer and the limitless expansion of the "originate to distribute" business model of financial intermediation that accompanied it. Credit institutions sold the credits they originated to the capital markets instead of holding them. This process of credit risk transfer was uncontrolled mostly due to repackaging. At the time the subprime crisis emerged the market for derivatives were relatively small in the emerging economy banking sectors which explains why they were not severely affected by the subprime crisis. Undoubtedly, if the originate-to-distribute business model had survived long enough the emerging market banks would have had their share of failures also.

Despite risk-weighted capital ratios that in most cases exceeded the regulatory minima, leverage was a key source of vulnerability going into the crisis. Besides, although VaR models have gained wide acceptance, they have been proven inadequate in covering tail risks or "Black Swan" incidents that brought the real risks. VaR models have been understood to be supplemented by forward-looking instruments such as stress tests

Table 1 Amounts Outstanding of OTC Derivatives by Risk Category and Instrument (Billion USD).

Risk Category/ Instrument	Dec 2007	Jun 2008	Dec 2008	Jun 2009	Dec 2009	Dec 2007	Jun 2008	Dec 2008	Jun 2009	Dec 2009
Total contracts	595,738	683,814	547,983	604,617	614,674	15,834	20,375	32,375	25,372	21,583
FX contracts	56,238	62,983	44,2	48,775	49,196	1,807	2,262	3,591	2,47	2,069
Forwards and FX swaps	29,144	31,966	21,266	23,107	23,129	675	802	1,615	870	683
Currency swaps	14,347	16,307	13,322	15,072	16,509	817	1,071	1,421	1,211	1,043
Options	12,748	14,71	9,612	10,596	9,558	315	388	555	389	343
Interest rate contracts	393,138	458,304	385,896	437,198	449,793	7,177	9,263	18,011	15,478	14,018
Forward rate agreements	26,599	39,37	35,002	46,798	51,749	41	88	140	130	80
Interest rate swaps	309,588	356,772	309,76	341,886	349,236	6,183	8,056	16,436	13,934	12,574
Options	56,951	62,162	41,134	48,513	48,808	953	1,12	1,435	1,414	1,364
Equity-linked contracts	8,469	10,177	6,155	6,615	6,591	1,142	1,146	1,051	879	710
Forwards and swaps	2,233	2,657	1,553	1,709	1,83	239	283	323	225	179
Options	6,236	7,521	4,602	4,906	4,762	903	863	728	654	531

(Continued)

Table 1   (Continued)

Risk Category/ Instrument	Dec 2007	Jun 2008	Dec 2008	Jun 2009	Dec 2009	Dec 2007	Jun 2008	Dec 2008	Jun 2009	Dec 2009
Commodity contracts	8,455	13,229	4,364	3,729	2,944	1,898	2,209	946	689	545
Gold	595	649	332	425	423	70	68	55	43	48
Other commodities	7,861	12,58	4,032	3,304	2,521	1,829	2,141	890	646	497
Forwards and swaps	5,085	7,561	2,471	1,772	1,675					
Options	2,776	5,019	1,561	1,533	846					
Credit default swaps	58,244	57,403	41,883	36,046	32,693	2,02	3,192	5,116	2,987	1,801
Single-name instruments	32,486	33,412	25,74	24,112	21,917	1,158	1,901	3,263	1,953	1,243
Multi-name instruments	25,757	23,991	16,143	11,934	10,776	862	1,291	1,854	1,034	559
Unallocated	71,194	81,719	65,487	72,255	73,456	1,79	2,303	3,66	2,868	2,44
Memorandum item										
Gross credit exposure						3,256	3,859	4,555	3,744	3,52

Source: www.bis.org.

and scenario analyses and those have to be part of the regulatory capital requirement models.

The Case of the Turkish Banking Sector: Strong Throughout the Crisis

If one puts it into plain words, the reason why the Turkish banking sector has been stronger than ever throughout the crisis is that the Turkish economy faced a severe banking crisis in 2001 resulting in the collapse of 24 banks followed by the enforcement of most advanced risk management regulations and establishment of a robust bank supervision environment.

As of the end of 2009, the Turkish banking system was in the process of bringing their risk systems into compliance with Basel II requirements. Banks representing 53% of the total assets of the sector are either mostly or fully compliant with the internal ratings-based (IRB) approach in credit risk; 83% of the system is compliant with advanced market risk methodologies; only 39% of the sector is compliant with counterparty risk requirements. Advanced operational risk methodologies are the weakest chain with only 30% of the total assets of the Turkish banking system being compliant.[1] With respect to standard methodologies, the entire system is fully compliant. Considering that no minimum standard currently exists for liquidity risk globally, Turkish regulatory liquidity risk limits have been in place since 2006 and the supervision of liquidity risk encompasses daily, weekly and monthly reporting to the supervisory authority by banks.

3. IMPLEMENTATION OF ENHANCED BASEL RULES

The latest version of the capital and liquidity reform package, which was announced at the end of July 2010, focused on the design of the definition of capital, the treatment of counterparty credit risk, the leverage ratio, and the global liquidity standard.

Definition of capital: The emphasis is on Tier 1 capital and common equity and retained earnings are taken as the core form of capital. Common equity and retained earnings are considered to be the basic measure for capital ratios and leverage ratios. The purpose of Tier 2 capital is to show the "gone concern" capital. Emerging market banks will require higher levels of

---

[1] Bankacilik Sektörü Basel II İlerleme Raporu-Şubat 2010.

capital. Hence, capital minima (Tier 1/total risk) should not actuate higher requirements than ascertained criteria for the banking sector in emerging economies. Regulatory adjustments including deductions from capital like minority interests, unrealized gains and losses, intangibles, and deferred tax assets should constitute a level playing field. The International Financial Reporting Standards (IFRS) rules are thought to be a significant substitute for differentiations in national accounting standards.

Leverage ratio: The leverage ratio was intended as a "backstop" measure to supplement risk-based ratios. Apart from being a non-risk measure, the leverage ratio is planned to be harmonized internationally. Emerging market economies heavily rely on their financial sector for achieving higher growth rates. This can be carried out by higher rates of credit growth. It is a well-known fact that financial institutions had excessive on- and off-balance sheet leverage while reporting strong risk-based capital ratios before the crisis. However, with respect to emerging market banking sectors any measures restricting their credit risk-taking capabilities and potential for borrowing for financial intermediation will lead to adverse macroeconomic consequences. From consumer financing to infrastructure financing, banking systems in emerging economies are the main vehicle for economic growth.

This is valid for the advanced markets also; according to a recent study "the Eurozone would feel the largest impact from the new Basel proposals, with growth cut by 0.9 percentage points per year".[2]

Procyclicality: The Basel II framework had an awareness of cyclical effects in capturing systemic risks. It elaborated on the issue with the requirement for long-term data sets to estimate probabilities of default, the introduction of downturn loss given default estimates, and the appropriate calibration of the risk functions, which convert loss estimates into regulatory capital requirements.[3] As for the emerging markets, the required data is scarce compared to that for the advanced markets and the adjusted probability of defaults and loan provisions considered together with capital add-ons proposed in Pillar 2 will result in double counting. Forward-looking provisioning will be an issue with regard to the differences in accounting systems.

---

[2] *Financial Times* (2010), "Basel Rules Threaten Growth, Say Bankers", 11 June, p. 32.
[3] Strengthening the Resilience of the Banking Sector, BCBS, Consultative Document, p. 74.

Liquidity standards: Basel II did not ascertain liquidity standards. There is only one document outlining the principles prepared by the Basel Committee for Banking Supervision (BCBS).[4] The new rules developed two minimum standards for liquidity. One is the 30-day liquidity coverage ratio (LCR) and the other is a long-term ratio, the net stable funding ratio (NSFR). The LCR being a short-term ratio requires banks to maintain a minimum standard of high-quality assets under the scenarios to be generated by supervisors. The eligible liquid assets for the LCR were defined by the BCBS. The assumptions behind the scenarios may not reflect the actual market dynamics in emerging economies. Run-off rates and such parameters should be derived from empirical studies. Narrowing the definition of eligible assets for the LCR may not be consistent with the emerging market economies where one will not see many complex products and practices. As for the NSFR, which is directly related with the banking sector's long-term function of maturity transformation, its main objective is to ensure that banks use stable sources to fund their activities.

Implementation timing: Timing should be based on a careful assessment of the macroeconomic conditions and the state of resilience of the global financial industry on the proposed date. This is important for level-playing-field issues, but equally important to ensure consistent, high-quality, and effective standards across the global system.

Emerging markets: The banking sector is the leading actor for economic growth in emerging markets. The implementation of the enhanced rules in emerging markets should be maintained by the same encompassing principles set at the international level. On the other hand, it is crucial that implementation takes into account the latest progress of regulation and supervision in emerging markets and accommodates the necessary degree of flexibility to adapt to local market conditions.

4. RISK MEASUREMENT OF FINANCIAL INSTRUMENTS IN TRADING AND BANKING BOOKS

The portfolio approach in risk management helps in the assessment and management of risk and risk-reward balance. A bank's balance sheet can

---

[4]Principles for Sound Liquidity Risk Management and Supervision, September 2008 (www.bis.org/publ/bcbs144.htm).

be divided into different portfolios on the basis of shared risks, and the methods for calculating the risk of these portfolios can be differentiated and the risk-reward balance can be tracked for each portfolio, which together make the risk management process easier. For this purpose risk factors should be defined for each instrument and the risks of these instruments should be monitored within their portfolios.

Bank portfolios can be grouped as shown below according to their liquidity profiles, hence their accounting code line-up.

Trading book: A trading book consists of assets which are subject to trade and appear on the asset side of the balance sheet and derivative trades for speculative purposes. As these assets are considered to be available for sale for income generation, risks related to these portfolios arise from the change in the prices in the market. As a result, changes in interest rates, exchange rates, option deltas, and commodity prices affect the market value of the trading book. Therefore, market risk arising from the expectation of the effects of market prices on the portfolio is employed when computing the risk on the trading book.

Banking book: Securities held for maturity, customer loans, and derivative deals for hedging purposes constitute the credit portfolio. Instruments in these portfolios bear credit risk because of their exposure to counterparty risk. In addition to that, the interest rate sensitivity of these instruments because of revaluation is examined within structural interest rate risk.

Equity investments: Banks can own stock in other companies for income generation or strategic purposes subject to regulatory limits. Equities of entities listed on a stock exchange are accounted with their market value while the rest of the investments are accounted with their book value. Dividends received from subsidiaries are accounted as extraordinary income in the income statement. Risks associated with a change in market valuations and dividends of subsidiaries are defined as investment risks. Depreciation in the value of a subsidiary translates into a decrease in equity for banks.

Real estate portfolio: Banks can obtain real estate either for physical needs or as a result of collecting receivables stemming from problem loans. Price changes in real estate markets lead to changes in the value of the real estate book. According to the banking laws, in general, real estate assets acquired through the collection of receivables should be liquidated within a certain

Table 2 Portfolios and Risk on Balance Sheet.

Portfolio/Risk Source	Risk
1 Trading book	Market risk
2 Banking book	Structural interest rate risk
2a Credit portfolio	Credit risk and structural interest rate risk
2b Subsidiary portfolio	Investment risk and structural interest rate risk
2c Real estate portfolio	Real estate price risk
3 Maturity mismatch	Liquidity risk
4 Process mismatch	Operational risk

time frame. Within this period of time, changes in the value of the real estate book can generate income or losses for banks.

Allocated credits, subsidiaries, and real estate holdings in assets and liabilities compose the banking book. An example of portfolio structure and associated risks are listed in Table 2.

IFRS-9: Financial Instruments can be used as a guide to decide if a financial instrument is evaluated within a trading or banking book. That decision is important as it determines risk assessment of the instrument and its placement in the risk measurement. IFRS-9 employs enhanced requirements for the classification and measurement of financial assets. All recognized financial assets are measured at either amortized cost or fair value. It uses two primary measurement categories for financial assets. A debt instrument that collects the contractual cash flows as only payments of the principal and interest generally has to be measured at amortized cost. On the other hand, instruments for speculative purposes have to be measured at fair value through profit or loss. In that sense, IFRS-9 makes clear how to determine the risk classification of an instrument, and its proper risk assessment technique.

As our focus is investment risk, we examine the importance of model risk in market risk and the effects of assessment methodologies on investment decisions.

Critical Issues in Market Risk Assessment

Market risk arises from the price changes in financial assets covered by the trading book of a bank. In the literature and market practices, market risk is measured by employing the VaR methodology. The following critical questions should be addressed to the analysts who examine the risk of a portfolio or trading book of a bank.

> *What is the technique employed to capture the volatility in market risk factors?*

The volatility in interest rates, equity, and option prices can be computed by EWMA, normally distributed GARCH and its variants (such as EGARCH, GARCH-M, TGARCH-M, etc.), asymmetrically distributed GARCH, normal mixed GARCH, or Markov models which account for regime change. The choice among these options and its compatibility with the subject of economic activity is crucially important. For example, normal GARCH models are doomed to fail in high-volatility economic settings where negative price movements create higher volatility. In these types of market, the volatility in risk factors should be computed using GARCH models which capture asymmetric distribution or Markov models which incorporate regime changes.

> *Which method of computing VaR is employed?*

Historical simulation, Monte Carlo, and variance-covariance models are often used to calculate VaR. Regulators do not interfere with the banks' choice as long as it is among these three options and validated. Therefore validation reports should be covered during bank analysis. Besides, the analyst should check whether the method chosen is in compliance with the bank's economic setting and its activity base. For example, a bank heavily exposed to derivative products should implement Monte Carlo simulations instead of historical simulation. Historical simulation has a tendency to fail in complex scenarios with highly volatile and/or thin markets. If the analyst feels that a more suitable method is possible she should compute VaR with both methods and compare the outcomes.

> *Is there a concentration within risk factors?*

Banks compute VaR for each of the following sub-categories: interest rate, FX rate, equity, and options. Any concentration and its implications during possible price movements should be carefully considered. At this point the importance of a risk-focused approach is revealed as only the nominal portfolio size of the above sub-categories is not informative enough. The important aspect is the risk associated with these portfolios. The bond portfolios of two banks can be equal in size but the differences in the bonds' maturity, currency, and issuer can create huge differences between their risks. Therefore risk-adjusted concentration analysis is much more valuable than nominal book magnitude.

Is there a rational balance between risk and return?

Optimizing the rational risk-return balance is the most important aspect of modern risk management. There, risk-adjusted return on capital (RAROC) analysis is crucial. The risks undertaken should be in line with expected returns on both individual risk factors and on the portfolio as a whole. Furthermore, banks should check whether their risk-return balance is in line with both their economic capital structure and regulatory requirements.

Is the bank's current market risk in compliance with its risk appetite and its business plan?

The growth strategies and methods employed by banks to achieve their targets are shaped by their economic surroundings as well as the decisions made by their boards. The board sets a level of risk appetite considering the business plan, demands from the execution side, economic conditions, profit targets, human capital, and other similar factors. The harmony between this risk appetite and the actual risks a bank faces defines the profitability, asset growth, and possible deviations from desired essential financial ratios.

Magnitude of VaR, its deviation and breaches

After careful consideration of the previous questions, the final task is to monitor the historical course of VaR. The crucial issue here is to back-test these findings and, in case a deviation exists in forecasted VaR, to reveal the causes of these deviations, and check whether these deviations are correlated with instances of high volatility and the number of breaches. If these deviations coincide with periods of high volatility, the methods used for computing VaR should be revised. The number of breaches is important for capital adequacy calculations. Banks with a history of larger than legal breaches are penalized with higher capital requirements.

Banks limit their market risk with VaR and early warning VaR limits. Breaches of these limits and their causes, whether they are extra positions taken or a change in risk factors, should be carefully examined during audits. Banks which breach these limits should be cautioned. Breaches caused by movements in risk factors imply that the expected return remains unmoved while the risks associated with it are increased, therefore causing a higher potential for loss. Breaches caused by a nominal increase in positions suggest that there is an increase in the risk appetite of the bank.

5. MODEL RISK IN PORTFOLIO MANAGEMENT

In classic portfolio management, the returns and covariance matrix of the portfolio are obtained from an estimation process containing the estimation error in practice. Especially in the case of multi-period optimization, the covariance matrix estimation might have noise such that changes in the matrix create changes in optimal allocations. However, using any mean-variance optimization model has certain difficulties in practice. Jobson and Korkie (1981), Jorion (1986), and Michaud (1989) provide evidence that disregarding uncertainty creates unstable mean-variance portfolio allocations. Fabozzi *et al.* (2007, p. 208) list three main drawbacks of mean-variance portfolio management, namely, (i) sensitivity to estimation error, (ii) effects of uncertainty in the input parameters, and (iii) large data requirement necessary for estimating the inputs for the portfolio optimization framework. First, they follow Broadie (1993) who introduces the terms true frontier, estimated frontier, and actual frontier to refer to the efficient frontiers calculated using the true expected and unobservable returns, estimated expected returns, and true expected returns of the portfolios on the estimated frontier. They argue that the estimated frontiers overestimate the expected return for any risk level on the actual and true frontiers. What is more, the actual frontier lies far below the true frontier, indicating that the optimal mean-variance portfolio is not always a proper or mean-variance efficient portfolio. As the true expected return is unobservable, it is not easy to be certain how far the actual expected return may be from the expected return of the mean-variance optimal portfolio, and at the end, we may have an underperforming portfolio with respect to its risk level. In this context, as securities with large expected returns with low risk are overweight, and vice versa, intolerable estimation errors occur in optimized portfolio weights (Fabozzi *et al.*, 2007, p. 211). Bawa, Brown, and Klein (1979) argue that even a minor change in the expected return estimates can create a fatal portfolio choice. For those reasons, Michaud (1989) refers to mean-variance optimizers as "error maximizers".

As model risk should always be kept in mind, it is preferable to have an internal model for capital management, in addition to regulatory capital.

Fig. 1 Components of Economic Capital.

6. CONCLUSION: REGULATORY CAPITAL VERSUS ECONOMIC CAPITAL

Economic capital is commonly defined as an equity reserve used by banks to absorb unexpected losses. The amount covering those losses is determined by each bank internally at a confidence level. The confidence level set reveals a trade-off between debt holders' protection and providing high returns to shareholders. Economic capital is distinct from regulatory capital. Economic capital should reflect the loss distribution of a bank for all its major risk factors. In contrast to regulatory capital, which includes credit risk, market risk, and operational risk, economic capital might include other risk components that might create loss in capital (Fig. 1).

The most significant risk component in economic capital is asset-liability management (ALM) risk arising from mismatch in assets and liabilities on the balance sheet. Especially in emerging markets in which long-term funding is restricted, interest rate margins are sensitive to fluctuations in interest rates. Independent of the markets, the recent global crisis has shown that banks should be able to jump start their capital in addition to their capital adequacy ratio in times of need.

Economic capital is considered to be a powerful business management tool. Apart from being a consistent risk metric, it could be used in performance measurement, and asset and business allocation, that is to say risk budgeting. Portfolio managers should be aware of the possible amount of loss in their portfolios in extreme cases.

Irrespective of the complexity of regulations and supervision intensity, it is the bank that knows its own risks best and the ways to manage them. In that sense, economic capital estimation and economic capital allocation (risk budgeting) across businesses within a bank are among the most powerful tools for management.

To conclude, we argue that capital and risk management is an art that should be supported by quantitative measurement techniques. Risk management is a flexible process and its success depends on controlling unexpected losses in case of a crisis.

REFERENCES

Bailey, A. (2006). *First Philosophy: Fundamental Problems and Readings in Philosophy*, London: Broadview Press.

Banks, E. (2002). *The Simple Rules of Risk: Revisiting the Art of Financial Risk Management*, New York: John Wiley & Sons.

Bawa, V., Brown, S. and Klein, R. (1979). *Estimation Risk and Optimal Portfolio Choice*, Amsterdam: North-Holland.

Broadie, M. (1993). "Computing Efficient Frontiers Using Estimated Parameters." *Annals of Operations Research*, 45:21–58.

Chandrasekharan, P.C. (1996). *Robust Control of Linear Dynamical Systems*, San Diego, CA: Academic Press.

Eichengreen, B. and Bordo, M.B. (2002). "Crises Now and Then: What Lessons from the Last Era of Financial Globalization?" NBER Working Paper 8715.

Fabozzi, F.J., Kolm, P.N. and Pachamanova, D. (2007). *Robust Portfolio Optimization and Management*, London: John Wiley & Sons.

Ferrucci, G., Herzberg, V., Soussa, F. and Taylor, A. (2004). "Understanding Capital Flows to Emerging Market Economies." *Financial Stability Review*, 16:89–97.

Jobson, J.D. and Korkie, B. (1981). "Performance Hypothesis Testing with the Sharpe and Treynor Measures." *Journal of Finance*, 36:888–908.

Jorion, P. (1986). "Bayes-Stein Estimation for Portfolio Analysis." *Journal of Financial and Quantitative Analysis*, 21:293–305.

Michaud, R. (1989). "The Markowitz Optimization Enigma: Is 'Optimized' Optimal?" *Financial Analyst Journal*, 45(1):31–42.

Chapter 2

PRODUCT VaR MODELLING

Rituparna Das

1. DEFINITION AND CLASSIFICATION OF INVESTMENT PRODUCTS

An investment product may be defined as a contract sold by some financial institution (FI), which provides an avenue for deployment of funds with an expectation of future cash inflow. Such cash flow may be in the form of an annuity, i.e. a fixed sum, or depending on conditions in the financial markets and the surrounding macroeconomic system, a variable sum in successive periods — say, monthly, quarterly, semiannually or annually. An investment product is also known as a security, for example, stocks (i.e. shares or equities), bonds, etc. One should be cautious that the term "security" has other uses in financial transactions, like collateral against a bank loan, which the bank may claim on default by the borrower.

As per the amount of cash flow, investment products are classified into fixed income products and variable income products. Buyers of such contracts may be an individual, a corporation, an FI or a government agency. An individual may buy a monthly income scheme (MIS) from a post office; a corporation or an FI may buy a fixed deposit (FD) from a bank; a government or a private enterprise may buy from a bank provident fund (PF) scheme for its employees. In any of the above contracts, if a fixed sum or percentage of the principal is promised to be paid by the seller of the contract, it will be called a fixed income product. For example, a bank like State Bank of India (SBI) or HSBC Singapore may promise a fixed interest rate to the deposit holders. Such rates are available on the websites of the

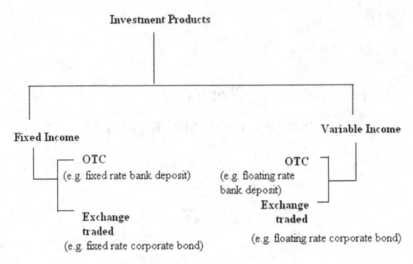

Fig. 1 Classification of Investment Products.

banks. On the other hand, some bank like Citibank may offer a floating rate of interest on deposits. In such a case it is a variable income product.

Depending on the nature of purchase of the contract, such contracts are classified as over-the-counter (OTC) products and exchange-traded (or simply "traded") products. In the case of OTC products, transactions take place between the buyer and seller in the presence or absence of a third party like a broker; here the buyer and seller know each other and hence on many occasions such products are customized and non-transferable. The PF scheme is one such example in the absence of a broker whereas shares of unlisted companies are an example where a broker or investment bank as a third party is often required. But, in the case of a corporate bond or a share of a company listed on the stock exchange (SE), which is sold or bought on the terminal of the SE, the buyer and the seller are anonymous there, the SE being the central counterparty. The product here is transferable. This is called a traded product. Such a product may be of the fixed income category or variable income category because some bonds offer fixed rates while others offer floating rates. The above classification is shown in Fig. 1.

Risks of investment products are classified into two categories: issuer risk and investor risk.

Issuer risk: An issuer faces market risk in the form of adverse movements in market interest rates and exchange rates.

Market interest rates are risk-free benchmark rates of yield like the long-term government securities rate or short-term Treasury bill (T-bill) rate. If the market rate of interests decreases, the issuer faces the risk of interest loss in the case of fixed-income products in the absence of a call option and enjoys a interest rate differential (or spread) if the market rate of interests increases, but at the same time faces the risk of early redemption, if there is any put option, since investors are likely to incur losses because of the fixed income category of the product. This is common for fixed-rate bank deposits and for fixed-rate corporate bonds with a put option.

Interest rates on rate-sensitive assets (RSA) and rate-sensitive liabilities (RSL) are not the same and the difference between them is net interest income (NII) on the balance sheet of a bank or FI. If RSA rates rise less or fall more than that of their RSL counterparts, there is a possibility of NII shrinking, a phenomenon which poses a challenge to asset-liability management (ALM).

If cash flows from a security are promised to be paid in foreign currency, the investor may suffer losses owing to adverse movements in the exchange rate. This is called exchange rate risk. The Russian government suffered similar losses in 1998.

Investor risk: It is necessary to distinguish between an investor and a trader here. An investor holds a security till maturity or for the long term and earns periodical cash flow like interest or dividends. The investor does not aim at short-term capital gain. An investor faces the risk of default by issuers on timely payment of interest and/or redemption of the principal amount on maturity. This is called credit risk. Hence, most regulators

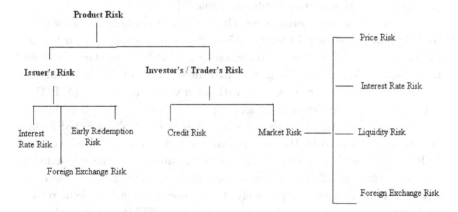

Fig. 2 Types of Product Risk.
Note: Conventionally the term "market risk" applies to the investor/trader, not to the issuer/borrower.

examine the credit rating of the issuer before permitting an issue. An investor can buy a product from the issuer in the primary market or from a trader in the secondary market.

A trader aims at short-term capital gain. Her job is buying at a certain price from the primary or secondary market, then trying to sell at a higher price in the secondary market and thus book a trading profit. She faces market risk in the forms of price risk and liquidity risk. It may happen that the price of the product is too low in the secondary market to yield any gain. This is price risk. On the other hand, there may be no buyer at all for some products (e.g. low-coupon long-term bonds). This is liquidity risk. Market risk may arise from the macroeconomic system or from the issuer herself. Availability of high-coupon bonds of the same maturity issued by an entity with a similar credit rating may cause liquidity risk; this is called systemic risk. On the other hand, liquidity risk may emanate from factors specific to the issuer herself. Then it is called non-systemic risk. There are several instances where the issuers declare themselves bankrupt and the bonds issued by them became illiquid, thereby leading to a series of bankruptcy of the investors. Figure 2 delineates the above discussion.

2. VALUATION OF INVESTMENT PRODUCTS

There is little difference between the price and the value of an investment product. Hence the terms "valuation" and "pricing" are often used synonymously. There are three values (or prices) of an investment product: book or acquisition value, intrinsic value and market value.

Book value or acquisition value: This is the past market value at which a security is acquired; acquisition value is different from acquisition cost, since the latter includes brokerage and commission in addition to the acquisition value; acquisition costs exist in the investment menu of the asset side on the balance sheet where reporting without marking to market (MTM) is permitted by the regulator in Basel I regime but not in Basel II regime.

Intrinsic value: This is the present value (PV) of all expected future cash flows discounted by the required rate of return (RoR). The investor's RoR is the issuer's cost of capital and at the same time the opportunity cost of investment offered by the market to the investor in the absence of any better alternative; alternatively it is also called market yield, return on investment, reference rate, yield to maturity (YTM), benchmark rate, discount rate or occasionally simply yield. The PV is called the theoretical value since the present value calculation is done as per different models expounded by economists like Keynes, Modigliani, Miller and Gordon. The RoR is decided by a host of factors like prevailing benchmark rates, inflation rate, economic growth rate and industrial output growth rate.

Market value: This is the price paid or to be paid by the investor or the trader currently, recently or in the past. The current market value is also called the spot price. The spot price is decided by demand and supply forces. A complete implementation of the Basel II framework requires the banks to report their investment book to the regulators in terms of market value. For traded products the last traded price (LTP) of the product becomes available to the members of the clearing agencies in the evening of every business day, e.g. the volume-weighted average LTP of a 91-days T-bill maturing on 30 July 2010, displayed on the website of the Clearing Corporation of India was 98.67 INR as on 25 June 2010.[1] In the US similar work is done by Fixed Income Clearing Corporation.

Since both the book value and the market value are prices determined by the forces of supply and demand, principles of valuation do not have much to do with them except for their use as past time-series data in research and forecasting by economists, and hence centre on the theoretical value, i.e. PV. PVs are nothing but expected figures. If all investors are assumed to be identically rational, an increase in an investor's PV of a particular product implies the same for others also. This is called "consistent rational expectation". Such an expectation would be the driver of the rise in demand and hence the rise in the spot price of the product and bring about equality between the PV and the spot price. So knowledge of how to calculate the PV is useful to both the sellers and buyers of investment products.

The discussion of PV calculation starts with the concept and valuation of a discount product. A discount product means an investment of a sum for some particular period in order to obtain a greater sum at the end of that period and there is no interim cash flow. Examples are discount deposits, commercial papers (CP) and certificates of deposit (CD) offered by banks, FIs and non-bank financial companies (NBFCs), and zero-coupon bonds (ZC) like T-bills offered by the central/federal government. If we take the above example of a 91-day T-bill with one month and five days left to mature, one has to invest 98.67 INR as on 25 June 2010 for a period of one month and five days in order to get 100 INR on 30 July 2010. Hence the PV

---

[1]Available at http://ccilindia.com/CCIL/DATA/Market%20Statistics/G-Sec%20Settle ment/Daily%20volume%20wise/CCIL-106-25062010.pdf.

as on 25 June 2010 of 100 INR to be available as on 30 July 2010 is in this
case 98.67 INR. Since the period from 25 June 2010 to 30 July 2010, both
days inclusive, is 0.97 years, denoting the annualized rate of return or yield
by r, we can write $98.76 \times (1+r)^{0.97} = 100$. Solving for r gives $r = 27.31\%$;
this is a case of equality between the spot price and PV if the investor's
calculated PV was found to be exactly 98.67 INR. Since T-bills are issued
by the sovereign it is generally risk-free save exceptions like there in Russia
and Argentina.[2] If the investor does not find any higher yield offered by
another risk-free product of similar maturity, 27.31% would be her RoR.

A discount product has a single cash inflow to the investor on
redemption. There are other products which offer multiple cash flows to
the investors from time to time like coupon-paying bonds issued by private
corporates as well as governments, non-discount deposits offered by banks,
stocks, MIS offered by banks as well as post offices and mutual funds. In
order to calculate the PV of such a product with the help of the knowledge of
pricing a discount product we relax the assumption of a single cash flow and
instead (i) assume that each future cash flow is the mature value of a distinct
discount product, (ii) calculate the PV of all the above separate discount
products, and (iii) sum up all the above PVs; the resultant numerical figure
is called the PV of the product offering multiple or periodical cash inflows
to the investor.

Illustration

Let us consider the traded bond iShares Barclays Capital Euro Corporate
Bond 1–5 which has a term to maturity (TTM) of 4.17 years as on 25
June 2010, a semiannual (SA) coupon of 5.03% and a redemption value of
€1000.[3] If the TTM and date of acquisition, purchase or settlement (DoS)
are known, the date of maturity (DoM) could be calculated by the trial
and error method, applying the MS Excel (XLS) formula "=yearfrac(earlier
date, later date)". The date may be typed in either format '25 June 2010'
or '06/25/2010'. Here, the TTM of 4.17 years means a DoM of 27 August
2014. The benchmark 10-year yield in London was 2.59% on the same
day.[4] Table 1 is the schedule of cash flows and their PVs from the above
product.

---

[2] Available at http://research.stlouisfed.org/publications/review/02/11/ChiodoOwyang.
pdf, http://fpc.state.gov/documents/organization/39301.pdf.
[3] Available at http://uk.ishares.com/en/rc/funds/IE15.
[4] Available at http://www.businessweek.com/news/2010-06-25/european-yield-spreads-
widen-on-concern-debt-crisis-deepening.html.

Table 1 Schedule of Cash Flows and PVs.

Date of Coupon	Period	Cash Flow (€)	PV (€)
27-Aug-10	1	25.15	24.8284713
27-Feb-11	2	25.15	24.51105316
27-Aug-11	3	25.15	24.19769303
27-Feb-12	4	25.15	23.88833904
27-Aug-12	5	25.15	23.58293997
27-Feb-13	6	25.15	23.28144525
27-Aug-13	7	25.15	22.98380498
27-Feb-14	8	25.15	22.68996987
27-Aug-14	9	1025.15	913.051632
		Clean price	1103.015349
		Accrued interest	16.76666667
		Dirty price	1119.782015

Working notes: $(5.03\%/2) \times 1000 = 25.15$; $24.82847 = 25.15/(1 + (2.59\%/2))^1$

Table 2 Schedule of Cash Flows and PVs.

Date of Coupon	Period	Cash Flow (€)	PV (€)
27-Aug-10	1	25.15	24.82602043
27-Feb-11	2	25.15	24.50621434
27-Aug-11	3	25.15	24.19052795
27-Feb-12	4	25.15	23.87890819
27-Aug-12	5	25.15	23.57130269
27-Feb-13	6	25.15	23.26765973
27-Aug-13	7	25.15	22.96792827
27-Feb-14	8	25.15	22.67205792
27-Aug-14	9	1025.15	912.2407913
		Clean price	1102.121411
		Accrued interest	16.76666667
		Dirty price	1118.888078

The interpretation of Table 1 is that when the market is offering 2.59%, the bond is offering 5.03% and the buyer has to compensate the seller by paying €92.149 more than the par value (same as the principal value, face value or redemption value). Suppose the coupon rate is 2.59%; now if we calculate the PV of the bond, the total PV would be €1000. Applying the same argument, if the coupon rate is lower than the market yield, the seller has to compensate the buyer by charging a price less than par. The next day, on 25 June 2010, the market yield rose to 2.61% and the price plunged (Table 2).

Above is the manual method of calculating the PV. In XLS there is a handy formula "=price(DoS, DoM, rate, yield, redemption, frequency)" for every €100 of face value to calculate the price; in this formula "rate"

Table 3 Accrued Interest, Clean Price and Dirty Price.

DoM	26-Jun-10
DoM	27-Aug-14
Rate	5.03%
Yield	2.61%
Redemption	100
Frequency	2
Price	109.4982115
Price for 1000	109498.2115
Accrued interest	16.76666667
Dirty price	109514.9781

means the annualized coupon rate. This gives the clean price, i.e. the sum of the PVs of all future cash flows. But the buyer is getting the first coupon after two months of purchase though she did not hold the bond for the preceding six months. Hence she has to pay the interest for four months to the seller. This is called the accrued interest (AI) or the broken period interest. The sum of the AI and the clean price is called the dirty price. Here, AI = €5.03% × (4/12) × 1000 = €16.77. The worksheet would look like Table 3.

Here, price means clean price per €100 face value. There will be a little difference between the results from these two methods because of rounding discrepancy.

The reader should note that the above result is yield-sensitive, i.e. the PV may not be the same if the market yield is assumed to be different from the benchmark 10-year rate in London. The rate of discount may vary from case to case. Different users, e.g. institutions, economists and researchers, apply different benchmark rates as market yields, e.g. the LIBOR in the UK, the federal fund rate in the US, the 10-year government security rate in India, the 91-day T-bill rate in Uganda work as benchmark rates for different users.

The price of a portfolio of bonds is the weighted average of the prices of the individual bonds in the portfolio, the weights being the proportions of the respective bonds in total investment. The relationship between the price of a bond and the market yield is shown in Fig. 3.

Similar arguments could apply to an ordinary stock from which dividends may be expected but redemption value is nil because of the legal nature of the contract embedded in the product. One can refer to the distinction between fixed income and non-fixed income categories of products here. For fixed-income non-discount products like bonds, there

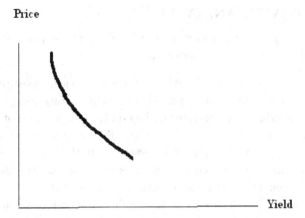

Fig. 3 Price of a Bond and Market Yield.

is a uniform periodical cash flow starting after the acquisition period and continuing till the redemption period in the form of coupons. This is known as annuity. In the case of non-fixed-income products like an ordinary stock, even if there are periodical dividend payments, their amounts may not be uniform; there may be the case of growing dividends or intermittent non-payment of dividends in any period. A floating-rate bond is another case of a non-fixed-income product. In this case the coupon is reset at the end of every period following some benchmark rate and hence the bond is repriced as if it were a new product acquired at the end of a period and to be held for only the next one period so that the question of holding it for a long time or till maturity does not arise.

The price of a stock may vary directly or inversely with the market index. The market index or stock index is the volume-weighted average price of a number of selected stocks. There are country-specific national indices, like Kenya's NSE 20-Share Index, as well as global indices like the S&P Global 100. There are several models of calculating the PV of a share offered by the economists, like those of Modigliani–Miller and Gordon, but unlike a fixed-rate bond, the PV often is not equal to the spot price or LTP.

The market value of a mutual fund is its net asset value (NAV). For calculating the present value, we can divide mutual funds into two fundamental categories: (i) equity-linked and (ii) debt-linked. The equity-linked funds may be valued as stocks are valued and the debt-linked funds are valued as bonds are valued. There is a mixed category where the fund is linked to both equity and debt and could be bifurcated into the equity-linked part and the debt-linked part and accordingly valued.

3. SENSITIVITY ANALYSIS

Sensitivity analysis means ascertaining why and how the price of a product varies. We find in the above section that

(i) bond prices vary inversely with yield; the numerical measure of such a variation is known as duration (D) or modified duration (MD) and is different for different bonds depending on the combination of the TTM, coupon rate and market yield; we shall discuss D in this section;

(ii) stock prices vary directly or inversely with the relevant index; the numerical measure of such a variation is known as equity beta, denoted by the Greek letter β and is different for different stocks depending on the profile and performance of the issuing companies; we shall discuss β in this section.

Duration

Duration (D) has three definitions depending on the nature of requirement. Risk management personnel in corporates, banks and FIs are interested in defining duration as the percentage fall in the price of a plain vanilla option-free bond following a 1% or 100-basis-point (one basis point is 0.01%) rise in market yield.

$$D = -\frac{\frac{\Delta P}{P}}{\frac{\Delta y}{1+y}}$$

The formula for D is written as above. Because of the inverse relationship between price and market yield, the minus sign is incorporated in the formula for D. There is an XLS formula for calculating D. One has to type in any cell of the worksheet the following text: "=duration(DoS, DoM, rate, yield, frequency)". The date has to be typed as "June 26, 2010"; this will appear as "26-Jun-10".

If somebody purchases the iShares Barclays Capital Euro Corporate Bond 1-5 on June 26, 2010, the formula for the duration is "=duration(26-Jun-10, 26-Jun-14, 5.03%, 2.61%, 2)". The worksheet would look like Table 4.

The market price of the bond per unit is €109.1 × 10 = €1091 approximately at a market yield of 2.61%. It is interpreted as follows: If the market yield rises by 100 bps, the market price of the bond would change by 3.69%. If a bank holds a portfolio of one million units of the above bond, the pre-shock value of the portfolio is 1091000000 and the post-shock value is

Table 4   Worksheet for Calculating Duration.

DoS	26-Jun-10
DoS	25-Jun-14
Rate	5.03%
Yield	2.61%
Redemption	100
Frequency	2
Duration	3.68682578
Price	109.1292987

Table 5   Calculating Loss after Upward Yield-Shock.

DoS	26-Jun-10	DoS	26-Jun-10
DoM	25-Jun-14	DoM	25-Jun-14
Rate	5.03%	Rate	5.03%
Yield	2.61%	Yield	2.63%
Redemption	100	Redemption	100
Frequency	2	Frequency	2
Price	109.1292987	Price	109.0498913
		Loss	0.079407451

1090000000, i.e. the MTM portfolio depreciates by 1 million approximately. The XLS worksheet would look like Table 5.

This is called price risk when it is predicted but has not happened yet; it is called loss if it has already happened. Thus, in the risk management literature D is a tool for predicting the movement of bond price in response to yield shock. The tool works as follows: $\Delta P = -D * P * \Delta y/(1+y)$, where D denotes duration, P denotes bond price, Δ denotes change, y denotes market yield and * is a multiplication sign. Computed ΔP is negative when the market yield is expected to look up; it is called price risk. The price-yield relationship has been depicted in Fig. 3.

The duration of a portfolio is the weighted average of the individual Ds of the bonds in the investment portfolio, the weights being the proportions of individual bonds in the total portfolio. It has been empirically found that the magnitude of D differs for the same bond following wild fluctuations in the market yield. Change in the price of a bond is more if the market yield falls substantially, say, by 200 bps than the change if the market yield rises by 200 bps. Graphically the yield-price relationship is not linear; rather, it is curvilinear. It is a blessing also for the bond investor. This feature is absent with stocks. When the market yield falls continuously, the bond price increases more than expected in terms of D and when the market yield rises continuously, the bond price decreases less than expected in terms of

D. This feature is known as convexity. It denotes the rate of change in duration in response to robust yield shocks. A more convex portfolio enjoys a higher rate of return than a less convex one whenever there is any yield shock.

Investors are concerned with the second definition of D. Here D is defined as the length of the post-acquisition period, at the end of which the acquisition cost is recovered. This period is shorter than the TTM. During the rest of the period of the TTM after recovery of the acquisition cost, the value of the cash flow is considered to be surplus over the acquisition cost. The recovery of the acquisition cost is ascertained by equating the acquisition cost to the present value of the sum of (i) the sum of the compound values of the reinvested coupons at the end of the duration period, compounding having been done at the rate of market yield; (ii) the predicted resale value at the end of the duration period using the same rate of market yield; and (iii) the AI for the period between the last coupon date and the resale date.

Both the definitions of D have the same measure. This means that if the aforesaid iShares Barclays Capital Euro Corporate Bond has a duration of 3.68 as per the first definition, the recovery period is 3.68 years. Let us verify whether the investment of 109.1292987 on June 26, 2014, is recovered by April 5, 2010, approximately after 3.68 years. The steps are as follows:

(i) The date of resale, liquidation, trade or disposal is obtained by applying XLS formula "=yearfrac(...)".

(ii) Each coupon is invested at a compound rate of 2.61% for the difference between the coupon date and the resale date.

(iii) The clean resale price on the resale date is obtained by applying XLS formula "=price(...)".

(iv) The AI is calculated for the broken period between the resale date and the coupon date prior to the resale date.

(v) The sum total of the aggregate coupon reinvestment compound amount (1238.45), the clean price of resale (109.98) and the AI (16.32) is calculated.

(vi) The PV of the above sum is calculated to be 1238.26.

(vii) The difference above PV and current investment is calculated to be 119.38.

The worksheet would look like Table 6.

In this model, the assumption is that there exists a single rate at which all compounding and discount are done, which in this case is 2.61%. This

Table 6 Worksheet for Calculation of Recovery of Investment in Duration Years.

Coupon date	Coupon	TTM	Coupon investment compound value	
27-Aug-10	25.15	4	27.88025489	
27-Feb-11	25.15	3.5	27.52338823	
27-Aug-11	25.15	3	27.17108945	
27-Feb-12	25.15	2.5	26.82330009	
27-Aug-12	25.15	2	26.47996243	
27-Feb-13	25.15	1.5	26.14101948	
27-Aug-13	25.15	1	25.806415	
27-Feb-14	25.15	0.5	25.47609345	
27-Aug-14	1025.15	0	1025.15	
			1238.451523	Sum
		Clean Price	109.9832802	on 5/4/2010
		AI	16.32421296	
		Total future cash flow	1364.759016	
		PV	1238.268717	
		Investment	1118.888078	
		Surplus	119.3806394	

assumption is refuted on many grounds, e.g. it denies risk premium, term premium, etc. Nevertheless D is a popular measure of risk in fixed-income products.

The third use of D is for academicians, modelers and economists. D is defined as the weighted average TTM, the weights being the proportions of the PVs of the individual cash flows of different periods in the total PV, i.e. price. Each cash flow here is treated as redemption of a ZC having a TTM equal to the length of the time period from the purchase of the bond to the occurrence of the cash flow; the YTM of the above ZC is the same as the discount rate of the bond. A distant cash flow, e.g. the coupon after five SA periods is less important than the coupon after two SA periods since money is locked for a shorter TTM in the latter case and hence entails less loss than the former if the market yield rises right after acquisition of the bond. This logic theoretically applies to all non-ZC investments where cash flows are known or already estimated, e.g. loans and project finance. An example is given in the worksheet in Table 7.

Practitioners and regulators find the modified duration (MD) in lieu of duration more useful because of the absence of the factor $1/(1 + r)$; the formula for MD is

$$MD = -\frac{\frac{\Delta P}{P}}{\Delta y}$$

Table 7 Calculation of Duration with Weighted Average Formula.

Column 1 Date of Coupon	Column 2 TTM	Column 3 Cash Flow (€)	Column 4 PV (€)	Column 5 weight (w)	Column 2 × Column 5 TTM*w
27-Aug-10	1	25.15	24.82602043	0.022525667	0.022525667
27-Feb-11	2	25.15	24.50621434	0.022235494	0.044470989
27-Aug-11	3	25.15	24.19052795	0.021949059	0.065847177
27-Feb-12	4	25.15	23.87890819	0.021666314	0.086665255
27-Aug-12	5	25.15	23.57130269	0.021387211	0.106936053
27-Feb-13	6	25.15	23.26765973	0.021111703	0.126670217
27-Aug-13	7	25.15	22.96792827	0.020839744	0.145878209
27-Feb-14	8	25.15	22.67205792	0.020571289	0.164570311
27-Aug-14	9	1025.15	912.2407913	0.827713519	7.449421671
		Clean price (Sum)	1102.121411	1	8.212985549

Note: Here D is 8.2 SA years or 4.1 years. The clean price is manually calculated to be 1102.12 per 100 face value, but in XLS applying the price formula gives a price of 109.13 and hence the duration is less in the XLS duration formula. The difference between the results is because of differences in rounding.

MD is believed by some practitioners to give a more accurate prediction in cases where (i) interests are received in compound rate and (ii) there is robust yield shock.

Necessity of Modified Duration

Sound understanding of valuation, sensitivity analysis, etc., of investment products call for a knowledge of quantitative techniques, a reasonably high level of numerical ability and conversancy with XLS-based software. A sizeable chunk of employees of banks and FIs in the emerging economies by and large lack the above expertise. It is not easier to introduce them to the concept of D as the first derivative of the price-yield equation; rather, it is easier to make them understand the concept of MD as a formula for calculating price shock: Price shock = MD × pre-yield shock price × yield shock, or technically $\Delta P = MD * P * \Delta y$ compared to the formula for D where yield shock is represented by $\Delta y/(1 + y)$.

Both D and MD work for option-free bonds. For an option-embedded bond, the sensitivity measure is effective duration (ED) because of a different price-yield relationship. For a callable bond, when reference rates fall, in order to save interest loss, the issuer can call back the bond and this feature arrests the price hike so that the price-yield curve looks like Fig. 4. The call option imposes a cap on the price of a callable bond.

In the case of a putable bond, when reference rates rise, in order to save interest loss, the buyer can ask for redemption so that the fall in price is restricted and the price yield curve looks like Fig. 5.

The put option sets a floor price for a putable bond.

This is the reason why a different measure of sensitivity is suggested:

$$ED = \frac{P_- - P_+}{2P_0 \Delta_y}$$

Here P_- is the new price after a positive yield shock, e.g. 1%, whereas P_+ is the new price after a negative yield shock of the same absolute magnitude (1%) and P_0 is the initial price.

If we assume our bond is callable, then $P_- = 113.188$, $P_+ = 105.24$, $P_0 = 109.129$ at the initial $y = 2.61\%$. The worksheet looks like Table 8 and Table 9.

Equity Beta (β)

The sensitivity of a stock to changes in the stock index is measured as β. It is the slope coefficient of regression of the return on a share on the

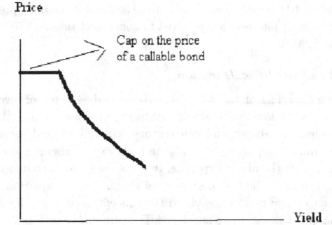

Fig. 4   Price-Yield Relationship of a Callable Bond.

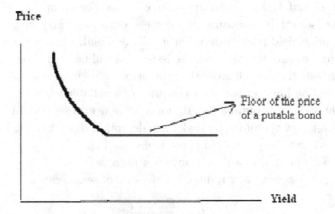

Fig. 5   Price-Yield Relationship of a Putable Bond.

return of the relevant index where the intercept is interpreted as a risk-free
rate and denoted by r_f. Let us consider the stock FCCY (1st Constitution
Bancorp) listed on NASDAQ. If we run a regression of FCCY's average
annual return for the year t on the average annual return of the NASDAQ
Composite Index for the year t based on monthly data for 10 years from
June 2000 to May 2010, the slope coefficient is 25%. The regression equation
is $r_{\text{FCCY}(t)} = r_f + \beta r_{\text{NASDAQ}(t)} + \varepsilon = 25\%\ r_{\text{NASDAQ}}$, since the risk-free
rate is zero in the US (perhaps following the American belief "no risk,
no gain") unlike in India where the risk-free rate varies between 11% and

Table 8 Price Before Yield Shock.

DoS	26-Jun-10
DoM	25-Jun-14
Rate	5.03%
Yield	2.61%
Redemption	100
Frequency	2
Price	109.1292987

Table 9 Price After Upward Yield Shock.

DoS	26-Jun-10
DoM	25-Jun-14
Rate	5.03%
Yield	3.61%
Redemption	100
Frequency	2
Price	105.2415679
DoS	26-Jun-10
DoM	25-Jun-14
Rate	5.03%
Yield	1.61%
Redemption	100
Frequency	2
Price	113.1885208

Now $ED = 4.336$.

4% depending on the TTM. Here ε is interpreted as the random error having a standard normal distribution with the same variance for every period t; it represents the fluctuation of $r_{\text{FCCY}(t)}$ around the regression line and cancels out on average. The risk-free rate means the YTM of the products issued by the sovereign. Bonds and stocks issued by government undertaking corporations, bonds issued by government and deposits in public sector banks are considered to be risk-free products. Graphically the above regression is given Fig. 6.

The above linear relationship between return on any security x and return on market portfolio m can be generalized and expressed as $r_x = \alpha + \beta r_m$. This is called the security characteristic line. The most popular version of the linear relationship involving β is CAPM.

The CAPM (capital asset pricing model) is $E(r_x) = r_x + \beta[E(r_m) - r_x]$, where E is to be interpreted as "weighted average of", the probabilities of

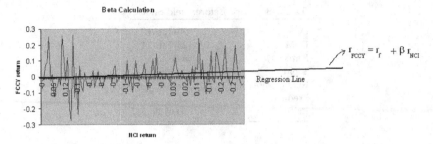

Fig. 6   Beta Calculation in CAPM.

occurrence of different numerical values of the return being the weights here.

Portfolio return is the weighted average return of individual stocks, the weights being the proportions of individual stocks in the portfolio. The β of a portfolio is the slope coefficient of regression of portfolio return on the relevant index return.

4. PROBLEM OF AGGREGATION AND EMERGENCE OF VALUE-AT-RISK

The Investment portfolio of a bank or an FI consists of heterogeneous categories of assets like shares and bonds with different measures of risk. So it is difficult to obtain the measure of risk of the aggregate portfolio. Further, existing measures of risk like D, MD and β do not provide the probability (denoted by p) of occurrence of the risk event. In this circumstance a different measure of risk of the aggregate portfolio with a certain p has been devised by JP Morgan. It is called value-at-Risk (VaR).

5. DEFINITION AND MEASURE OF VaR

VaR is defined as the maximum loss on investment during a particular period like a day or a month with a particular p. It is an improvement over other risk measures in the sense that it applies to all categories of investment products and predicts the maximum loss with a p value of 95% or 99% and accordingly enables the investor make loss provisions in advance.

The underlying assumption in VaR calculation is that daily portfolio returns follow an independent and identical normal distribution (ND) with an average of zero and a non-zero SD. This assumption is criticized on the grounds that in real life the probability density of return follows some other distributions than ND like beta.

VaR can be measured using three methods: (i) the delta normal method, (ii) the simulation method and (iii) the historical method.

Delta Normal Method

The delta normal method is based on the concept of standard normal distribution (SND). It assumes that the asset markets are perfect and the daily returns on every €1 investment follow an independent and identical SND. In this method the lower limits of 95% or 99% confidence intervals, i.e. symmetric p area under the SN curve, are taken as the measure of maximum daily loss on €1 investment and for every 1% SD. For 99% p, the maximum loss amount is €2.32; for 95% p it is €1.64. Hence for an MTM portfolio €100 and an SD of 2%, the 99% daily loss is €2.32*100*2%. It is recommended by regulators all over the world to take at least the last 1,000 days' return data for the investment portfolio starting from the most recent past (i.e. the business day preceding the day of calculation of VaR) for the purpose of computing the maximum probable loss for today. But this method is not popular among practitioners, particularly those in emerging economies, mainly because this method needs knowledge of statistics and because SD is dependent on change in scale, i.e. the day the entire stock market crashes, the SD value becomes smaller, representing less market risk, which is wrong.

This method does not need any software for calculating VaR. The XLS formula for the average is "=average(number, number 2, ...)", for SD is "=stdev(number, number 2, ...)" and for variance is "=var(number, number 2, ...)". The reader should distinguish between "var" and "VaR". The former or "VAR" is short for "variance" whereas the latter is short for "value-at-risk".

Simulation Method

This method is useful for those institutions which are suffering from lack of an adequate database and also those which have adequate databases but are interested in building alternative scenarios by creating artificial samples with the same p distribution parameters and then comparing VaR figures. This method is also not popular among practitioners in emerging economies because it requires knowledge of statistics.

It should be noted at this stage that VaR calculation following different methods yields different results from the same sample. If there is a sample size of 1,000 available, there is no need for the simulation method except for back testing. In VaR calculation the simulation method is used if the sample size is below 1,000. It is necessary to back test the VaR calculated following a particular method with the help of simulated samples. Simulated samples mean samples generated by the random number generation tool in XLS by feeding the calculated average and SD from the existing real life sample into the ND menu.

Historical Method

This is the most popular method because it does not require knowledge of statistics or the use of statistical software. Anybody with high school-level numerical ability can use this method after a short guidance. In this method the return figures are arranged in ascending order and then the 0.5 percentile return figure is chosen as the daily VaR on €1 investment.

In order to illustrate the above methods we have considered a USD portfolio consisting of 60% investment in iShares DJ Asia/Pacific Select Dividend 30 and 40% investment in iShares FTSE/Xinhua China 25 for the period from June 22, 2006 to July 15, 2010. The length of the period is chosen in a way to obtain exactly 1,000 daily portfolio return figures. Once we have the sample, we can calculate the portfolio VaR as on July 16, 2010. To make it simple, suppose the MTM portfolio is valued at $10 billion. The SD of return is 1.99%. The delta normal 99% daily VaR is $2.32*1.99%*10 billion = $46,166,057 = $46.17 million.

In order to obtain the historical VaR we arrange the return figures in ascending order and locate the 99th percentile between the fifth and sixth figures starting from the minimum return. It is 1.54%. Now the portfolio VaR is $1.54%*10 = $15.4 million.

Now let us back test the above results with simulation in XLS. The sample has a mean of 0.04% and a SD of 1.99%. Next we generate an artificial sample with XLS and locate the historical VaR after arranging the sample in ascending order. It comes up to 51.7 million. It may be different in another simulated (i.e. artificially generated in XLS using the ND tool of random number generation) sample. One approach is to run the simulation 10,000 times and select the maximum VaR. Selecting the average VaR is another approach because providing capital equivalent to the maximum size of the simulated VaRs has a huge opportunity cost.

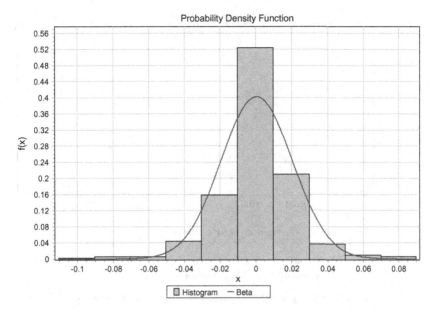

Fig. 7 Probability Density Function of Daily Returns.

Finally we fit the distribution of the real sample in a fitting and simulating software, e.g. EasyFit of MathWave Technologies or BestFit of Palisade Corporation. We get a beta distribution with parameters $\alpha_1 = 2430.7$, $\alpha_2 = 1830.9$, $a = -1.4956$, $b = 1.1273$. The graph is given in Fig. 7.

6. NEED FOR EXTREME TAIL LOSSES (ETL)

What we saw above is that the central assumption of a normal p distribution in the VaR model hardly works in real life. It may follow the Cauchy distribution with fat tails. A second criticism of VaR is that prediction of loss in the left tail of the ND curve beyond the lower limit of 99% confidence interval remains unknown, though losses may be severe in an extremely stressed scenario. Hence it is suggested to calculate the ETL. It is an average of the losses in the tail area of the ND curve between 99.5% and 100%. This area may be sliced into 5, 10, 20 or more parts as per the wisdom of the analyst. For example, we sliced it into five parts, 99.6%, 99.7%, 99.8%, 99.9% and 100%, and then calculate the VaR for each of these and divide the sum of the VaRs by five.

The concept is explained in Fig. 8.

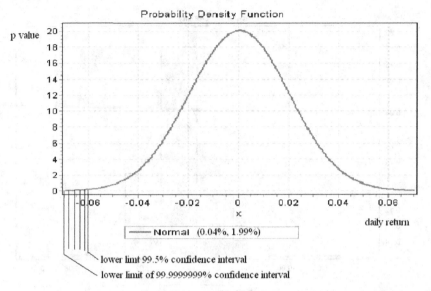

Fig. 8   Slicing of Left Tail Area into Five Equal Sub-Areas.

Table 10   Slicing of Left Tail Area into
Five Equal Sub-Areas.

p	=normsinv(p)	VaR ($)
99.60%	2.65207338	52776260.3
99.70%	2.74778741	54680969.4
99.80%	2.87817212	57275625.1
99.90%	3.09025258	61496026.4
100.00%	7.93597294	157925861
	Sum	384154743
	Average	76830948.5

Table 11

p	=normsinv(p)	VaR ($)
99.55%	2.61205686	51979931.6
99.60%	2.65207338	52776260.3
99.65%	2.69684891	53667293.2
99.70%	2.74778741	54680969.4
99.75%	2.80704162	55860128.2
99.80%	2.87817212	57275625.1
99.85%	2.96775204	59058265.5
99.90%	3.09025258	61496026.4
99.95%	3.29055993	65482142.6
100.00%	7.93597294	157925861
	Average	67020250.4

It is to be noted that the lower limit of the 100% confidence interval does not make any statistical sense and hence in lieu of 100%, we take 99.99999999999%. The XLS formula "=normsinv(p)" gives the lower limit value with the p value inserted. The XLS worksheet is given in Table 10.

The ETL measure comes up to $76.8 million.

For 10 slices of the aforesaid tail the worksheet looks like Table 11.

The ETL measure comes up to $67 million, much less than the previous one. Thus, the larger the number of slices, the smaller the ETL magnitude.

REFERENCES

Allen L., Boudoukh, J. and Saunders, A. (2004). *Understanding Market, Credit and Operational Risk: The Value at Risk Approach*, Malden, MA: Blackwell, Chapters 2 and 3.

Basel Committee of Banking Supervision (1995). An Internal Model-Based Approach to Market Risk Capital Requirements, available at http://www.bis.org/publ/bcbs17.htm.

Choudhry, M. (2004). *Advanced Fixed Income Analysis*, Oxford: Elsevier Butterworth-Heinemann, Chapter 10.

Cvitanic, J. and Zepatero F. (2004). *Introduction to the Economics and Mathematics of Financial Markets*, Cambridge: MIT Press, Chapter 5.

Damodaran, A. (2002). *Investment Valuation*, New York: Jon Wiley & Sons, Chapter 4.

Holton, G.A. (2003). *Value at Risk Theory and Practice*, California: Academic Press, Chapter 1.

Hull, J.C. (2009). *Options, Futures and Other Derivatives*, Singapore: Pearson Education, Chapters 4 and 20.

Jorion, P. (2007a). *Financial Risk Manager Handbook*, New Jersey: John Wiley & Sons, Chapters 2, 10 and 11.

Jorion, P. (2007b). *Value at Risk*, New York: McGraw-Hill, Parts I, II and III.

Marrison, C. (2002). *The Fundamentals of Risk Measurement*, New York: McGraw-Hill, Chapters 4 and 6.

Moix P.V. (2001). *The Measurement of Market Risk*, Berlin: SpringerVerlag, Chapters 2 and 4.

Robb, J.A. (2008). Fat-Tailed Distribution, available at http://www.fattails.ca/distribution.html.

Saunders, A. and Cornett M.M. (2006). *Financial Institutions Management: A Risk Management Approach*, New York: McGraw-Hill Irwin, Chapters 8, 9, 10, 11, 15, 17.

Steven, A. (2003). *Financial Risk Management*, New Jersey: John Wiley & Sons, Chapter 5.

Chapter 3

IS IT ALL ABOUT DISCLOSURE? REGULATING STRUCTURED FINANCIAL PRODUCTS AFTER THE LEHMAN BROTHERS MINIBONDS SAGA[*]

Wei Shen

1. INTRODUCTION

Although it has been almost three years since the collapse of Lehman Brothers Holdings Inc. (LBHI) in September 2008, shockwaves from its demise are still reverberating through the world of retail structured products in Asia. The sudden collapse of the Lehman Brothers Group, one of the world's foremost banks trading in credit and interest rate products and securities, was the most influential and direct incident of the financial tsunami causing not only distress among millions of local and international investors but also widespread concerns in the society particularly as to the financial impact on individual investors of minibonds. In Hong Kong, more than 43,700 individual investors bought approximately HK$20 billion worth of Lehman minibonds,[1] and suffered losses of billions of dollars, and regulators such as the Hong Kong Monetary Authority (HKMA), Hong Kong's *de facto* central bank, received more than 21,000 complaints in 2008 alone relating to the mis-selling of minibonds[2] and referred some cases

[*]The author wishes to thank Mr Gao Pengcheng for his comments on an earlier draft of this article.
[1]SFC estimate, available at http://www.invested.hk/invested/en/html/section/products/structured/unlist_cls.html.
[2]Yam, J. (2008), "Chief Executive's Statement" in *HKMA Annual Report 2008*, pp. 9–10. By 18 February 2011, investigation into 99% complaints have been completed and 14,377 complaints were settled through settlement agreements. HKMA Progress of the HKMA's

involving complaints of alleged mis-selling to the Securities and Futures Commission (SFC), the independent statutory body in charge of regulating Hong Kong's securities market. The minibonds crisis also sparked political turmoil and triggered a large number of mass protests and demonstrations in Hong Kong.

This article will review the Lehman minibonds saga from both the legal and policy perspectives. The rest of this article is structured as follows: Section 2 analyses the structure, nature and inherent risks of the minibonds. The claimed mis-selling practice is discussed in Section 3 by looking into the statutory and common law rules. Lack of full disclosure is diagnosed as the main cause of the Lehman minibonds saga. In Section 4, however, it will be pointed out that disclosure is not the sole regulatory flaw attributable to the minibonds saga. Dealing with complexity, weaknesses of credit ratings and artificial freedom of contract in the context of complicated financial markets are all important in improving the regulatory regime and financial market. A preliminary conclusion follows in Section 5.

2. WHAT ARE LEHMAN MINIBONDS? STRUCTURE, NATURE AND INHERENT RISKS

The term "minibonds" is somewhat misleading for at least some investors. Minibonds are not corporate bonds linked to the issuing bank or a blue-chip company's equity. Nor do they perform like conventional bonds. Instead, they are highly complex and high-risk structured derivative products tied to an underlying security, i.e., a credit of certain specified reference entities, traded in specialized markets. The term "mini" refers to the smaller minimum denominations, as low as US$5,000 in certain cases. These bonds were sold so that they would be affordable to retail investors. Lehman minibonds are made up of complicated structured derivatives, with embedded leverage to increase the yield of the instruments. Due to their complexity, minibonds, like other structured financial products, are sold to institutional or sophisticated investors in many jurisdictions as credit-linked notes. However, minibonds were distributed over-the-counter as retail products to retail or lay investors in Hong Kong in 2003 when the SFC

Investigation in Lehman Brothers-related Cases, http://www.info.gov.hk/hkma/eng/press/2011/20110218e3-index.htm.

relaxed certain prospectus rules for unlisted securities in February 2003[3] and other jurisdictions in Asia such as Singapore, Taiwan and Macau. The sale of minibonds was successful and US$4.6 billion in claims were issued by 19 intermediaries including bank and securities dealer distributors, some of them prominent players, with Lehman being the most successful one with a 35% market share.

In Hong Kong, minibonds linked to the insolvent US investment bank Lehman Brothers Holdings Inc. were issued by Pacific International Finance (PIF), a special purpose investment vehicle incorporated in the Cayman Islands, which was formed for Lehman's use and subject to no restrictions on borrowing.[4] As indicated by the SFC on its website, a total of 36 series of minibonds were issued by PIF in Hong Kong.

Lehman Brothers Commercial Corporation Asia, acting as the arranger, arranged for the minibonds issued by PIF to be distributed by the retail banks to retail investors in Hong Kong. For instance, the coordinating distributor for Minibond Series 36 was Sun Hung Kai Investment Services Ltd. and the minibonds were distributed by KGI Asia, Chong Hing Bank and Sun Hung Kai Investment Services Ltd. The holders of the minibonds were entitled to receive a coupon payment on a periodic basis.[5] Taking Minibond Series 36 as an example, the investors would receive a "coupon" at a rate of 5.5% in exchange for "taking the risk that any one of seven companies would default on their reference debts."[6] The arranger selected some US dollar-denominated underlying assets, which were purchased by PIF with the proceeds of sale as the collateral. These assets, held by HSBC Hong Kong as a trustee, included tranches of collateralized debt obligations (CDOs),[7] various securities such as liquidity funds or money market funds,[8]

---

[3]HKMA (2008), "Report of the Hong Kong Monetary Authority on Issues Concerning the Distribution of Structured Products Connected to Lehman Group Companies," 31 December, p. 1.

[4]Minibonds prospectuses and other source documents posted SFC's website.

[5]When minibonds were sold to retail investors, "gifts" of inexpensive consumer products or supermarket coupons were also given to the investors.

[6]Webb, D. (2008), "Lessons from Lehman Minibonds," available at http://www.webb-site.com/articles/lehmanlessons.asp, 20 October.

[7]CDOs are debt securities collateralized by conventional securities issued by named reference entities, and use credit default swaps to mimic the behaviour of the collateral pool, which is a mixed pool of mortgage loans and/or other income-generating assets owned by an SPV. Schwarcz, S. (2008), "Protecting Financial Markets: Lessons from the Subprime Mortgage Meltdown," *Minnesota Law Review*, 93(2):4–5.

[8]See the section "Information about the Underlying Securities" in the issue prospectus for Octave Notes Series 12 minibonds.

and other asset-backed securities from Lehman with credit risks matching the reference entities.[9]

The collateral for each minibond series is kept separately by a custodian and provides security for the noteholders' claims, equalling the minibond issue amount at inception.[10] The collateral varies between the series. Some of them are backed by debt obligations of Lehman Brothers while others are backed by CDOs, which can be backed by further collateral such as bonds of a single financial institution or a money market fund. The CDOs are not only collateral but also synthetic securities, similar in intent, as they may include further swap arrangements with Lehman Brothers, which are subject to termination due to the filing of petition. Where Lehman Brothers is owed a payment on termination of the swap arrangements, some of the proceeds of the collateral may be paid to Lehman Brothers. In this case, Lehman Brothers or its liquidator has no other right to take the collateral.

The minibonds were embedded with a credit default swap (CDS).[11] PIF entered into an interest rate or interest basis swap agreement with Lehman Brothers Special Financing Inc. (LBSF), a wholly owned subsidiary of Lehman Brothers Inc., as a swap counterparty.[12] The function of the swap is to create a single revenue stream matching the minibond coupon dates. PIF would pay LBSF a sum equal to the interest and other income it received

---

[9]Prior to the bursting of the US housing bubble, CDOs and other parts of the capital markets provided more than half the credit to US consumers and businesses, and a large amount in Europe too. See Van Duyn, A. "SEC Charges Reveal More On Practices In Structured Finance," *Financial Times*, 24 June 2010, pp. 25.

[10]The collateral may be shared by the holders of different tranches of that minibond series.

[11]In a typical CDS, a credit seller, the first party, agrees to assume the credit risk of certain debt obligations of a specified borrower or other obligor in exchange for a fee from the credit buyer, the second party. In the case that a "credit event", i.e. default or bankruptcy, occurs in respect of the obligor, the credit seller will pay the credit buyer an amount calculated in reference to the post-default value of the debt obligations. Alternatively, the credit seller may buy the debt obligations for their full face value from the credit buyer. For details, see Schwarcz, S. (3rd ed. 2002 & Supp. 2006), *Structured Finance: A Guide to the Principles of Asset Securitization*, New York: Practicing Law Institute, §10:3.1, pp. 10–16. In practice, "naked" CDSs are often regarded as a kind of insurance policy against a bond defaulting, which has been blamed by regulators for exacerbating the financial crisis, e.g., more recently, the sovereign bonds crisis in some EU member states. See Peel, Q., Masters, B., Jones, S. and van Duyn, A. (2010), "Call For Derivatives Rule Reform," *Financial Times*, 11 March 2010, pp. 2.

[12]As to how these swaps worked, the minibonds prospectus often contained a section "Information about the Swap Arrangements for the Notes" explaining the swap arrangements, e.g. p. 67 of the issue prospectus for Octave Notes Series 12 minibonds.

for the collateral. In return, PIF would receive from LBSF fixed payments equal in aggregate to the interest due on the minibonds.[13] Lehman Brothers Holdings, as the swap guarantor, guaranteed the obligations of LBSF under the swap agreement.[14] In this sense, PIF, based on the CDS, leveraged its collateral by selling credit protection to Lehman, and received fees to enhance the revenue available to service the notes. Through the CDS, the most common form of credit derivative used to acquire or protect credit risks, "minibonds investors were putting up cash to underwrite compound credit default swaps."[15]

Payment of the principal amount on the minibonds was linked to the performance of certain "reference entities" identified in the relevant prospectus. The reference entities differed from series to series. Earlier series were linked to one entity or 150 companies while more recent issues had between six and eight reference names.[16] The return on each issue is a function of the credit standing of specified borrowers. According to the swap agreement, if any of the reference entities suffered certain "credit events" such as bankruptcy, involuntary reorganization, failure to make payment on specified indebtedness or restructuring of specified indebtedness, PIF would be obliged to deliver all of the collateral to LBSF in return for the payment by LBSF to PIF of the "credit event redemption amount", which would be used to compensate the minibond holders for any shortfall in recovering the debt from the reference entity. In this sense, a swap is similar to an insurance contract in which the buyer pays a premium to the insurer in return for compensation upon the occurrence of the event insured against, i.e. the credit risk of the reference entity. The credit event redemption amount was calculated on the basis of the market value of the reference entity's obligations, depending on the non-occurrence of specified events.[17]

---

[13]For example, the swap arrangement includes credit default swaps to enhance the interest payable under Minibond Series 36; see the section "Information about us and how Our Notes are Secured" on pp. 19–21 of the issue prospectus.

[14]Lehman Brothers Holdings was also the guarantor of the collateral for some early series of minibonds.

[15]A credit default swap seller takes on the risk of the reference entity and may shift the risk by repackaging the swap into minibonds and selling the same to the lay investors.

[16]For example, Octave Notes Series 12 has eight reference entities including the PRC, Standard Chartered Bank, DBS Bank, Oversea-Chinese Banking Corporation, HSBC Bank, Swire Pacific, MTR Corporation and Lehman itself. Minibond Series 36 is credit-linked to seven reference entities: CLP Power Hong Kong, CNOOC, DBS Bank, HSBC Bank, Hutchison Whampoa, MTR Corporation and Standard Chartered Bank.

[17]The specified events include a company or sovereign credit event, a mandatory redemption event or an issuer event of default. See the section "Risk Factors" in

The amount can be adjusted based on the termination value of the other components of the swap agreement and the market value of the collateral.

As soon as any of the reference entities suffered a credit event, the notes would be redeemed immediately at a discount to their face value, and the holders of the minibonds would lose a portion of their principal amount. This loss would be greater if LBSF were owed any amount upon termination of the swap agreement or if the market value of the collateral were less than its stated principal amount. Upon a redemption event, Lehman would exercise a call option to redeem the notes early without compensating the holder for reinvestment losses. In addition, the minibonds would cease to accrue interest upon occurrence of the credit event, but the amount received by the issuer from LBSF would not be payable to the holders of the minibonds until the minibonds' stated maturity date. This means that the investor recovers much less of his investment if the reference entity defaults.

The stated maturity date was typically three to six years after the issue date. If no reference entity suffered a credit event before the stated maturity date, and no other redemption event occurred, the holders of the minibonds would be entitled to receive a payment on the maturity date equal to the liquidation value of the collateral. An event of default on an asset included in the collateral, or a reduction of the principal amount of an asset in accordance with its terms, a feature common to many asset-backed securities, could result in a partial redemption of the minibonds, at a loss to the holder of the minibonds. Subsequently, a default by one entity at the centre of a tangled web of derivative contracts could trigger a failure of the entire financial system.

All minibond issues contained a condition that Lehman's parent remained solvent. The bankruptcy of a counterparty or guarantor under a CDS can trigger the termination of outstanding swap contracts. Once swaps were terminated, the minibonds were subject to mandatory redemption even if reference entities did not suffer any credit event, and investors would suffer a substantial loss, which explains how the collapse of Lehman Brothers (which may not be one of the reference entities) made investors unable to

---

the issue prospectus for Octave Notes Series 12 minibonds, pp. 76–85. A company or sovereign credit event means the occurrence of one of the following events with respect to a company and its successors: bankruptcy, failure to pay, restructuring; with respect to the sovereign entity and its successors: failure to pay, restructuring, repudiation/moratorium. *Ibid.*, p. 35.

fully redeem their investment.[18] PIF had a theoretical choice to terminate the swap contracts or seek replacement counterparties.[19] Prolonging the swaps avoids a mandatory sale of collateral and may improve recovery in the long run but may be infeasible due to a falling market. Termination forces a sale of collateral, leaving minimal proceeds for distribution to minibond holders net of PIF payments due to Lehman and noteholder trustees.

Lehman Brothers Holdings Inc., the Lehman Brothers Group's listed parent, and LBSF filed a petition under Chapter 11 of the US Bankruptcy Code with the US Bankruptcy Court of the Southern District of New York on September 15 and October 3, 2008 respectively. Eight Lehman companies have been put into liquidation in Hong Kong, including Lehman Brothers Asia Limited.[20] When the petition was filed, Lehman Brothers was the fourth-largest US investment bank with a history of over 150 years and a perennial credit rating of A or above. No one would have foreseen that a bank of this standing would collapse overnight. The collapse of the Lehman Brothers Group is truly one of the most unpredictable and unfortunate consequences of the global financial tsunami.

The filing of a bankruptcy petition constituted an event of default under swaps.[21] After the termination of the swap arrangements, the minibonds would become subject to early redemption unless the trustee for the minibonds directs otherwise, and the collateral would be sold in the market. The amount payable to the holders of the minibonds upon early redemption would equal the liquidation proceeds of the collateral "adjusted to take account of any payment which is due to, or due from, LBSF or PIF on termination of the swap arrangements and for the costs, fees and expenses of making such a sale."[22] The amount of the proceeds depends on such factors as the current market value of the collateral underlying the particular series

---

[18]The issue prospectus of Minibond Series 36 highlighted on p. 22 this reason, (saying that "[the issuer] has the right to terminate the swap agreement if...that swap counterparty or Lehman Brothers Holdings Inc. suffers specified insolvency-related events...").

[19]Replacement of counterparties to sustain swaps, as a choice, was discussed in relation to Singapore minibonds. This was very challenging to implement due to Lehman's liquidation filing, leaving little substance in the institution, and needed strong state support.

[20]HKMA, *supra* note 3, p. 7.

[21]The filing by Lehman of a petition under Chapter 11 of the US Bankruptcy Code constitutes a company credit event, for instance, under the issue prospectus for Octave Notes Series 12 minibonds.

[22]The issue prospectus for Octave Notes Series 12 minibonds, pp. 49–63. Page 2 of the issue prospectus for Minibond Series 36 explained the way to calculate the termination payment:

of minibonds.[23] Lehman Brothers and its subsidiaries have no control over the early redemption of the minibonds of a particular series and the sale of collateral, termination of swap arrangements and eventual distribution of proceeds to holders. When LBHI went bankrupt, the value of minibonds was significantly less than their principal amount. As a result, a lot of retail investors lost all or a significant portion of their investment. This marked the start of the minibond saga in Hong Kong.

Derivatives often connote speculation and risky investment. Minibonds are no exception. Given the structure of minibonds as outlined above, a retail investor is actually exposed to multiple risks: the credit quality of the reference entities, the credit quality of LBSF as a swap counterparty, interest rate risk, liquidity risk, currency exchange rate risk, and the risk that the underlying collateral may fall in value and so on. Even if no reference entity has suffered a credit event, upon termination of the swap agreement, for example, due to the insolvency of LBSF, a holder of minibonds would be exposed to the credit risk of LBSF to the extent that any amount was payable by LBSF, and would also be exposed to the market value of the collateral, which would need to be sold to redeem the minibonds. Much of the collateral, like that of Minibond Series 36, reportedly consists of CDOs, other asset-backed securities or other obligations that are worth far less than their original principal amounts. Holders of the minibonds would eventually be exposed to the decline in the market value of the collateral at maturity or upon an earlier redemption event even if Lehman Brothers Holdings and its subsidiaries had remained solvent. In a practical sense, minibonds are more like bonds issued by the

---

The amount of any termination payment will be based on the cost of entering into a swap transaction with the same terms and conditions that would have the effect of preserving the economic equivalent of the swap agreement. A termination payment could be a substantial amount. For example, exchange rates or interest rates may change so that when the termination amount is calculated it would be expensive to enter into swap arrangements at that time which give the parties the same cashflows as under the swap arrangements which we agreed at the time we issue our Notes.

Also see a leaflet issued by Lehman Brothers Asia Ltd. dated 17 September 2008 on the SFC website.

[23] From an economic perspective, the value of the deal depends on three complex characteristics of the underlying assets pool: the rate at which borrowers prepay (redeem their mortgage early); their propensity to default; and the loss severity (the proportion of the debt that cannot be recovered if a borrower defaults).

reference entity together with the risk attached thereto. However, unlike a bond, the minibond holders are subject to the operational risk of the issuer, an SPV incorporated solely for the purpose of issuing minibonds, and the trustee, holding no assets other than its issued capital and the assets which back the minibonds in question. Indeed, the minibonds are simply a conduit for the coupon payments between the swap counterparty and the investors.

3. MIS-SELLING PRACTICES UNDER STATUTORY AND COMMON LAW RULES

Thousands of Lehman minibond holders in Hong Kong claimed that they had bought the minibonds under the conception or misconception that minibonds were conservative and low-risk investment products, and that the distributing banks or brokers had misled or deceived retail investors into investing in minibonds.

Regulatory Framework and Statutory Rules

Under Hong Kong law, the sale of risky products such as Lehman minibonds by a salesperson of a financial institution does not need to be approved either by the SFC or HKMA so long as this salesperson's employer is registered with the SFC at the corporate level.[24] As a matter of fact, none of Lehman's arms has held a Hong Kong banking license, and Lehman's subsidiaries were licensed by the SFC to engage in corporate finance and securities advisory, and securities and futures dealing.[25] In selling products to customers, distributing banks and brokers need to abide by the SFC Code of Conduct which requires them to consider the suitability of the investment for their clients. In this regard, a salesperson must seek information from his client concerning the client's financial situation, investment experience and investment objectives relevant to the provided products or services. The intermediaries also need to make sure that the client understands the nature and risks of the products and has sufficient net worth to assume the risks and bear potential losses arising from the trading of products. Disclosure of risks in the form of warning statements must be made and the recommendation to or solicitation of the client must be reasonable in

---

[24] A salesperson at a brokerage must be licensed with the SFC at the individual level.
[25] The SFC is the regulator bearing the duty to "maintain the status of Hong Kong as a competitive international financial centre" and to supervise the investment selling activities of brokers.

all circumstances. These rules apply to all intermediaries, banks and non-banks selling minibonds to the retail public in Hong Kong. Failure to abide by these rules may constitute mis-selling.

The minibonds prospectus was authorized by the SFC under the Companies Ordinance, some sections of which are applicable to debentures. The basic requirement is that full disclosure of the products be made in the prospectus concerning the debenture except some exempted circumstances under which the disclosure requirement is not strictly implemented by the SFC under the Companies Ordinance.[26] On its face, the Companies Ordinance takes a disclosure-based approach, which is different from the merit-based regulations. Accordingly, the SFC is not obliged to consider the suitability of the product for the investors. As a matter of fact, each series of minibonds received the SFC's exemptions from the Companies Ordinance prospectus requirements, providing that the distributor had made buyers confirm they had read and understood the issue and program prospectuses in either English or Chinese. The similar "umbrella" programmes cover most concessions granted to many issues, some of which were based on the negotiations between arrangers and the SFC. The SFC prospectus exemptions related in all cases to the information on Lehman.

However, the way the SFC characterized and dealt with minibonds is highly questionable. As minibonds were not bonds or debentures, the SFC could have characterized minibonds as investment products. In this case, the sale of minibonds falls in the regulatory scope of the Securities and Futures Ordinance. The SFC might have exercised its discretion to examine the suitability and merits of the selling of minibonds by the distributing banks or by brokers to retail investors. Accordingly, the SFC could have required the modification of the products and advertisement materials. Similarly, the HKMA appears to have failed to properly supervise the selling practices of the banks and brokers.[27]

The SFC categorized mis-selling into two classes.[28] First, an investor may be given materially wrong information about a financial product which leads the investor to make an investment decision that he would not have made if the correct information had been provided. The second type of mis-selling occurs when an investor ends up investing in a product that is

---

[26]Johnstone, S. (2009), "Hong Kong Minibonds Scandal: Regulator Accountability," *International Financial Law Review*, 28(5): 35–38.

[27]The Hong Kong Monetary Authority is responsible for monitoring the investment selling activities of banks in accordance with the SFC's Code of Conduct.

[28]The SFC's *Enforcement Reporter* (Issue 60), October 2008.

not suitable given his financial position, investment objectives, expectations and risk tolerance level.

Common Law Rules

Can Lehman minibond holders recover damages for the alleged mis-selling of minibonds? The duty of care imposed on banks giving advice to potential customers has been established for half a century since the case *Woods* v. *Martins Bank Ltd.* (1959)[29] and approved by the House of Lords in *Hedley Byrne & Co. Ltd.* v. *Heller & Partners Ltd.* (1964).[30] In Hong Kong, the leading authority is the Court of Appeal case of *Susan Field* v. *Barber Asia Ltd.* (2003).[31]

Field was an inexperienced investor and made this known to her financial advisor, Barber Asia, in the first place, and said she wanted to invest her savings in a conservative way. Barber Asia advised her to invest in conservative insurance funds. However, Field was later advised by Barber Asia to take a riskier investment strategy and to gear up her existing investment by having a loan denominated in Japanese yen (carrying a low rate of interest), being backed up by the existing investment as collateral, for a new investment scheme denominated in pound sterling (at a gearing factor of 2.5 times the original investment principal). The loan proceeds would be converted into pound sterling for investment in a sterling money market fund which ran a higher interest rate. The purpose of this repackaging of Field's investment was to take advantage of the low interest rate for yen-denominated loans. The yen, however, strengthened. As a result, compared to the pound sterling-denominated investment, the corresponding liability under the yen loan increased and Field suffered a loss. In this case, Barber Asia never received any fees from Field for its advisory services. Instead, the parties agreed that Barber Asia would receive commission from companies whose products Field had acquired through Barber Asia.

The court noted that Field and Barber Asia did not enter into any contract, express or implied. Nevertheless, the court still found that Barber Asia had been negligent in providing financial advisory services to Field due to its failure to heed Field's clearly stated desire to take a conservative rather than a risky investment strategy, and to warn Field of the existence

---

[29] 1 QB 55.
[30] AC 465.
[31] HKCU 712 (Court of First Instance, HCA 7119/2000, 17 June 2003; affirmed on appeal [2004] 3 HKLRD 871).

and nature of the risks involved in the repackaged investment products.[32] Therefore, Barber Asia breached its duty of care owed to Field. The court confirmed that a duty of care is likely to arise if an investment advisor "assumes the responsibility of providing advice to a plaintiff, and knows or ought to know that the plaintiff is likely to rely on that advice". The court went on to list the "pertinent factors" taken into account to determine such duty of care. These factors include

> the relative skill and knowledge of the parties, the context in which the advice is given, whether the giver of the advice is doing so completely gratuitously or is getting a reward whether in some direct or indirect form, and whether or not there are any express disclaimers of responsibility (which would negate any assumption of responsibility by a defendant).[33]

The play of these pertinent factors, as the case *Williams* v. *Natural Life Health Foods Ltd.* (1998)[34] indicated, depends on the exchanges (which, as Lord Steyn pointed out, must include statements and conduct) between the parties, which is an objective enquiry. Any change to these "pertinent factors" can be decisive in the ruling. For instance, should the investment scheme have been low-risk and/or commensurate with Field's low risk appetite, the result could have been different.

Based on *Susan Field* v. *Barber Asia*, financial advisors should always ensure that their advice is consistent with the investment objectives of the investor and that all of the risks have been adequately explained to and understood by the investor. *Susan Field* v. *Barber Asia* seems to suggest that a mere general introduction of the products is not sufficient to discharge the duty of care owed by the advisor to the investor.

Back to the Lehman minibonds saga; one difference between the two cases is the nature of minibonds. What Field purchased at the outset was a conservative product as confirmed by the court. It was the subsequent investment strategy that exposed Field to fluctuations in the currency exchange rate which gave rise to a higher risk. Minibonds, however, are inherently risky. This difference may not outweigh the similarity between Susan Field and minibond holders: They were all conservative but the

---

[32]The court applied to the financial advisory context general principles which govern the duty of care set out in *Henderson* v. *Merrett Syndicates Ltd.* (1995) 2 AC.
[33]Deputy Judge Barma SC, 155.
[34]2 All ER 577, Lord Steyn, 582.

products offered to them were high-risk investment products, or at least riskier than was suitable for their investment appetites.

Another technical but subtle difference is the introductory material available to the investors. Field was not provided with any introductory brochure for the high-risk investment strategy. Minibonds were sold with prospectuses. Arguably, the banks and brokers could try to wash their hands by saying that the minibond holders made their investment with sufficient knowledge of the nature and existence of the risk in purchasing minibonds. Lord Steyn's "objective test" shed some light on the minibonds case: "the impact of what a defendant says or does must be judged in the light of the relevant contextual scene".[35] The minibonds were distributed in the non-transparent over-the-counter market and targeted retail investors, the majority of whom are not professional investors or intermediaries and whose participation in any issue is modest. Therefore, it is hard for the retail investors to make a sophisticated investment decision though it may be made on an informed basis. For instance, the retail investors have not much idea about the secondary market prices and know little about Lehman Brothers and its subsidiaries. In particular, the sale of minibonds to elderly and unsophisticated investors is likely to be problematic. A normal level of disclosure may not fit this particular group of investors' needs as they may need more investment education. The distributing banks and brokers should have communicated the investment risks to these investors in an explicit and understandable fashion. Nevertheless, most of these investors were told that the minibonds could serve as their retirement pension funds. Given the complex "contextual scene" of minibonds, banks and brokers should have explained the complex nature and inherent risk of minibonds to the investors.

In determining whether the banks had been negligent in giving investment advice, Gloster J identified some factors in the case of *JP Morgan Chase Bank* v. *Springwell Navigation Corp.* (2008)[36] such as

> the contractual context (including the terms of the relevant contractual documents and disclaimers, and the absence of any written advisory agreement); what, if anything, was said to the advisee by the bank's representatives when he was introduced to the adviser; the actual role played by the adviser (including the purpose for which he was giving the advisee

---

[35] *Ibid.*
[36] EWHC 1186 (Comm).

recommendations or advice) over the relevant period; the extent
of the advisee's financial experience or sophistication; the extent
of the advisee's reliance on the various advisers, including the
extent to which it was foreseeable that he would rely upon them
for the investment advice the investor alleges it should have
been given; and the regulatory background.[37]

In essence, these factors are in line with Lord Steyn's "objective test",
which may not necessarily shed light on the factual dispute in the minibonds
saga.

Both *Susan Field* v. *Barber Asia* and *JP Morgan Chase Bank* v. *Springwell
Navigation Corp.* imposed a duty of care on financial advisors such as Barber
Asia and JP Morgan which not only sold financial products or services but also
provided investment advice to the customers. Can banks and brokers succeed
in pushing away their liabilities in arguing that they only made financial products available to the customers without advising them? In other words, is a
salesperson of financial products also subject to a duty of care to the buyers?
Gloster J made it clear in *JP Morgan Chase Bank* v. *Springwell Navigation
Corp.* that a salesman still owes a duty of care to the client, that is, a "reasonable care not to recommend a highly risky investment without pointing out
it was such."[38] Lindgren J concurred with this ruling in *NMFM Property* v.
Citibank (No. 10) by pointing out that

> the fact that the advisers were agents for the investor and were
> promoting investment in units in the property trust ... does not
> mean that the investors could not reasonably have relied upon
> them not to recommend an investment that involved a risk of
> financial loss, at least without warning them of that risk.[39]

Therefore, a salesperson still owes a duty of care to customers but the
level of duty of care imposed on a salesperson appears lower or narrower
than that applicable to an advisor.

---

[37] *Ibid.*, 53.

[38] *Ibid.*, 108.

[39] *NMFM Property* v. *Citibank (No. 10)*, 525–526. "Beyond reasonable doubt" has been
considered by Judge Garry Tallentire in hearing a case brought by Lehman minibonds
holders against a former personal financial services manager at Bank of China (Hong
Kong) for seven misinterpretation charges. Chiu, A (2011), "Bank Manager Acquitted
in Minibond case," South China Morning Post, 19 February, at A3. Incredible, unreliable
and inaccurate evidence given by alleged victims was also a key factor that the judge
ruled in favor of the defendant.

Investigation of the mis-selling practices also needs to focus on the manner in which minibonds were sold, in addition to the written marketing materials for minibonds. For instance, minibonds were sold at subway stations and sometimes even cross-sold into the time deposit investors' hands. A sound selling practice should include a clear and complete introduction of the nature and characteristics of the investments and other options available to the customers. The financial institutions should act in the investors' best interests by knowing the investors, ensuring adequate due diligence, making reasonable recommendations, helping clients make informed decisions, and employing competent staff with appropriate training. Further, the management of the financial institutions bear the primary responsibility for ensuring the maintenance of appropriate standards of conduct and adherence to proper procedures in accordance with the SFC Code of Conduct.[40] As a matter of policy and "good practice", it may be advisable for financial institutions to make available a presentation explaining in plain terms the risks of investing in certain products to the prospective customers when selling these complex financial products.

4. REGULATING STRUCTURED FINANCIAL PRODUCTS: SOME "MINI" REGULATORY OPTIONS

Facing increasing public blame over the regulatory failure, the Hong Kong government proactively put forward a repurchase scheme endorsed by the Hong Kong Association of Banks on behalf of the distributors of Lehman minibonds. Sixteen distributing banks[41] offered to buy back the

---

[40]Ching, F. (2008), "Regulators have Let Down Investors Badly," *South China Morning Post*, 4 November, p. 16.

[41]They are (in alphabetical order) ABN AMRO Bank N.V., Bank of China (Hong Kong) Limited, Bank of Communications Co., Ltd. Hong Kong Branch, Bank of East Asia Limited, Chiyu Banking Corporation Limited, Chong Hing Bank Limited, CITIC Ka Wah Bank Limited, Dah Sing Bank Limited, Fubon Bank (Hong Kong) Limited, Industrial and Commercial Bank of China (Asia) Limited, MEVAS Bank Limited, Nanyang Commercial Bank Limited, Public Bank (Hong Kong) Limited, Shanghai Commercial Bank Limited, Wing Hang Bank Limited, and Wing Lung Bank Limited.

minibonds at their mark-to-market[42] value.[43] The repurchase scheme was agreed on by both the SFC and HKMA as part of a global settlement of regulatory investigations. The HKMA, together with the Hong Kong International Arbitration Centre (HKIAC), also offered to provide the investors with a mediation and arbitration platform. The HKMA and the banks concerned will share the fee in a 50:50 split to cover the qualified candidate's arbitration or mediation costs. In order to be qualified for the scheme, the investor has to have made a complaint to the HKMA which has reviewed it and referred it to the SFC for consideration; alternatively, either the HKMA or the SFC has to have made a filing against the bank or bank officer concerned. These actions, however, in essence, neither clarify the level and scope of the duty of care of the banks and brokers selling minibonds to retail investors nor address any concerns, i.e. the obligations of distributors of financial products, surrounding the claimed mis-selling practice. These solutions merely provided the retail investors some shortcut routes to satisfy their partial claims.

In response to the multitude of issues arising from the minibonds crisis, the SFC published its "Consultation Paper on Proposals to Enhance Protection for the Investing Public" on 25 September 2009.[44] Inadequate disclosure has been diagnosed to be the root of the Lehman minibonds saga. The central proposal made in the consultation paper was to enhance the disclosure regime by requiring that all products include user-friendly

---

[42]In its simplest form, a securities account must be adjusted in response to a change in the market value of the securities. An investor may buy securities on credit from a securities broker-dealer. In order to secure the purchase price, the buyer may pledge the securities as collateral. The broker-dealer can require the investor to maintain a minimum collateral value, thereby guarding against the price of the securities falling to the point where their value as collateral is insufficient to repay the purchase price. When the market value of the securities falls below this minimum, a "margin call" will be issued by the broker-dealer asking the investor to deposit additional collateral to keep up with the minimum. Failure to deposit additional collateral in the form of money or additional securities may trigger a default and the broker-dealer can foreclose on the collateral. The overall purpose of requiring investors to "mark to market" is to reduce risks. Bodie, Z., Kane, A. and Marcus, A. (2008), *Essentials of Investments*, McGraw Hill, pp. 71–72.

[43]The repurchase proposal, however, encountered difficulties in its implementation after the issue of a cease-and-desist order from Lehman Brothers' US counsel to HSBC Hong Kong, as a result of the "automatic stay" imposed by Lehman Brothers' US bankruptcy filings. It is not clear to what extent Chapter 11 bankruptcy proceedings in the US may preclude buy-back efforts in Hong Kong.

[44]Also see SFC (2009), "Consultation Paper on Possible Reforms to the Prospectus Regime in the Companies Ordinance and the Offers of Investment Regime in the Securities and Future Ordinance", (October).

short-form summary disclosures or concise "key facts statements" no more than four pages long (excluding charts and graphics), which may make the disclosure documents more accessible to the average investor. This section will discuss whether the strengthening of the disclosure regime as such is an effective regulatory technique to address the inherent risks exposed in the minibonds saga.

Why Full Disclosure of Minibonds is Insufficient

Policy makers and regulators often view financial markets as an agglomeration of rational investors, who make optimal resource allocation and wealth maximization decisions so long as they are supplied with sufficient information on all relevant aspects of products like securities and well-structured economic incentives. Based on this modern finance theory, full disclosure is the exclusive focus of financial and securities regulations.[45] Almost all the regulators made a great effort to ensure the availability of a vast volume of pertinent information in the public domain.[46] The underlying rationale of this regulatory technique is that full disclosure helps investors to evaluate the merits of an investment so that they are adequately protected. It is a basic tenet that investors have the ability to make their own evaluations which do not require more costly and time-consuming governmental merit analysis of the products offered in the market.[47]

The rational investor hypothesis reshaped modern financial regulation which has extended the disclosure paradigm from prevention of market abuse to retail investor protection. For instance, under the third pillar of Basel II, timely informed rational actors are assumed to be capable of acting as supervisors and enforcers of prudential regulations such as capital adequacy rules.[48] As this argument goes, had rational investors been given higher-quality information they would have approached structured credit securities with caution and would not have been overexposed to the risks

---

[45]Hazen, T. (2005), *The Law of Securities Regulation*, §8.1[1][B] and §1.2[3] (explaining that "the focus on disclosure was based on the conclusion that sunlight is the best disinfectant").

[46]The SEC, for instance, has proposed a new regulatory framework for the securitized market to require disclosure of pool level or asset level data for each loan. See van Duyn, A. (2010), "SEC Charges Reveal Move On Practices In Securitized Finance," *Financial Times*, 24 June 2010, pp. 25.

[47]*Ibid.*, §1.2[3][A].

[48]Basel Committee on Banking Supervision, "International Convergence of Capital Measurement and Capital Standards: A Revised Framework," updated November 2005.

involved in structured products such as CDOs since a large volume of information allows them to calculate the risk and return possibilities of an investment and make informed investment decisions.

Instead of incomplete disclosure, the major reason for the minibonds saga actually was product complexity, which not only increased the amount of information but also meant the disclosures were insufficient and the digestion of disclosed information difficult. The retail investors were supplied with a large volume of information about the structured financial products. Disclosure documents ordinarily consist of a prospectus and a prospectus supplement, which are hundreds of pages of impenetrable legal prose. However, the structure of minibonds is so complex that they are incomprehensible to individual investors. The majority of investors do not have the resources to evaluate such information with a degree of certainty. The market failed to understand what was disclosed and appreciate the implications of such disclosed information, in particular, the inherent risks involved. Compared to intangible benefits, tangible high costs involved in produce research and risk analysis[49] may have pushed away any attempt to collaborate on risk analysis.[50] Under the given circumstances, full disclosure became insufficient and the product complexity caused the retail investors to be unable to understand and operate products in the market.[51] Lack of understanding always leads to failure to draw proper conclusions and make sensible investment decisions, which in turn creates market failure or corporate scandals.[52] Thus, the Lehman minibonds saga exposed many of the limits of disclosure as an effective regulatory tool in the context of financial markets.

The emergence of complex structured financial products is the result of the division of and competition in the financial industry. Modern financial institutions comprise banks, insurance houses and securities firms whose functions become increasingly overlapped and interconnected. On one hand, banks try to expand the boundaries for permissible non-banking activities.

---

[49]MacKenzie, D. (2010), "Unlocking the Language of Structured Securities," *Financial Times*, 19 August 2010, pp. 20 (discussing the use of Intex, a graphics-based computerized tool for designing deals and analyzing risks, which may cost one bank about US$1.5 million a year).

[50]Barboza, D. (2002), "Complex El Paso Partnerships Puzzle Analysis," *New York Times*, 23 July, p. C1.

[51]For a technical account of defining deals' Intricate cash flow rules, see MacKenzie, D., *supra* note 49.

[52]Gordon, J. (2002), "What Enron Means for the Management and Control of the Modern Business Corporation: Some Initial Reflections," *University of Chicago Law Review*, 69(3):1233, 1238–1239.

Other financial services firms like insurance and securities companies, on the other hand, show the tendency of being operated profitably and demonstrate the inherent value proposition presented by banks, such as stability, structure, security and safety, which are appealing to customers and by extension their money.[53] In order to adapt to the competitive environment, financial institutions create innovative investment products for distribution to their customers. In addition to traditional products such as shares, futures, funds and bonds, products can be structured to include foreign currency, commodities, or residential mortgages in the form of fixed-income securities, interest rate swaps,[54] equity derivatives, credit derivatives, warrants, minibonds and investment-linked insurance products. The complexity in financial products and markets is also a natural response to the "demand by investors for securities that meet their investment criteria and their appetite for ever higher yields"[55] so that the risks can be more easily transferred and traded, thereby promoting efficiency, efficacy and depth in financial markets. The market players become more innovative in offering innovative products, thereby maintaining their competitiveness, earning higher returns[56] and offsetting the rapid decline of profit margins.[57] Innovation in designing products, structuring pools of financial assets, and using special-purpose vehicles allows financial service providers to access low-cost financings without having to rely on banks and other financial intermediaries.[58]

As financial products have become more complicated and speculative in nature, market standards and practices may have to encounter dynamic risks and unanticipated defaults, sometimes a form of market abuse. In particular, the complexities of innovative financial products obscure the ability of market participants to sense and judge risks and consequences.

---

[53]Divanna, J. (2002), *Redefining Financial Service: The New Renaissance in Value Propositions*, Palgrave Macmillian, pp. 9–10.

[54]Rathbone, J. (2010), "Derivatives Reform is Set to Punish the EV Property Sector," *Financial Times*, 21 July 2010, pp. 22 (claiming that the interest rate swap by far is the most common derivative used for hedging).

[55]Green, P. and Jennings-Mares, J. (2008), "Letter to the Editor," *Financial Times*, 4 July, p. 14.

[56]Bethel, J. and Ferrel, A. (2007), "Policy Issues Raised by Structured Products," in Fuchita, Y. and Litan, R. (eds.), *New Financial Instruments and Institutions: Opportunities and Policy Challenges*, Brookings Institution Press, pp. 167, 171.

[57]Hu, H. (1993), "Misunderstood Derivatives: The Causes of Informational Failure and the Promise of Regulatory Incrementalism," *Yale Law Journal*, 102(6):1457, 1497.

[58]Schwarcz, S. (2002), "Enron and the Use and Abuse of Speical Purpose Entities in Corporate Structures," *University of Cincinnati Law Review*, 70:1309, 1315.

Ordinary investors may not be aware of or fully understand the potential risks attached to the products and complex terms and conditions, especially when sales intermediaries do not explain the risks in an appropriate manner. The risk and return from structured products are related to three main issues: the volatility of the future value of an underlying asset, the uncertainty of future events, and the exposure of the product. As each type of investment is subject to market forces, in essence, the more leveraged a portfolio product is, the greater are the assumed risk and the expected reward.[59] In terms of minibonds, the interests of the minibond issuers are no longer aligned with the interests of the owners of the minibonds. Therefore, there is legitimate concern that the minibonds indicated and fostered moral hazard on the part of the issuers, which may have resulted in lax product offering and market practice standards.[60] Derivatives are used more often in Hong Kong in order to manage foreign exchange risks, which fluctuate over time. Conventional mathematical models used to estimate the dynamic correlation are at best approximations. It is likely that innovative product suppliers may default at a much higher rate than anticipated.

The complexities of financial products also contribute to contagion since the products are so sophisticated, specialized and complicated that they do not have a liquid trading market. In the absence of a flow market, these financial products can only be effectively valued through highly complex mathematical models or assumptions.[61] The wrong assumptions can easily create a chaotic response from the investors who may quickly lose confidence in the products. In addition, complexity facilitates fraud in the case of complex asset-backed securities transactions like minibonds. This is because the asset-backed products are so complicated that even a bankrupt company may well package its assets to be sellable securities.[62]

---

[59]Chorafas, D. (2005), *Wealth Management: Private Banking, Investment Decisions, and Structured Financial Products*, Butterworths, available at http://www.ebookee.cn/ Wealth-Management-Private-Banking-Investment-Decisions-and-Structured-Financial-Products_188863.html.

[60]This moral hazard concern is real in the context of the subprime mortgage crisis. Henry, D. and Goldstein, M. (2007), "The Bear Flu: How It Spread," *Business Week*, 31 December, p. 30.

[61]Shah, N. (2007), "Can Wall Street be Trusted to Value Risky CDOs?" *Reuters*, 14 July, available at http://www.reuters.com/article/reutersEdge/idUSN0929430320070714 (pointing out that models used to value illiquid assets can "break down rather dramatically during abnormal times because the assumptions underlying the models fail").

[62]Schwarcz, S. (3rd ed. 2002 and Supp. 2006), *Structured Finance: A Guide to the Principles of Asset Securitization*, §1:1, pp. 1–2.

Therefore, the investors are unable to rely much on the issuer's public reputation for financial integrity and governance to monitor the economic performance of products. The minibonds *per se* adopt an indirect holding structure in which intermediary entities are used to hold debt and equity securities on behalf of the owners or investors. For instance, issuers of the securities record ownership as belonging to one or more depository intermediaries which then record the identities of other intermediaries such as banks or brokerage firms that buy or sell interests in the securities.[63] The economic effect of this structure is that credits become more available to less creditworthy borrowers. From the regulatory perspective, this indirect holding structure exacerbates uncertainty by reducing transparency: it is not easy for outsiders such as retail investors to readily determine the ultimate owners or credit exposure of the underlying assets of securities.[64]

Market failure may be aggravated by the complexities of modern financial markets through human interactive behaviour due to some socio-psychological factors such as bounded rationality, strategic trade behaviour, and cognitive biases. For instance, bounded rationality explains risk-taking investment behaviours in purchasing minibonds, which competed with conventional financial instruments in offering more economic benefits but came attached with more risks, being purely speculative and economically similar to gaming instruments. A complex financial product like minibonds may compromise or even frustrate the investors' ability to draw a sensible conclusion from the interactivities among market participants and further predict market movements or consequences. Due to the investors' tendency to herd or take a more opportunistic strategy, some investors may not have the capacity or desire to use the disclosed information in a rational manner. Herding has been recognized as one of the main amplifiers of the financial crisis[65] as it is linked to the agency problem and places a very powerful limitation on rational reaction to disclosed information.[66] Investor overconfidence and rising market prices may also lead investors to ignore the warning signals in the disclosed data in favour of

---

[63]Schwarcz, S. (2001), "Intermediary Risk in the Global Economy," *Duke Law Journal,* 50:1541, 1547–1548.

[64]*Ibid.,* 1583.

[65]UK FSA (2009), "The Turner Review: A Regulatory Response to the Global Banking Crisis," March.

[66]Avgouleas, E. (2009), "The Global Financial Crisis, Behavioural Finance and Financial Regulation: In Search of a New Orthodoxy," *Journal of Corporate Law Studies,* 9:121–157.

over-reliance on credit ratings. Noises are likely to arise in the market when irrational investor behaviour interferes with market efficiency.[67] As a result, market participants invest and trade as much in reaction to the expected behaviour and strategy of others,[68] which in turn affects, positively or negatively, market stability.

In the context of minibonds, the complexity aggravated the market failure through the interconnectedness of market participants. The wide use of financial instruments such as credit default swaps to hedge against the risk on the investments *de facto* linked many financial institutions as "counterparties".[69] A subsidiary of Lehman appeared to have significant exposure to other market participants in the Lehman group on CDS contracts. Its lack of assets to pay its liabilities on the swap contracts may have damaged other market participants' ability to honour the swap contracts and therefore their reputation. Due to the interconnectiveness of various contracts and parties, bankruptcy or other failures of a given market participant, together with information failure on the counterparty's financial condition and contingent exposure, can cause other participants to default on their obligations to other market participants, which may eventually put enormous strains on the financial system and lead to a domino-effect collapse of the entire financial market.[70] This counterparty risk[71] is further complicated by the lack of a trading system for the derivative transactions which are essentially contract-based private transactions and traded over-the-counter.[72]

---

[67]Hazen, T. (1991), "The Short-Term/Long-Term Dichotomy and Investment Theory: Implications for Securities Market Regulation and for Corporate Law," *North Carolina Law Review*, 70:137, 157.

[68]Anderson, L. and Holt, C. (1997), "Information Cascades in the Laboratory," *American Economics Review*, 87:847, 847.

[69]Boyle, P. and Boyle, F. (2001), *Derivatives: The Tools That Changed Finance*, Risk Books, London, p. 7.

[70]Schwarcz, S. (2008), "Markets, Systemic Risk, and the Subprime Mortgage Crisis," *Southern Methodist University Law Review*, 61(2):198–200.

[71]The counterparty risk is "real" in the sense that it is believed to be integral to the failure of credit markets in the subprime crisis. Schwarcz, S. (2009), "Keynote Address: Understanding the Subprime Financial Crisis," *South Carolina Law Review*, 60:549, 562.

[72]Van Duyn, A. (2010), "Derivative Dilemmas," *Financial Times*, 12 August 2010, pp. 5 (reporting that according to the Bank of International Settlements, 3.4% of derivatives were traded on exchanges and the rest, US$614,674 billion worth, were traded in private markets).

How Can the Disclosure Regime be Improved Given the Increasing Complexity?

The disclosure regime must be improved together with the financial product complexity, or vice versa. Given the growing complexity in the financial markets, there is a clear need to devise strategies that make the disclosure regime actually work under actual market conditions. Financial transactions are becoming more complex largely as a result of the growing utility of securitization, various forms of credit risk transfer, and financial derivatives. These legitimate transactions present problems of completeness of disclosure, not only for retail users but also for professional intermediaries. The following examples in the case of the Lehman minibonds well indicate the flaws and weaknesses of the existing disclosure regime.

- The prospectus and other marketing materials were supposed to explain the complex structure of the minibonds in a sense that investors could understand. This, however, was not the case. For instance, the Lehman prospectus and sales materials contained such warnings that minibonds were "not principal protected". This cautious language was indeed unreliable because it is by definition true of any debt obligation that is not cash-collateralized.
- In most debt and equity issues, the prospectus should include information as to the use of transaction proceeds. The information can be disclosed in broad terms without any compliance covenants.[73] However, the purpose of Lehman's interest in issuing minibonds was not disclosed in the prospectuses except that the SPV would receive a "small fee" in the transaction.
- In the minibonds transactional arrangement, Lehman was central, being an arranger, swap counterparty, guarantor, seller and valuer of collateral, SPV sponsor and credit protection buyer. Nevertheless, this multiple-function role was scarsely mentioned in the sales material and rarely explained clearly in formal disclosure documents. Lehman could have argued that financial and other information concerning its standing was readily available elsewhere, and needed no repetition in documents for each single issue. The information disclosed in the sales material and prospectus seems to switch the focus from the main credit risk and Lehman's centrality in the transaction, as arranger, commercial

---

[73] Hong Kong Companies Ordinance, Schedule 3.

beneficiary and legal owner of prior claims on collateral, to unfocused and pure introductory information.

- Information on Lehman contained in a separate 82-page base disclosure document merely comprised US statutory filings. Although other transaction documents were listed in the prospectuses available for inspection while minibonds were on offer or outstanding, it may be unreasonable or unimaginable that an unsophisticated buyer actually would visit Lehman's office in order to grasp and digest more relevant information from swap confirmations, master agreements, trustee agreements, exchange listing rules, details of SPV collateral, or credit protection sold by the SPV. It is questionable whether the transaction risk and purpose were plainly presented to the investors as even professional or institutional investors could not have valued the minibonds by simply referring to the information supplied to the buyers in prospectuses and marketing materials.

- The sale of each issue of minibonds was supported by documents in length and style conventional for complex securities. For example, the sale of Series 36 involved a 54-page issue prospectus in English and a 51-page issuer program prospectus with substantially identical content, and a pricing supplement with the final terms. The lengthy prospectuses as such actually created obstacles for a retail investor to carefully digest and enquire into the mechanics of the minibonds.

- The minibonds marketing materials may have contained some "bluff" information. For instance, one 2005 issue contained this slogan:

> "Just as pyramids are a long-standing symbol of strength, the Minibond Series 16 combines the strength of Hutchison Whampoa and five well-known financial institutions to let you invest with peace of mind".

In this scenario, the distributing banks and brokers may have already misled at least some uneducated or unsophisticated retail investors and disregarded the client's needs and risk appetite.

Disclosure in relation to minibonds and other complex financial instruments must satisfy at least two criteria. Disclosed information must be as complete as possible, clearly presented to investors so that they are able to make an informed investment decision. Products must carry warnings that make clear their speculative nature so that the inherent risks can be properly evaluated by investors. Accordingly, some measures may be taken to improve the current disclosure regime. For instance, a complete disclosure should at least include adequate product descriptions, a balanced picture of the product, and more importantly, upfront, prominent and adequate warnings of all risks. The nature of the underlying transaction must be clearly explained in plain terms. An initial movement in this regard was made when the HKMA required at the end of 2008 the banks to re-label products containing CDBs.[74] While changes to the disclosure regime are necessary in order to restore investor confidence, the debates on how much information needs to be released about loans, and when, and also whether prices at which securities are traded need to be reported, still continue. All these subtle issues in relation to price and loan level transparency deserve careful thinking and planning in the policy-making process.

When complexity impairs disclosure, efforts must be made to address the complexity.[75] One way of dealing with it is to make disclosure more approachable by strengthening the abstractions and simplifications. Regulatory reform tackling the product complexity issue could require more meaningful regulatory warnings and the standardization of marketing material, which would be of assistance to investors, retail or professional, in comparing competing financial products. Lack of standardization inherently poses considerable difficulty in filling the gaps between market expectations and market reality, and in properly evaluating the risks of structured products with any degree of accuracy. Sensible steps taken in this area could also be to increase product standardization and enhance clearing and settlement infrastructure. These measures could improve the transparency of the market for structured credit securities and further improve retail investors' processing and digestion of product information. However, the attempt to limit uncertainty by standardizing financial products and transactions as well as transactional materials may not be a timely regulatory tool to keep up with the development of the complex derivatives market due to rapid changes in the market condition. In addition, standardization may block innovative efforts taken by the market participants to adapt themselves to changing and competitive markets.

In the field of prudential regulation of investment banks and structured products, the effectiveness of the disclosure regime may increase if relevant

---

[74]Young, T. (2008), "Hong Kong Regulators on Defensive over Minibonds," *AsiaLaw*, Hong Kong, November.

[75]Along with regulatory action, market players must be deemed to have taken appropriate and responsive actions to make products simpler. 60% of total structured product volumes in Hong Kong's private banking industry are now comprised of equity-linked notes with a maturity of one month. Simpler, more liquid and more transparent products such as warrants, exchange traded funds, and other listed products are gaining popularity after the Lehman minibonds saga. See Cookson, R. (2010), "Caution Sees 'Bells and Whistles' Products Wane," *Financial Times Weekly Review of the Fund Management Industry*, 10 May 2010, pp. 4.

rules are adapted to actual market conditions and disclosure is utilized as a supplement to strict protective rules, e.g. business activity barriers. Disclosure can be buttresses as cost-effective, supplemental protections that minimize information asymmetry or mitigate its consequences. For instance, there should be mandatory disclosure of commissions in the sale of investment products so that the investors are aware of the profitability of the selling practice and can compare it with the profit he may obtain by purchasing and selling the products. This is an effective way of reducing agency costs stemming from the conflict between the interests of individuals and the institutions for which they work. The SFC has indicated its plan to amend the Code of Conduct to require distributors to disclose to customers monetary and non-monetary benefits that they receive.[76] In competitive markets such as highly contested financial markets, institutions, i.e. prescriptive regulations, still matter to the formation of information and private incentives.[77] While the protective regulation in banking markets focuses on the imposition of dynamic pre-provisioning obligations, i.e. capital adequacy regulation and credit flow restrictions, the exposed risks in connection with structured financial products call for the imposition of limits on the use of securitization by investment and commercial banks,[78] and a further separation of commercial banking from investment banking.[79] These protective rules effectively restrict the types of activities a financial institution may undertake and restrain its risk-taking appetite.

Although disclosure has become the cornerstone of modern financial regulation, it is not a perfect option. Indeed, disclosure is an expensive or intrusive regulatory technique for both securities and structured product issuers and financial firms. Periodic or mandatory disclosure involves an array of professionals like auditors, lawyers and compliance officers who are assigned to process and verify disclosure information. This effectively increases the level of difficulty in curing the agency problem as banks' and shareholders' concerns are markedly different and banks care more about making money than correcting prices through arbitrage trading and

---

[76]SFC Consultation Paper.

[77]Smith, V. (1962), "An Experimental Study of Competitive Market Behavior," *Journal of Political Economy*, 70:111.

[78]Avegouleas, E. (2009), "The Global Financial Crisis, Behavioural Finance and Financial Regulation: In Search of a New Orthodoxy," *Journal of Corporate Law Studies*, 9:149–150.

[79]UK FSA (2009), "The Turner Review: A Regulatory Response to the Global Banking Crisis," March, pp. 43, 94.

risk management controls. Due to the highly complex and fast-moving environment of global financial markets, regulators may make the wrong choice concerning the kind of data and information that has to be disclosed or regulated or design the wrong supervisory focus concerning how to address the market actors' concerns. Thus, financial intermediaries were not necessarily requested to make a constructive assessment of the systemic implications of their market activities.

There are good reasons why disclosure can become a more constructive and effective regulatory technique in the context of financial markets given the indisputable benefits disclosure has brought in battling market abuse, fostering liquidity, and democratizing financial markets. While recognizing the importance of disclosure as a regulatory tool, the practical difficulty is to limit the information asymmetry so it does not exceed certain bounds. The limitations, weaknesses or flaws call for a rethinking of the disclosure paradigm in financial regulation. The question is how useful extensive disclosure of information will be to retail or unsophisticated investors, particularly for those lower down in the income and educational pyramid. In the context of structured products, the pre-eminence given to disclosure as a regulatory technique is unwarranted if the disclosed information cannot be properly processed or utilized by the investors in the decision-making process. In terms of financial regulations, disclosure cannot be enforced for the purpose of protecting the whole market from the risk of contagion. In the foreseeable future, disclosure will remain an effective and strong supervisory tool only if the content, volume and format of disclosure are adapted to actual market conditions. This requires a substantial overhaul of its processes, volume, timing and format. More importantly, disclosure should be used as a supplement to strict protective rules.

It also has to be noted that disclosure alone cannot solve the regulatory problems and defects. Take minibonds as an example. Minibonds are debt obligations or debentures,[80] where a holder's right to principal or profit is linked to the performance of financial or other assets that are contractually unconnected to the minibonds. Any single issue of minibonds specifies one or more reference variables whose uncertain outcomes dictate the return on the instrument. Banks arrange new issues to deliberately match their private clients' view on interest rates, asset prices or financial indexes. Structured notes are largely speculative while some products like minibonds can be designed to be more conservative. In substance, structured notes

---

[80]Companies Ordinance, s 2.

are proprietary instruments based on subjective financial modelling, which makes risk assessment or comparison impossible for non-specialists. This requires regulators and policy makers to give some thought to other means.

Gatekeeper Theory and Credit Ratings

Gatekeepers refer to professional persons including auditors, lawyers, securities analysts and those at credit rating agencies who provide verification and certification services to investors. They are regarded as reputational intermediaries and third-party monitors with the capacity to prevent misconduct by withholding support from wrongdoers.[81] It has been argued that it is the gatekeepers' failure in serving as a watchdog for the public that led to the array of financial scandals.[82] Therefore, part of the solution to cure the financial crisis or corporate failure is to improve the regulatory regime governing gatekeepers and their operational behaviours, which in turn improves corporate governance and financial regulations.[83] Each gatekeeper occupies a special position in the market that allows him to possess more information than the investing public about financial products and their suppliers. This market position gives the relevant gatekeepers

---

[81]Kraakman, R. (1984), "Corporate Liability Strategies and the Costs at Legal Controls," *Yale Law Journal,* 93:857–898; Gilson, R. (1984), "Value Creation by Business Lawyers: Legal Skills and Asset Pricing," *Yale Law Journal,* 94:239–313; Gilson, R. and Kraakman, R. (1984), "The Mechanism of Market Efficiency," *Virginia Law Review,* 70:549–644; Kraakman, R. (1986), "Gatekeepers: The Anatomy of a Third-Party Enforcement Strategy," *Journal of Law, Economics & Organization,* 2:53; Choi, S. (1998), "Market Lessons for Gatekeepers," *Northwest University Law Review,* 92(4): 916–966.

[82]Coffee, J. (2001), "The Acquiescent Gatekeeper: Reputational Intermediaries, Auditor Independence and the Governance of Accounting," Ctr. for Law & Econ. Studies, Columbia Law Sch., Working Paper No. 191, available at http://papers.ssrn.com/paper.taf?abstract_id=270944; Coffee, J. (2002), "Understanding Enron: It's about the Gatekeepers, Stupid," *Business Lawyer,* 57:1403–1420; Coffee, J. (2003), "Gatekeeper Failure and Reform: The Challenge of Fashioning Relevant Reform," Ctr. for Law & Econ. Studies, Columbia Law Sch., Working Paper No. 237, available at http://papers.ssrn.com; Coffee, J. (2003), "The Attorney as Gatekeeper: An Agenda for the SEC," *Columbia Law Review,* 103:1293–1316; Coffee J. (2006), *Gatekeepers: The Professions and Corporate Governance,* New York: Oxford University Press.

[83]For instance, right after the Enron scandal, many countries tightened rules regulating the auditing industry even though no academic research had proven a clear connection between audits and the quality of auditing work. The UK and US required firms to rotate the lead partner on an audit after five years, and defined "cooling off" periods for those joining an audit client. Italy put limits on audit firm tenure. For a brief historical account, see Hughes, J. (2010), "Lehman Case Revives Dark Memories of Euron Times," *Financial Times,* 25 March 2010, pp. 15.

a chance of giving a warning signal to the public when the information is different from that made public in the disclosure materials. According to the gatekeeper theory, gatekeeper failure exists when the gatekeeper verifies an issuer statement that it knows, or through reasonable effort could have known, is untrue or misleading. It is gatekeeper failure that reduces the reliability of the disclosure information and thus undermines the effectiveness of the regulatory institutions or means.

The role of credit agencies and their rating methodologies play an increasingly important role in financial regulations. While securitization and financial markets grew rapidly and products became more complex, investors demonstrated limited capacity for or interest in appreciating the disclosed information and calculating the attendant risks of structured products, but paid more attention to rigorous credit controls and valuation models. Investors often prefer to take a shortcut approach by over-relying on the fact that the structured financial products may be rated "investment grade", i.e. a rating of BBB– or better, by top rating agencies such as Standard & Poor's and Moody's.[84] In this sense, credit ratings are used by retail investors as substitutes for due analysis and full understanding of the investments. Institutional buyers and sellers of structured securities also used credit ratings as simplifying heuristics in order to price them without reliable price quotations.[85]

However, credit ratings have widely known shortcomings.[86] The credit rating agencies (CRAs) were criticized for handing out top-notch triple-A ratings to structured products,[87] relying too much on "market mood rather than fundamentals,"[88] and causing the financial crisis.[89] The issuers of the

---

[84]Schwarcz, S. (2002), "Private Ordering of Public Markets: The Rating Agency Paradox," *University of Illinois Law Review,* 1:6–8 (discussing ratings and the concept of "investment grade").

[85]IMF (2008), Global Financial Stability Report, "Containing Systemic Risks and Restoring Financial Soundness," April, p. 55.

[86]The President's Working Group on Financial Markets (2008), "Policy Statement on Financial Market Developments," March, p. 15.

[87]Anderlini, J. (2010), "Chinese Rating Agency Criticizes Western Rivals for Causing Crisis," *Financial Times,* 22 July, p. 1.

[88]Tait, N. (2010), "Brussels to Tackle Rating Agencies," *Financial Times,* 18 May 2010, pp. 6.

[89]van Duyn, A. (2010), "Dilemmas of Reforming the Rating Agencies," *Financial Times,* 11 June, p. 23 (reporting that Moody's alone rated US$4,700 billion of residential mortgage-backed securities between 2000 and 2007, and US$736 billion of CDOs); Tait, N. (2010), Ibid., *Financial Times,* 18 May, p. 6 (reporting that the European Commission is to launch pan-European centralized supervision of CRAs due to their role in the recent Greek

products used CRAs know-how and software in order to build baskets of
securities that would ensure an AAA rating. CRAs were subject to conflicts
of interest as the buyers of their ratings were the issuers whose products they
rated,[90] which promoted the practice of "ratings shopping".[91] CRAs bundled
together underlying debt obligations emanating from a multitude of obliga-
tors but did not make public the estimated correlation of obligations in the
asset pool.[92] CRAs did not take into account the marketability and liquidity
of a financial product in rating the asset value in the case of securities. While
the wide use of credit ratings as heuristics increases market efficiency, it also
sometimes exposes the market to bias and systematic error.[93]

Credit ratings can be easily misunderstood or misused, which substantially affects selling activities and investment behaviours in the financial
market. Many of the minibonds, for example, were "backed by" CDOs and
these CDOs were rated "AAA" at the time of the minibonds' issue. According to the Octave Notes Series 12 issue prospectus, Standard & Poor's
credit rating of Lehman Brothers Holdings Inc. as of 6 October 2006 was
A+. Lehman's issue prospectus for Minibond Series 36 made a reference to
historical default probability,[94] which suggests that the likely cumulative

---

debt crisis i.e. the introduction of a new planned pan-EU supervisory agency which will be
in charge of the registration and oversight of CRAs in Europe).

[90]Schwarcz, S. (2002), "Private Ordering of Public Markets: The Rating Agency Paradox,"
University of Illinois Law Review, 1, available at http://ssrn.com/abstract=267273 or
doi:10.2139/ssrn.267273.

[91]Anderlini, J., *supra* note 78 (reporting that China's largest credit rating agency had
criticized Moody's Investors Service, Standard & Poor's and Fitch Ratings for becoming
"too close to the clients they were supposed to be objectively assessing").

[92]In the US, SEC Rule 17g-5 requires issuers of asset-backed bonds to maintain websites
with all the information needed to rate the bond. Europe is considering similar rules. van
Duyn, A., *supra* note 79.

[93]Jolls, C., Sustein, C. and Thaler, R. (1998), "A Behavioral Approach to Law and Economics," *Stanford Law Review*, 50: 1471, 1777.

[94]The prospectus on p. 54 extracted a table from Standard & Poor's 2007 Global
Corporate Default Study and Rating Transitions showing the cumulative default history
for investment grade rating categories from one to three years. The relevant section
explains the default risk of an A-rated bond as follows:

> For example, take a bond which is rated A by Standard & Poor's. The
> table shows that the statistical likelihood of default on the bond, based on
> the cumulative historical default history of A-rated bonds between 1981
> and 2007, is 0.07% in the first year following issue, 0.18% in the second
> year, 0.3% in the third year, and so on.

historical rate of failure for triple-A collaterals is extremely low.[95] This indeed was a "tricky" assertion in conflating the default performance of all conventional AAA-rated debt issues with those of structured AAA CDOs since the historical default rate of a bond is not necessarily indicative of the risk that Lehman would be unable to meet its obligations under the swap arrangement. Besides, the words "backed by" seem to suggest that the amount of notes outstanding was matched by the value of the SPV collateral at any time during their life span, which is of course not true as a matter of fact.

Retail investors, unlike institutional investors, might not have found accurate and sufficient information in the market to make an informed investment decision since structured credit products were predominantly new products without long trading histories. A high rating such as "AAA" may have easily led retail investors to believe the products were of high standards with little risks. The complexity of structured products and the risks involved were simply beyond the comprehension of the retail investors. According to Lehman's Annual Report of 2007, its long-term credit ratings were A1 (Moody's) and A+ (Standard and Poor's), which were actually far better than some other bonds issued by local blue chips such as Swire Pacific and Hutchison Whampoa, which were rated A− only. To an outsider, the rating seems unstable and changeable within a short time span. Both Standard & Poor's and Moody's lowered the long-term senior rating of Lehman very quickly,[96] which made it difficult for retail investors to act correspondingly.[97] Rating agencies have not proved effective in the face of complexity or market failure. When rating agencies are heavily relied upon to provide an objective view, and the rating system is increasingly used as the main assessment tool, it is hard for the general public to understand the possibility of it being misused.[98]

Why do investors choose to substitute proper analysis and due diligence with a "subscription to a ratings publication"? There are several reasons.

---

[95] http://www.sfc.hk/sfc/html/EN/general/general/lehman/lehman_structure_products. html.

[96] Hong Kong Monetary Authority (2008), Report of the Hong Kong Monetary Authority on Issues Concerning the Distribution of Structured Products Connected to Lehman Group Companies, 31 December, p. 5.

[97] It was argued that rating agencies contributed to the subprime mortgage meltdown by failing to downgrade securities backed by subprime mortgage on a timely basis.

[98] NcNab, H. and Taylor, P. (2008), *Consumer Credit and Risk Management*, Global Professional Publishing, p. 24.

The over-reliance on ratings is not surprising especially when the type of investment tool is generally accepted in the marketplace. Investors, in particular retail investors, are easily seduced by a simple but quick reference — ratings — to determine the suitability and creditworthiness of the products due to their complexity. Investors may choose to ignore the already known flaws and defects of credit ratings so that substantial research costs can be economized to facilitate transactions. In spite of its shortcomings, credit ratings could still be used by investors as a benchmark of value.

From a behavioural perspective, investors and other market participants rely more heavily on the representativeness heuristic other than any rational computations.[99] Investors' cognitive limitations and focus on short-term profit forced sophisticated investors to ignore the warning signals frequently given by CRAs concerning the true function of their ratings.[100] Had sophisticated investors paid attention to these warnings, they would have easily identified and incorporated them into the decision-making model and discounted the importance of credit ratings. Investors may misunderstand the mechanics of innovative financial instruments due to their complexity. In this regard, extensive market disclosure may be useful to eliminate moral hazard and to fashion appropriate incentives so that investors and creditors become *de facto* monitors of banks and financial institutions. However, it is less constructive in preventing institutional failures or safeguarding systemic stability. These may explain why an incredible amount of blind trust was placed on the ratings of CRAs, which had grown more to be powerful than anyone intended.[101]

In the light of the increased gatekeeper failure of the recent decades, it has been pointed out that four factors contribute to systemic breakdown: (i) agency problems within the gatekeeper firm themselves; (ii) imperfect competition within the gatekeeper industry; (iii) a decline in the value of reputational capital that leads managers and gatekeepers to agree to lower verification standards; and (iv) reduced exposure to litigation where the risk of liability for gatekeepers declined substantially in the 1990s, given the fact that litigation can be a very expensive way to change behaviour, particularly for accountants. Some studies suggest that expanding the scope or level of their liability, however, will induce gatekeepers to monitor managers

---

[99]The representativeness heuristic is used by individuals to evaluate probability.

[100]CRAs often insist that ratings measure default risk only rather than the likelihood or intensity of downgrades or mark-to-market losses.

[101]IMF (2008), Global Financial Stability Report, "Containing Systemic Risks and Restoring Financial Soundness," April, p. 56.

and prevent them from committing misconduct.[102] In short, the gatekeeper theory has demonstrated the importance of enlisting gatekeepers, including rating agencies, to prevent corporate fraud and market failure.

As rating agencies constitute a public good, assisting individual investors in assessing the creditworthiness of complex securities, it is important to improve credit rating capabilities.[103] The rating agencies have made an attempt to improve credit rating capabilities by implementing various procedural review steps.[104] The improvement of the rating agencies may not only partly solve the asymmetric-information problem but also increase the quality of their "private certification" via ratings of securities. One way to improve the rating system is the mandatory disclosure of the cross-correlations and asset value which will help the investors' self-assessment.

Restoring the Freedom of Contract Doctrine in Financial Transactions?

The minibonds were not listed and intentionally liquid, and at no time would their value not be opaque. To a non-retail intermediary, these features suggest that minibonds are inherently costly and only for hedging purposes rather than utility investments. Accordingly, non-retail actors would negotiate with the arranger or issuer before accepting uncompensated credit risk or partially disclosed core terms or transactional structure. Although negotiation may not avoid any potential loss in the end, informed or balanced negotiation and contracting at least guarantee fairness and transparency in the transacting process. Unfortunately, retail investors are not able to have such leverage in this process.

In financial transactions, retail investors are more disadvantaged due to the general reluctance of the courts to interfere in commercial bargains, partly because of the vagueness in financial regulations and partly because of the complexity of the transactions. In particular, an innovative financial investment contract may take the market more time to digest risk factors

---

[102]Hamdani, A. (2003), "Gatekeeper Liability," *Southern California Law Review*, 77: 53–121.

[103]Schwarcz, S., "Protecting Financial Markets," *supra* note 7, p. 10, n. 31.

[104]Standard & Poor's (2008), "Descriptions of New Actions to Strengthen Ratings Process and Better Serve Markets," February 7, http://www2.standardandpoors.com/spf/pdf/media/Leadership_Action_Details.pdf.

and reach price equilibration.[105] A doctrine of contractual unconscionability has been proposed to fill the gap where there exist intrinsic bargaining imbalances.[106] Accordingly, the court may be more willing to void bargains made between parties that are highly unequal and subject to information asymmetries that cannot be readily eliminated by the supply of additional data or supporting material. As a result, the party who has "information processing disabilities" may expect to have some remedies in the court ruling.

Freedom of contract only makes sense when bargaining clarity prevents an instrument from becoming unconscionable. In complex financial transactions, special knowledge and experience may be required or needed for investors to make an appropriate evaluation of the contract as a financial instrument in making a fair bargaining.[107] In order to protect retail investors in complex financial transactions, the courts should be more open to contractual unconscionability, which could offer an incentive for regulatory reforms. The forthcoming regulatory reforms must set standards for contractual behaviour in financial markets. Standardizing contracts is obviously a regulatory technique that some countries are trying to introduce into play.[108] The US Dodd-Frank Wall Street Reform and Consumer Protection Act is heading towards this objective by, among others, pushing derivative products on to clearing houses so that the financial system is less vulnerable to the default of a major financial dealer.[109] Financial regulators can only conduct its supervisory and investigatory functions more effectively where the marketing rules are clear, consistent and uniform. In addition, the regulatory reforms also need to ensure contractual completeness, i.e. the purpose and speculative nature of the complex financial transaction being made explicit to all investors under all expected circumstances. For example, a statutory pre-execution cooling-off period could be introduced to safeguard investors by providing them with a reflection period. This would allow retail buyers to have more time to

---

[105] Gilson, R. and Kraakman, R. (1984), "The Mechanisms of Market Efficiency," *Virginia Law Review*, 50:549, 585, 615–616.
[106] See generally Trebicock, M. (1993), *The Limits of Freedom of Contract*, Cambridge, MA: Harvard University Press; Collins, H. (1999), *Regulating Contracts*, New York: Oxford University Press.
[107] The Unconscionable Contracts Ordinance only applies to goods and services.
[108] Peel, Q. *et al.*, *supra* note 12.
[109] Van Duyn, A. (2010), "Derivative Dilemmas," *Financial Times*, 12 August 2010, pp. 5.

consider their investment decisions and actions.[110] The doctrine of freedom of contract is only sensible if it is not misapplied. Therefore, to tackle market abuse, a rewriting of bankruptcy laws may need to be introduced to limit the influence of "empty creditors" who have bought credit default protection that exceeds their underlying credit exposure.[111] Apart from lending more legal leverages to retail investors, considerations should be given to the establishment of legal mechanisms to enable consumers or investors to assert their legal rights, e.g. class action mechanism and contingency fees.

5. THE WAY FORWARD: SOME PRELIMINARY CONCLUSIONS

The Lehman minibonds saga revealed weaknesses and defects in the existing regulatory regime, even though regulators have defended themselves over accusations of a failure to monitor banks and brokers to trade and sell Lehman minibonds,[112] and could potentially have wide ramifications on sales practices throughout Hong Kong's financial industry.

The foundational aim of modern financial regulation is an investor protection ethic exemplified by an array of financial and securities regulations such as the US securities law. Unlike its US counterpart under which strict disclosure requirements make structured notes sales to US retail investors impossible, the Hong Kong Securities and Futures Ordinance only categorizes professional investor classes, leaving retail investors as the residual[113] and vulnerable under the investor protection regime. Non-Hong Kong legislation, i.e. US rules,[114] usually defines sophisticated investors by their scale of experience or wealth. The EU Directive on Markets in Financial Instruments takes a similar approach, not only imposing an obligation on the regulated firm to know its clients but also allowing investors to elect their status for the scope of instruments that they may purchase.[115] The UK Financial Services and Markets Act 2000 is largely

---

[110]HKMA (2008), "Report of the HKMA on Issues Concerning the Distribution of Structured Products Connected to Lehman Group Companies," December, p. 76; SFC (2008), "Issues Raised by the Lehman Minibonds Crisis: Report to the Financial Secretary," December, p. 9.

[111]Peel, Q. *et al.*, *supra* note 12.

[112]Young, T. (2008), "Hong Kong Regulators on Defensive over Minibonds," *AsiaLaw*, November.

[113]Securities and Futures Ordinance, Sch 1.

[114]15 UCC 2A(1), §77b.

[115]Directive 2004/39/EC.

aligned with the EU approach. Meanwhile, it states that investor protection will be tempered by a concern for contractual freedom.[116] This appears to be the position taken by Hong Kong regulators such as the SFC,[117] which believed the risk of the notes was slight or immaterial and the prospectus exemptions were justifiable.[118]

Hong Kong operates a "disclosure-based" regime for authorizing structured products. In theory, the efficient market hypothesis may not apply to complex securitization transactions (which are *sui generis*) or debt markets (which were often issued in private placements[119] and do not have a secondary market).[120] However, the so-called "semi-strong" form of the efficient market hypothesis lends authority to the belief that the stock prices "instantaneously reflect all publicly available information relevant to the value of traded stocks".[121] Disclosure offers other benefits to corporate governance and financial regulation. For instance, disclosure is used as a regulatory means to enhance the separation of ownership and control, i.e. breaking the management monopoly over corporate information.[122] Less consideration is given to the question of whether investors and market actors are actually able to digest all of the disclosed information and make wise investment decisions. This alerts us to the fact that improving the disclosure regime alone cannot prevent the systemic collapse of the financial system as a whole.[123] Efforts should also be devoted to dealing with the

---

[116]s 5(1).

[117]The SFC chief executive commented in the Legislative Council that "the requirement [for structured note buyers] is to understand the features of the product" and "[buyers] should ask 'why does it pay me more than the normal deposit of the bank?'" LC Paper No. CB(2)216/08-09, p. 37.

[118]On the same occasion, the SFC chief executive commented that "these products were backed by triple-A collaterals and the likely cumulative historical rate of failure for triple-A collaterals over the past 25 years between 1981 and 2006 is 0.09 percent for the first three years." LC Paper No. CB(2)216/08-09, p. 37.

[119]Bethel, J. and Ferrell, A. (2006), "Policy Issues Raised by Structured Products," p. 12, available at http://lsr.nellco.org/harvard/olin/papers/560 (explaining that CDBs are overwhelmingly privately placed).

[120]Stern, Y. (2001), "A General Model for Corporate Acquisition Law," *Journal of Corporation Law*, 26:675, 709 (claiming that the studies show that the bond market is not efficient); McDaniel, M. (1988), "Bondholders and Stockholders," *Journal of Corporation Law*, 13:205, 242 ("there is evidence that the market for corporate bonds is not very efficient").

[121]O'Kelley, C. and Thompson, R. (1999), *Corporations and Other Business Associations*, New York: Aspen, pp. 170–171.

[122]Cox, J. *et al.* (2004), *Securities Regulation*, New York: Aspen, p. 246.

[123]Schwarcz, S. (2008), "Systemic Risk," *Georgetown Law Journal*, 97:193, 206.

regulation of credit ratings, complexity of financial products and freedom of contract.

Dividing the regulatory functions and responsibilities for supervising intermediaries' conduct of business between two or more regulators is not an integrated and purposive design, and, due to the gaps and overlaps in this multiple-regulator system, has manifestly failed to respond to the global credit crisis.[124] Consideration could be given to allocating regulatory duties to a single regulator. One model the Hong Kong government may consider is an integrated regulator approach, under which all financial services are regulated in all aspects by a single regulator. Some elements of the "twin peaks" model, adopted in Australia, could be brought into Hong Kong to improve some aspects of the present regulatory structure. Under this "twin peaks" model, one regulator, the Australian Securities and Investment Commission, is responsible for supervising the conduct of business, and the other, the Australian Prudential Regulatory Authority, for supervising capital adequacy. In other words, two authorities regulate and supervise two aspects of financial activities: conduct of business on the one hand, and safety of business on the other. Compared to this "twin peaks" model, Hong Kong's regulatory regime's shortcomings are obvious. The division of regulatory responsibilities has not been clearly drawn between the SFC and HKMA, both of which can walk away or take actions to deal with one or some aspects of the minibonds saga. Eventually, no authority will take full responsibility for the saga.[125]

A sound and solid legal and regulatory system and the rule of law are the cornerstones of Hong Kong as an international financial centre. However, no system can remain stagnant forever. It is clear that the present regulatory structure in Hong Kong may not work as well as expected in response to the growing complexity of financial markets and products such as minibonds, CDOs and CDSs.[126] The minibonds saga provides

---

[124] *Ibid.*

[125] Hong Kong Government (2008), "Task Force to Tackle Financial Tsunami," 15 October, available at http://news.gov.hk. (The HKMA tried to strengthen the supervisory framework for the liquidity risk management of authorized institutions by amending the methodology for calculating capital adequacy ratios in accordance with the latest guidelines and recommendations of the Basel Committee on Banking Supervision. Meanwhile, the HKMA tried to strengthen stress tests, capital planning and management of off-balance-sheet exposures, and encourage a more complete disclosure of risk information.)

[126] The popularity and use of these new products are diminishing. See van Duyn, A. (2010), "More Turmoil Looms in CDO Market," *Financial Times*, 21 June, p. 11.

an opportunity for Hong Kong not only to address the weaknesses and flaws highlighted by the saga but also to consider its long-term role and competitiveness in the international financial system as a wide array of regulatory reforms have been put in place in other jurisdictions.[127] The regulatory landscape has developed rapidly in recent years to cope with the proliferation of financial derivative products.[128] The US introduced sweeping financial regulatory laws partly aimed at damping down on the vast over-the-counter derivatives markets. The European Commission is planning to call for a register of all derivatives trade, and further force more of these transactions out of exchanges and into centralized clearing houses, which guarantees clearer stands between each party and helps safeguard the financial system against a default.[129] With widespread clearing, investors will be able to know about mispricing before it turns out to be a disaster. Germany has introduced a bar on "naked" short selling in German stocks, euro-zone governance bonds and credit default swaps linked to these bonds. China has postponed a plan to introduce CDSs to its domestic market due to the derivatives' contribution to the global financial crisis.[130] The government, rather than the private sector, has the incentive to be informed of systemic risks,[131] and more importantly, deal with the deficiencies in the market design and infrastructure which exacerbates the misuse of financial instruments. The legislature, regulatory authorities and industry players must enhance the regulatory system and bring it in line with the rapid developments in the financial market.

[127]Rathbone, J. (2010), "Derivatives Reform Is Set to Punish the EU Property Sector," *Financial Times*, 21 July, p. 22 (reporting the passage of the Alternative Investment Fund Managers Directive); Luce, E. (2010), "Obama Signs Bill to Overhaul Wall Street," *Financial Times*, 22 July, p. 1 (reporting the passage of the Dodd-Frank Wall Street Reform bill brought the most sweeping overall of Wall Street regulation in place).

[128]Masters, B. and Murphy, M. (2010), "Suspense Over," *Financial Times*, 19 August 2010, pp. 5.

[129]Grant, J. and Grene, S. (2010), "Asset Managers Say OTC Fees Will Hit Savers," *Financial Times*, 2 August 2010, pp. 14.

[130]Anderlini, J. and Cookson, R. (2010), "China Postpones CDS Launch," *Financial Times*, 31 May 2010, pp. 16.

[131]Hu, H. (1993), "Misunderstood Derivatives: The Causes of Informational Failure and the Promise of Regulatory Incrementalism," *Yale Law Journal*, 102:1457, 1502.

Chapter 4

REGULATION OF OVER-THE-COUNTER
DERIVATIVES IN AUSTRALIA*

Paul Latimer

1. INTRODUCTION

Derivatives are listed and traded on financial markets (like ASX 24 — formerly the Sydney Futures Exchange), or they are traded person-to-person over-the-counter (OTC). Due to the global financial crisis of 2007–2009, derivatives have become household words, with calls for improved OTC regulation.

There is no direct Australian regulation of OTC financial products. Instead, OTC derivatives are regulated indirectly by Australia's "three peaks" system of market regulation by the Australian Securities and Investments and Commission (ASIC), the Australian Prudential Regulation Authority (APRA) and the Australian Competition and Consumer Commission (ACCC). In addition, there is industry self-regulation through the standards of trade associations like AFMA and ISDA. This regulation is underpinned with provisions for market misconduct at common law and under the relevant legislation.

Data from APRA, ASIC and the Reserve Bank of Australia confirms that Australian financial markets and financial products including OTCs are well-regulated, subject to further improvements to operational and risk management practices, and that they may have been less

---

*An earlier version of this chapter as at February 2009 was published in the *Australian Journal of Corporate Law*, 23:9.

affected by the financial crisis than equivalent markets in some other countries.

2. DERIVATIVES IN THE NEWS

Derivatives provide an important method of managing risk in financial markets.[1] Derivatives are listed and traded on financial markets like ASX 24 (formerly called the Sydney Futures Exchange, a subsidiary of the Australian Securities Exchange), or they are traded person to person over-the-counter. The volume of the global and "virtual"[2] OTC market — described by some as the Wild West of trading[3] — far exceeds the market for exchange-traded derivatives.[4]

OTC derivatives[5] are contracts which are customized to the needs of a client. They include equity, fixed-income and credit derivative products including derivative instruments like credit default swaps (CDSs).[6] OTC

---

[1]Derivatives are financial contracts which derive their value from an underlying market. They attract both hedgers and speculators who enter the market to gamble on the future price of assets — forwards, futures (such as exchange-traded derivatives traded on regulated exchanges like ASX 24 or LIFFE), options and swaps. Exchange-traded derivatives are standardized in standard amounts and for standard periods. A futures contract is made when a buyer and a seller are contracted to exchange the underlying asset when the contract matures, or close out the contract by offset. An option gives the owner the right but not the obligation to buy or sell the underlying asset. Derivatives derive their value from primary assets like commodities, currency and equities. The future price of the asset is unknown.

[2]See, e.g. Das, S. (2006), *Traders, Guns & Money, Knowns and Unknowns in the Dazzling World of Derivatives*, Harlow: FT Prentice Hall, p. 53.

[3]Partnoy, F. (2003), *Infectious Greed: How Deceit and Risk Corrupted the Financial Markets*, New York: Times Books, p. 18.

[4]Reported to be USD59 trillion in the Bank of International Settlements' estimate of total notional premiums under credit default swaps at the end of 2007, cited by Cooper, J. (2008), "Putting the 'Mort' Back in Mortgage — A Pocket Guide to the Global Credit Crisis," ASIC, 22 August, para 7, at asic.gov.au. Reserve Bank statistics show that total OTC trading has risen from USD3.8 billion in 1995 to USD29.5 billion in 2007, comprising interest rate derivatives (forward rate agreements, swaps and options) and foreign exchange derivatives (currency swaps and options): The Australian Foreign Exchange and Derivative Markets, *Reserve Bank Bulletin*, January 2008, at www.rba.gov.au, accessed 1 September 2010.

[5]Also called exotic derivatives, because their pricing is not transparent, and the aftermarket is either illiquid or nonexistent. The financial institutions which add value by creating complex, customized OTC solutions may hedge these exposures using the standardized exchange-traded OTC derivatives.

[6]Security-based swap agreements are excluded from the Securities Act 1934 (US) s 3A (swap agreements), added by the Gramm–Leach–Bliley Act (15 USCS §78c note), passed in 1999, which repealed part of the Glass–Steagall Act of 1933 by allowing competition between banks, insurance companies and securities companies.

derivatives are far more flexible than exchange-traded derivatives. They are

> individually negotiated, bilateral notional amount agreements
> including swaps, providing for cash flows based on move-
> ments in interest, currency, equity, commodity or other indices
> (or a combination thereof), and swap-related products which
> are, or have certain characteristics similar to, options (including
> caps and floors and OTC options on those indices or on
> securities or commodities themselves).[7]

It is true that OTC markets "operate on an ad hoc basis with no regulatory infrastructure, and as such, the 'market' is simply a collection of individual transactions".[8] OTC markets are not self-regulated by the rules of a formal exchange, but the perception that OTC markets are "unregulated" overlooks the regulation of the major market players in different ways and the codes of conduct in many OTC markets.[9] For these reasons, OTC markets can give rise to uncertainty and risk aversion.[10] Finance theory and experience demonstrate that OTC markets are not transparent and have minimal price transparency.[11]

Derivatives markets attract both hedgers and speculators so that each can hedge their bets against an uncertain future price by making a contract for future trading at today's price by buying or selling a derivative contract. A CDS is an OTC product designed to manage financial risk which allows a debt holder to hedge the risk by insuring against credit risk (default). Speculators may buy into the market and gamble on changes in prices. The debt holder (the buyer of the swap) swaps the risk of the debt for the

---

[7]Henderson, S.K. (1999), "Credit Derivatives," in Hudson, A. (ed.), *Credit Derivatives: Law, Regulation and Accounting Issues*, London: Sweet and Maxwell, p. 2.

[8]MacNeil, I.G. (2005), *An Introduction to the Law on Financial Investment*, Oxford and Portland, Oregon: Hart, p. 286. This is picked up in MiFID, Art 4 (Definitions) cl 1(2)(14):

> "Regulated market" means a multilateral system operated and/or
> managed by a market operator, which brings together or facilitates
> the bringing together of multiple third-party buying and selling
> interests in financial instruments — in the system and in accordance
> with its nondiscretionary rules — in a way that results in a contract,
> in respect of the financial instruments admitted to trading under its
> rules and/or systems, and which is authorised and functions regularly
> and in accordance with the provisions.

[9]ICAP (2008), "White Paper: The Future of the OTC Markets," 10 November, para 1.1, at http://www.icap.com, accessed 1 September 2010.

[10]Brown, C. and Davis, K. (2008), "The Sub-Prime Crisis Down Under," *Journal of Applied Finance*, 18:1, 16, 27.

[11]See, e.g. Das, S., *Supra* note 2, pp. 6, 126.

creditworthiness of the issuer (the seller of the swap). The seller receives payments from the buyer. In return, the seller of the swap will be obliged to pay the buyer if there is a specified event like bankruptcy or default by the buyer.

Hedgers and speculators are exposed to financial risk, and losses with derivatives could be unlimited. In the view of Warren Buffett, derivatives are "financial weapons of mass destruction carrying dangers that, now while latent, are potentially lethal".[12]

OTC derivatives are designed for the individual customer and may be based on any amount, tenor, maturity date or product. In contrast, exchange-traded derivatives are standardized in contract size, expiry date and approved products (the "underlyings"). They are issued when a person enters into the legal relationship that constitutes the financial product.[13]

Each party to an OTC contract enters its own contract. Because there is the risk of default, each party must assess the creditworthiness of the other party and its ability to perform its obligations through the life of the trade. Because OTC derivatives are negotiated privately, they fall outside direct regulation by regulators such as the Australian Securities and

---

[12]Buffett, W.E. (2003), Chairman's letter, 21 February, in Berkshire Hathaway Inc. *2002 Annual Report*, 15. There were reports that European auctions to settle CDS claims linked to the collapse of three Icelandic banks were successful: *Financial Times* (US edition) (2008), 7 November, p. 22.

The former financial services firm, Lehman Brothers Holdings Inc., filed for Chapter 11 bankruptcy protection in the US in September 2008. This was reported to be the largest bankruptcy in US history. Before this, ISDA had provided risk mitigation provisions (such as netting and collateral), legally enforceable under the ISDA Master Agreement, to assist in the event of any counterparty failure. ISDA had provided for a special OTC derivatives trading session on Sunday, 14 September 2008, to permit parties to reduce their market risk ahead of the then potential bankruptcy filing by entering into transactions with other participants.

On 21 October 2008, creditors of Lehman Brothers who had acquired CDSs to hedge against the risk of a Lehman bankruptcy were scheduled to settle those accounts. One of these was American International Group (AIG), a major public company which had issued many of the Lehman CDSs. The amount of the settlement was reported in the media to be between USD100 billion and USD400 billion. This was a gross figure; the net payments required in the settlement of the Lehman CDSs was USD5.2 billion.

There is the danger of systemic risk and a "domino effect" if a firm with large OTC derivatives positions goes into bankruptcy. This is the reason the US Fed provided JP Morgan with a short-term line of credit to assist the purchase (rescue) of Bear Stearns, a very large player in the OTC market for CDS.

[13]*Corporations Act 2001* (Cth) s 761E(3), item 3. This is the main Australian legislation affecting the OTC market. It is national, one-stop regulation passed by the government of the Commonwealth of Australia, operating Australia-wide.

Investments Commission (ASIC).[14] In the words of the then ASIC deputy chairman:

> these contracts are privately negotiated and trade in non-transparent and largely unregulated markets. The mechanisms for weighing up the overall risks of these instruments have been shown to be inadequate and their complexity has meant that almost all institutions have not fully appreciated their potential risks.[15]

In contrast, exchange-traded derivatives on regulated financial markets are regulated by ASIC under its legislative powers, subject to the jurisdiction of the courts and the legal system. This includes ASIC's accountability to the federal parliament. ASIC regulation, such as it is, is indirect by means of ASIC powers over "financial products",[16] including its licensing power.

Further differences between exchange-traded and OTC derivatives involve the following risks:[17]

(i) Legal risk: Settlements of OTC derivatives may be delayed and payment netting may not be recognized by the laws of some countries. Trading may be slowed down by the need to obtain legal opinions. In contrast to OTC derivatives, exchange-traded derivatives are usually subject to a very detailed legal framework.

(ii) Price risk: An exchange-traded derivative can be closed out because exchange markets are liquid. It may not be possible to close out an OTC derivative because it may not be possible to ascertain a representative price if an OTC derivative is exotic and if there are no buyers.

---

[14] *Australian Securities and Investments Commission Act 2001* (Cth) (ASIC Act); asic.gov.au. Further regulation affecting exchange-traded derivatives includes the reporting obligations to AUSTRAC under the Anti-Money Laundering and Counter-Terrorism Financing Act 2006 (Cth). A person who acquires or disposes of a derivative as defined in the Corporations Act (a "reporting entity") must report this to AUSTRAC, as exchange-traded derivatives are included in s 6 as a "designated service" (s 6; items 33(b) and 35 of Table 1).

[15] Cooper, J., *Supra* note 4, para 7.

[16] *Corporations Act 2001* (Cth) s 763A.

[17] See, e.g. Harding, P.C. (2004), *Mastering the ISDA Master Agreements (1992 and 2002): A Practical Guide for Negotiators*, London: Pearson Education Ltd, pp. 3–4; Ward, V. (1993), "The Relationship with Exchange Traded Derivatives," in Cavalla, N. (ed.), *OTC Markets in Derivative Instruments*, London: Macmillan.

(iii) Settlement risk: Because the regulated financial market assumes the counterparty risk for each transaction once the initial trade has been made, it assumes responsibility for all payments for margins and margin calls. Settlement risk of exchange-traded derivatives is minimized as exchange regulation aims to ensure that the parties comply with their obligations within strict time limits.

3. INTRODUCTION TO REGULATION OF OTC DERIVATIVES IN AUSTRALIA

The definition of "financial product" in the Australian legislation[18] does not mention OTC derivatives by name. Instead, they are regulated indirectly by the *Corporations Act 2001* (Cth) and common law in at least eight different examples of OTC regulation, as discussed below. Many of these build on the research and give effect to the 50 recommendations in an Australian research report in 1997.[19]

In contrast to some other jurisdictions,[20] there is no direct Australian regulation of OTC financial products and OTC financial markets by ASIC. This does not mean that the market for OTC derivatives including CDSs in Australia is unregulated, as OTC derivatives are instead regulated indirectly by Australia's "three peaks" system of market regulation by ASIC, the Australian Prudential Regulation Authority (APRA) and the Australian Competition and Consumer Commission (ACCC).[21] The origins

---

[18] *Corporations Act 2001* (Cth) s 763A.

[19] Companies and Securities Advisory Committee (1997), *Regulation of On-exchange and OTC Derivatives Markets*, Final Report (CASAC Report), at www.camac.gov.au, accessed 1 September 2010. CASAC, originally set up in 1989, was renamed the Corporations and Markets Advisory Committee (CAMAC) in the financial services amendments as from March 2002.

[20] For instance, Canada; under the *Derivatives Act 2008* (Quebec) s 39, a dealer who engages in over-the-counter trading of a standardized derivative is deemed to operate a financial market. The Financial Services Authority's *London Code of Conduct for Principals and Broking Firms in the Wholesale Markets*, June 1999, sets out the principles and standards expected of broking firms in the wholesale markets, including OTC wholesale products as defined, at http://www.fsa.gov.uk/pubs/additional/lcc.pdf, accessed 1 September 2010.

[21] This fulfils one of Hudson's argument for reform — his call for a regulatory authority to consider the technical analysis of derivatives as well as the whole range of financial services products: Hudson, A. (1998), *The Law on Financial Derivatives*, London: Sweet & Maxwell, 2nd ed., p. 356; Hudson, A. (2009), *The Law of Finance*, London: Sweet & Maxwell, Chapter 32; see further links at http://www.alastairhudson.com, accessed 1 September 2010.

of Australia's three peaks go back several decades, but the system in its current form is the result of the consolidation of jurisdictions in the 1990s. As a result, and as discussed below, Australia has not faced a reassessment of OTC regulation as in many other jurisdictions.

4. OTC DERIVATIVES AND THE GLOBAL FINANCIAL CRISIS: PROPOSALS FOR NEW REGULATION

Derivatives have become household names due to the global financial crisis of 2007–2009 and the resulting loss of investor confidence and liquidity crisis. They are opaque and complex financial structures, and if in substantial numbers, have the potential to put companies at risk in periods of crisis. They have been identified as leading to build-ups in debt-triggering problems in earlier financial crises.[22] The omniscient comments of Hudson in 1998 hypothesized on the risk of derivatives trading destabilizing the world economy, wresting control of the economic tiller from the hands of national governments and contributing to the meltdown of the global financial system, giving rise to the need for a response from governments and the banking system.[23] Examination of the causes of and solutions to the world financial crisis has occupied the attention of many governments and regulators.

Commentators and politicians now talk of "highly complex and incorrectly rated financial instruments that packaged this debt and allowed it to circulate throughout the system in a high-stakes game of 'pass the parcel'";[24] "arcane instruments" like "synthetic collateralized debt obligation", "an amalgam of collateralized debt obligations" and "credit default swaps",[25] and "toxic assets".[26]

---

[22]See, e.g. International Organization of Securities Commissions (IOSCO) (1998), "Emerging Markets Committee, Causes, Effects and Regulatory Implications of Financial and Economic Turbulence", in *Emerging Markets, Interim Report*, September, p. 33, at www.iosco.org, accessed 1 September 2010.

[23]Hudson, A., *The Law on Financial Derivatives, Supra* note 21, pp. 352–353; not in the 4th ed., 2006.

[24]Sherry, N. (2008), "Has Australia's Corporate Law and Superannuation System Responded Well to the Global Financial Crisis?" Address to the National Press Club Canberra, 19 November, at http://minscl.treasurer.gov.au, accessed 1 September 2010.

[25]See, e.g. Morgenson, G. (2008), "How the Thundering Herd Faltered and Fell," *New York Times*, 9 December, p. 9.

[26]Guerrera, F. (2008), "Fed Takes $2.7bn Paper Loss on Bear," *Financial Times*, 24 October.

The global financial crisis turned the attention of the international regulatory community to OTC derivatives markets, with a flurry of research reports and proposals for new regulation of such markets, including the requirement that most derivatives be traded on markets and that they be cleared through clearinghouses.[27]

The G-20 world leaders[28] examined the world financial crisis in November 2008 in Washington DC, and issued a Declaration including an undertaking to

> request our Finance Ministers to formulate additional recommendations, including... strengthening the resilience and transparency of credit derivatives markets and reducing their systemic risks, including by improving the infrastructure of over-the-counter markets.

The G-20 leaders at the Pittsburgh summit in September 2009 recommended that standardized OTC derivative contracts be traded on exchanges or on electronic trading platforms. The summit further recommended that OTC derivative contracts be cleared through central counterparties by 2012, that they be reported to trade repositories, and that non-centrally cleared contracts be subject to higher capital requirements.[29]

This builds on the earlier G-20 recommendation that

> supervisors and regulators, building on the imminent launch of central counterparty services for credit default swaps (CDS) in some countries, should: speed efforts to reduce the systemic risks of CDS and over-the-counter (OTC) derivatives transactions; insist that market participants support exchange traded or electronic trading platforms for CDS contracts; expand OTC derivatives market transparency; and ensure that the infrastructure for OTC derivatives can support growing volumes.[30]

In tandem, the US President's Working Group on Financial Markets announced a series of initiatives to strengthen oversight and transparency

---

[27]Including recommendations of the Financial Stability Board (formerly the Financial Stability Forum) at http://www.financialstabilityboard.org, accessed 1 September 2010.
[28]The Group of Twenty (G-20) Finance Ministers and Central Bank Governors was established in 1999 to bring together systemically important industrialized and developing economies to discuss key issues in the global economy.
[29]G-20 (2009), Leaders' Statement: The Pittsburgh Summit, 24–25 September, available at http://www.pittsburghsummit.gov/mediacenter/129639.htm, accessed 25 February 2011.
[30]G-20 (2008), Declaration of the Summit on Financial Markets and the World Economy, November 15, Washington DC.

and to create a centralized market infrastructure for the OTC derivatives market, including credit default swaps:[31]

(i) The development of credit default swap central counterparties to reduce the systemic risk associated with counterparty credit exposures, to facilitate greater market transparency and to promote a more competitive trading environment including CDS exchange trading. This is discussed below. US regulators anticipate that one or more CDS central counterparties will commence operations in the near future.

(ii) The establishment of a Memorandum of Understanding (MOU) on consultation and information sharing regarding CDS central counterparties among the Federal Reserve Board of Governors, the Securities and Exchange Commission (SEC) and the Commodity Futures Trading Commission (CFTC). The then chairman of the SEC had announced a new MOU between the SEC, the US Federal Reserve and the CFTC to address credit default swaps.[32] This will improve investor protection with more transparency of the clearing agencies that may be established for credit default swaps.

(iii) Releasing a new set of policy objectives, possibly in legislation, to address the challenges of OTC derivatives and to report on the strengthening of the infrastructure of OTC derivatives markets, including the following policy objectives:

(a) Improve the transparency and integrity of the CDS market;
(b) enhance risk management of OTC derivatives;
(c) further strengthen the OTC derivatives market infrastructure, and
(d) strengthen cooperation among regulatory authorities.

Further, the Basel Committee on Banking Supervision[33] has recommended new requirements on counterparty risk to discourage OTC transactions and to move OTC derivatives contracts to on-exchange.

---

[31]US Department of the Treasury (2008), "PWG Announces Initiatives to Strengthen OTC Derivatives Oversight and Infrastructure," 14 November, at http://treas.tpaq. treasury.gov/press/releases/hp1272.htm, accessed 1 September 2010.

[32]US Securities and Exchange Commission (2008), "SEC Chairman Cox Statement on MOU with Federal Reserve, CFTC to Address Credit Default Swaps," 14 November, at http://www.sec.gov/news/press/2008/2008-269.htm, accessed 1 September 2010.

[33]The Basel Committee on Banking Supervision was created by the central bank governors of the Group of Ten nations as an informal forum to set supervisory standards and recommendations for best practice in banking supervision, with the purpose of encouraging convergence toward common approaches and standards http://www.bis.org/bcbs/index.htm, accessed 25 February 2011.

In addition, Basel II recommendations include strengthening the capital requirements for counterparty credit risk exposures arising from OTC derivatives to help strengthen banking institutions, and to increase incentives to move OTC derivative exposures to central counterparties and exchanges.[34] Basel II has also recommended requiring swaps dealers and major swap participants to be regulated by the SEC and the CFTC.

5. ANY LESSONS FOR AUSTRALIA FROM THE US ON THE REGULATION OF OTC DERIVATIVES?

At present, credit default swaps are generally not regulated in the US as either securities or insurance.[35] The decision not to regulate OTC derivatives was influenced by evidence from former Federal Reserve Board Chair Alan Greenspan in 2000 that regulation of the OTC derivatives market was not needed because

> OTC transactions in financial derivatives are not susceptible to — that is, easily influenced by — manipulation. The vast majority of contracts are settled in cash, based on a rate or price determined in a separate highly liquid market with a very large or virtually unlimited deliverable supply. Furthermore, prices established in OTC transactions do not serve a price-discovery function. Thus, even if the price of an OTC contract were somehow manipulated, the adverse effects on the economy would be quite limited. With respect to fraud and other unfair practices, the professional counterparties that use OTC derivatives simply do not require the protections that CEA provides for retail investors. If professional counterparties are victimized, they can obtain redress under the laws applicable to contracts generally.[36]

---

[34]Bank for International Settlements (2009), "Strengthening the Resilience of the Banking Sector — Consultative Document," December, at http://www.bis.org/publ/bcbs164. htm, accessed 1 September 2010.

[35]See, e.g. US Department of the Treasury (2008), *The Department of the Treasury Blueprint for a Modernized Financial Regulatory Structure,* Washington DC, March, p. 47, at http://www.treas.gov/press/releases/reports/Blueprint.pdf, accessed 1 September 2010. The Commodities Futures Modernization Act of 2000 (US) excludes OTC financial derivatives between sophisticated counterparties from regulation by the CFTC, the SEC or anyone else on the basis that they are not susceptible to manipulation. Hence the CFMA excluded OTC derivatives from commodities regulation, including antifraud provisions.

[36]Greenspan, A. (2000), "Over-the-Counter Derivatives," Testimony before the Committee on Agriculture, Nutrition and Forestry, United States Senate, 10 February,

This is no advance on the words of Rountree in 1993 that "(a) consistent regulatory framework is critical to the efficiency and long-term effectiveness of the derivative markets and it is in the interest of both the regulators and the participants to ensure that this objective is achieved".[37]

Attitudes are changing after the experience of the global financial crisis of 2007–2009. Chris Cox, the then chairman of the US SEC, was critical of the lack of regulation of the OTC derivatives market. He was critical of the "significant opportunities that exist for manipulation in the USD58 trillion CDS market, which is completely lacking in transparency and completely unregulated".[38] Three days later Cox stated that

> (u)nfortunately, as I reported to Congress this week, a massive hole remains: the approximately $60 trillion credit default swap (CDS) market, which is regulated by no agency of government. Neither the SEC nor any regulator has authority even to require minimum disclosure. I urge Congress to take swift action to address this.[39]

Australia's three peaks of market regulation contrast with the "alphabet soup" of US derivatives regulation watchdogs, which currently include the SEC, the CFTC, the Office of Thrift Supervision (OTS), the Federal Deposit Insurance Corporation (FDIC) and the Securities Investor Protection Corporation (SIPC). Add to these the "four horsemen of derivatives regulation",[40] and the distinctions in the US regulatory divisions of the

---

at http://www.federalreserve.gov/boarddocs/testimony/2000/20000210.htm, accessed 1 September 2010.

[37] Rountree, R. (1999), "Accounting and Regulation," in Cavalla, N. *Supra* note 17, p. 240. This is not a new issue in the US: e.g. Stout, L. (1999), "Why the Law Hates Speculators: Regulation and Private Ordering in the Market for OTC Derivatives," *Duke Law Journal*, 48:701.

[38] Cox, C. (2008), "Turmoil in US Credit Markets: Recent Actions Regarding Government Sponsored Entities, Investment Banks and Other Financial Institutions," Testimony before the Committee on Banking, Housing and Urban Affairs, United States Senate, 23 September, at http://banking.senate.gov/public/_files/COXTestimony92308.pdf, accessed 1 September 2010.

[39] Securities and Exchange Commission (2008), "Chairman Cox Announces End of Consolidated Supervised Entities Program," 2008-230, 26 September.

[40] Partnoy, F. (2001), "ISDA, NASD, CFMA, and SDNY: The Four Horsemen of Derivatives Regulation?" University of San Diego, Public Law Research Paper No 39, 29 November, available on SSRN. The four horsemen are the International Swaps and Derivatives Association (for OTC derivatives), the legal rules applied in arbitration of disputes by the National Association of Securities Dealers, the Commodity Futures Modernization Act of 2000 and the case law in the jurisdiction of the US federal judges in the Southern District of New York.

past between commercial banking, investment banking, insurance, private equity and hedge funds.

The Economist has described the SEC "as a cracked piston in a sputtering regulatory engine that dates back to the 1930s".[41] In the US, there is growing expression of the view that the US financial services regulation does not fulfil the needs of a fully integrated global financial system. There are calls for consolidation of regulators with the creation of a British-style "super-regulator" along the lines of the Financial Services Authority (or its successor).[42] For example, the then SEC chair has called for amalgamation of the SEC and the CFTC, which would result in regulation of financial products like credit default swaps that can currently be used as synthetic substitutes for regulated securities.[43] The chairman of the CFTC has called for a new "objectives-based" regulatory regime under three new primary authorities — a systemic risk regulator, a market integrity regulator and an investor protection regulator. Under the proposed risk regulator, traders of various OTC instruments would need to report market data to regulators when those products "begin playing a public pricing role or when their size creates the risk of a systemic event".[44]

CDS and CDS indices may cease to be traded over-the-counter and be moved to regulated exchanges. This could reduce counterparty risk and so increase transparency, or could the risk be managed by establishing clearing houses without the need to trade them on an exchange?[45] In the view of ICAP, the interdealer broker, an exchange solution "needlessly grants the exchange a monopoly on trade execution" which would lead to restricted access to clearing, increased costs and diminished flexibility.[46]

---

[41] *The Economist* (2009), "The Securities and Exchange Commission: Growing Insecurities," 15 January.

[42] Spitzer, E. (2008), "How to Ground the Street," *Washington Post*, 16 November, p. B01. New UK financial regulation is coming into focus: Treasury (2010), *A New Approach to Financial Regulation: Judgment, Focus, Stability* (Cm 7874) at http://www.hmtreasury.gov.uk/d/consult_financial_regulation_condoc.pdf, accessed 1 September 2010.

[43] Cox, C. (2008), "Building on Strengths in Designing the New Regulatory Structure," Speech at the PLI 40th Annual Securities Regulation Institute, New York, 12 November.

[44] Lukken, W.L. (2009), Keynote Address before FIA Futures and Options Expo, Chicago, Illinois, 11 November, at http://www.cftc.gov/stellent/groups/public/@news room/documents/speechandtestimony/opalukken50.pdf, accessed 1 September 2010.

[45] Grant, J. and Dickson, M. (2008), "CDS Trades 'Likely to Shift to Exchanges,' *Financial Times* (Asia ed.), 26 November, p. 27.

[46] ICAP White Paper, *Supra* note 9, para 1.5.

6. REGULATION OF OTC DERIVATIVES IN AUSTRALIA

OTC Self-regulation: AFMA/ISDA

Contracts in off-exchange or over-the-counter OTC derivatives are bilateral, privately negotiated contracts between counterparties. The contracts are not standardized and they are not made on an exchange (a financial market, a futures exchange).[47] Regulation of OTC contracts is based on "governance arrangements for OTC derivatives [that] are predominantly based on private sector-inspired practices of self-regulation and self-supervision".[48] OTC contracts take place in a self-regulatory framework involving trade associations in conjunction with government and regulators based upon shared transnational understanding which includes market practice (industry usage), conventions and standard documentation such as terms like those of the Australian Financial Markets Association (AFMA) and the International Swaps and Derivatives Association (ISDA).[49]

OTC derivatives exposure in Australia is relatively low by international standards, and is low in absolute terms, with the exception of interest rate and foreign exchange products.

---

[47]If they were standardized contracts, there would be a case for a public electronic exchange with full disclosure to overcome the private conversations and the absence of transparency evident with directly negotiated contracts.

[48]Tsingou, E. (2006), "The Governance of OTC Derivatives Markets," in Mooslechner, P., Schuberth, H. and Weber, B. *The Political Economy of Financial Market Regulation: The Dynamics of Inclusion and Exclusion*, Cheltenham, UK: Edward Elgar, p. 186.

[49]The AFMA webpage states that AFMA represents over 130 industry participants in the wholesale banking and financial markets, including Australian and foreign banks, securities companies, state government treasury corporations, fund managers, traders in electricity and other specialized markets and industry service providers, www.afma.com.au, accessed 25 February 2011. AFMA members are the leading participants in Australia's on-exchange and off-exchange financial markets, with a turnover of more than $81 trillion in 2006/2007; e.g. AFMA, *Guide to Australian OTC Transactions*. ISDA was formed in New York in 1985, originally with 10 members. ISDA has over 860 member institutions from 57 countries on six continents, which include most of the major institutions that deal in OTC derivatives, as well as many of the end-users like businesses and governmental entities which use OTC derivatives to manage financial market risk: www.isda.org, accessed 1 September 2010; Harding, *Supra* note 17, p. 19. Other relevant trade associations include the International Securities Lending Association (UK; ISLA; www.isla.co.uk, accesssed 1 September 2010) and the Securities Industry and Financial Markets Association (US; SIFMA; www.sifma.org), which have also been recognized by regulators, e.g. in the EU and the US, as a valid basis for netting exposures for the purposes of regulatory capital and risk reporting.

OTC trading is subject to regulatory oversight, along with risk management controls and the requirements of corporate governance and financial reporting. In addition, the conduct of swap participants within this self-regulatory framework is guided by the discipline of the market.

Australia's financial authorities have examined OTC derivatives markets following the recommendations of the Financial Stability Board to assess market practices.[50] This has included a survey of Australia's OTC derivatives landscape, with the conclusion that there remains scope for further improvements in operational and risk-management practices.[51] In particular, the report encourages industry participants to consolidate and to build on recent enhancements in market practice to continue to improve market transparency, to ensure continued progress in the timely negotiation of industry-standard legal documentation, to expand the use of collateral in order to manage counterparty credit risks, to promote Australian access to central counterparties for OTC derivatives products, to expand the use of automated facilities for confirmations processing, to expand the use of multilateral "portfolio compression" and reconciliation tools and to increase Australian influence in international industry forums.

Australian Market Licence (AML)

Under the former "on-exchange trading rule", futures contracts had to be traded on a licensed financial market holding an Australian Market Licence.[52] This had the effect of limiting the development of standardized OTC products

---

[50] *Supra* note 27.

[51] APRA (2009), Survey of the OTC Derivaties Market in Australia, 2–3 May, at http:// www.apra.gov.au / Media-Releases / upload / Survey-of-the-OTC-Derivatives-Market-in-Australia-report.pdf, accessed 1 September 2010.

[52] See Gengatharen, R. (2001), *Derivatives Law and Regulation*, Boston: Kluwer Law International, p. 14. Former Corporations Law s 1258, which replaced former Futures Industry Act 1986 (Cth) and State Codes s 128, stated that "An eligible futures broker shall not deal in a futures contract on behalf of another person unless the dealing is effected: (a) on a futures market of a futures exchange. . .". (The Corporations Law was a schedule to the Corporations Act 1989 (Cth), passed by the Commonwealth to apply in the ACT. It was adopted by each State and the NT under the name Corporations Law.) It was introduced in the 1986 Act in response to manipulative off-exchange practices directed mainly at retail investors: CASAC Report, *Supra* note 19, para 4.9. In the view of CASAC, it would not be practical to require all derivatives transactions to be effected on a licensed market or an exempt market (bearing in mind that derivatives is a much wider concept than futures): *Ibid.*, para 4.15. The former s 1258 became redundant with the licensing requirements for exchanges, now in the form of the AML licensing requirements for financial markets in financial products (s 767A) in the *Corporations Act 2001* (Cth).

or documentation to the former definition of a "futures contract",[53] a definition based on standardization. For an OTC derivative to fall within the definition of a "futures contract", the OTC market would have to be migrated to be traded on an organized market regulated by ASIC.

The former "on-exchange trading rule" is now superseded by current definitions. If OTC derivatives trading qualifies as a "financial market" (*Corporations Act 2001* (Cth) s 767A) trading "financial products" (s 763A), the operator of the OTC platform would need to be licensed by ASIC with an Australian Market Licence (s 791A). The definition of a financial product includes one of the purposes of an OTC derivative, namely, a facility for managing financial risk (s 763C).

The note to s 763C includes, as examples of managing financial risk, hedging a liability by acquiring a futures contract or entering into a currency swap. If either of these takes place person-to-person — not through a financial market — there would be no need for a licence. The Explanatory Memorandum made clear that "most transactions which are considered to form part of the informal 'OTC market'" are excluded from the financial market definition under s 767A(2)(a) if a party is "making or accepting . . . offers or invitations to acquire or dispose of financial products in circumstances that involve direct negotiation between the parties who each accept the counterparty credit risk".[54]

Licensing of financial markets serves the public interest to ensure *inter alia* standards of competence.[55] It also removes the independence and unaccountability of self-regulation. The *Corporations Act 2001* (Cth) sets out licensing preconditions in, for example, s 795B, which includes evidence of adequate operating rules and adequate arrangements for supervising the market.[56] The Operating Rules (Listing Rules, Market Rules) of licensed

---

[53] *Futures Industry Act 1986* (Cth) and State Codes s 4(1).

[54] Financial Services Reform Bill 2001, *Explanatory Memorandum*, para 7.15; also para 7.13.

[55] Set out in *Corporations Act 2001* (Cth) (Chapter 7: Financial Services and Markets). An entity must have an Australian Market Licence to operate a "financial market" which trades "financial products" that include financial investments (securities) and managing financial risk (derivatives) (s 791A).

[56] Building on the CASAC Report, *Supra* note 19, Recommendation 8:

> Any applicant for authorisation of a market that involves fungible derivatives transactions (that is, any standardised agreements that are fully interchangeable with substitute transactions of the same class) and from which retail end-users are not excluded should only be authorised to conduct a financial exchange.

financial markets, written by the financial market (SFE), are binding in contract.[57]

Once licensed, the operator of a financial market for derivatives is subject to ASIC regulation and oversight (e.g. ss 793C, 794D). This includes ASIC's power to investigate and collect information under the ASIC Act.

A market licensee is under many statutory obligations. It must ensure that the market is "fair, orderly and transparent".[58] If requested by ASIC, it must give information to ASIC regarding listed companies (s 792C), it must assist the Commission (s 792D) (including assisting surveillance checks by ASIC: s 912E), and it must give ASIC access to the market (s 792E).

Licensing gives rise to checks and balances, such as the obligation of ASIC to assess financial market compliance in its annual compliance reports (s 794C). A market licensee must lodge an Annual Compliance Report with ASIC (s 792F). In addition, the Act requires a licensee to provide an Annual Report detailing the extent to which the licensee has complied with its obligations under Chapter 7 of the Corporations Act and the *Corporations Regulations 2001* (Cth).

The Commonwealth Government ("the Minister") can give a formal direction to a financial market (s 794A) and to ASIC.[59] The Commonwealth Government ("the Minister") may call for a report on specified matters (s 794B). A market licensee may refer matters to (notification) the Commission (plus ASX/ASIC MOU).

Effective regulation of financial markets to maintain, facilitate and improve the performance of the financial system and the entities within that system[60] could justify the migration of more OTC contracts to an exchange-traded market. Incomplete markets are one cause of market failure, so such a move may overcome asymmetry of information, especially at turning points, when there may be sharp reductions in liquidity as a result of unexpected changes in conditions.[61] Trading OTC contracts on a licensed exchange

---

[57] *Corporations Act 2001* (Cth) ss 793A–793C. In effect, the operating rules, when they are "not disallowed" by the Minister (ss 793D–793E), are approved by the Commonwealth Government. These include the details of the SFE financial products set out in the Operating Rules of the Sydney Futures Exchange, Section 6 (Contract Specifications and Associated Rules), October 2008.

[58] *Corporations Act 2001* (Cth) s 792A(a).

[59] *Australian Securities and Investments Commission Act 2001* (Cth) s 12 (policy); s 14 (investigations).

[60] See *Australian Securities and Investments Commission Act 2001* (Cth) s 1(2)(a).

[61] Kearns, J. and Lowe, P. (2008), "Promoting Liquidity: Why and How?" *Lessons from the Financial Turmoil of 2007 and 2008*, Reserve Bank of Australia 2008 Conference, 14–15 July, at www.rba.gov.au, accessed 1 September 2010.

would also include settlement through a central counterparty (see *Clearing House* below).

Exempt Financial Markets

Some OTC markets involving foreign exchange contracts, foreign exchange derivatives, foreign exchange options and CDSs have been declared by ASIC to be exempt financial markets if the market involves professional investors and there is no involvement of retail investors. The market operator is spared some regulatory burden, but will need an Australian Financial Services Licence (AFSL), must lodge an annual report with ASIC and must undertake to cooperate with ASIC.[62]

Australian Financial Services Licence

There is overlap between market makers (who offer to trade with each other on a principal-to-principal basis) and dealers (who buy and sell financial products).

Australia regulates OTC transactions indirectly by requiring a person who carries on "financial services business" to have an AFSL. This brings them under ASIC regulation.[63]

---

[62] *Corporations Act 2001* (Cth) s 791C; listed under "Exempt Markets" on the ASIC website at asic.gov.au, accessed 1 September 2010.
This picks up on the following:

> CASAC Report, *Supra* note 19, Recommendation 1: The legislation should distinguish between wholesale and retail participants in derivatives markets...
> CASAC Recommendation 2: There should be no regulatory restrictions on retail participation in OTC derivatives markets, provided the safeguards for retail end-users recommended in this Report are implemented.
> CASAC Recommendation 23: (ASIC) should have a power to exempt parties whose activities might sometimes constitute market-making (sellers), but who are predominantly end-users, from the OTC market-maker licensing provisions.
> Market-making includes professional intermediaries like funds management, treasury operations and trustee corporations who will structure and enter either side of an OTC transaction as principal for their wholesale counterparties.

[63] *Corporations Act 2001* (Cth) s 911A. CASAC Report, *Supra* note 19, Recommendations 14, 20, 21, 22, 24, 25.

"Financial services business" includes providing "financial product advice". An OTC contract is a "financial product" (s 763A(1)(b)) because a person "manages financial risk" (s 763C). The Corporations Act gives acquiring a futures contract or entering a currency swap as examples of managing financial risk (s 763C note 1(b)).[64] Broad as it is, the definition of a "financial product" excludes exempt forward contracts, which are not cash-settled (s 761D(3), s 765A(1)(n)).

In addition, there are exemptions from the need for an AFSL in the case of "financial product advice" (including OTC trading) by APRA-regulated bodies (s 911A(2)(g)) (below), persons regulated by overseas regulatory authorities (s 911A(2)(h)) and foreign financial service providers providing a financial service in specified circumstances.[65]

Once licensed, a licensee is under many statutory obligations such as the core principle to observe the objective standard of acting "efficiently, honestly and fairly".[66]

Clearing House

In the case of exchange-traded derivatives in Australia, licensing of clearing and settlement facilities is provided for in the Corporations Act.[67] There may be counterparty risk in an OTC derivatives position because it is a private off-exchange contract between two parties where it may be impossible to know who is on the other side of a swap contract and what risks may be involved. If one party defaults, the other party would be left with a nonperforming contract.

One solution for counterparty risk is to interpose a clearing corporation between buyer and seller as the legal counterparty to both parties to localize risk. A clearing house for standardized contracts would eliminate the externalities of failure by providing risk management of both exposures so that if one party defaults, the other is not affected. The clearing house

---

[64]Baxt, R., Black, A. and Hanrahan, P. (2008), *Securities and Financial Services Law*, Sydney: LexisNexis, para 3.19.

[65]This is s 911A(2A) to s 911(2E), inserted by *Corporations Regulations 2001* (Cth) reg 7.6.02AG (Modification of section 911A of the Act). Many constitutional issues are raised by purported amendments to legislation enacted by regulations; also Baxt, R. *et al.*, *Supra* note 64, para 14.14.

[66]*Corporations Act 2001* (Cth) s 912A. ASIC has set out its views on the client money provisions in *Corporations Act 2001* (Cth) Pt 7.8 Div 2 with reference to derivatives: Consultation Paper 114, *Client Money Relating to Derivatives*, August 2009.

[67]*Corporations Act 2001* (Cth) Part 7.3. This is one of Hudson's arguments for reform — his call for a clearing house in the case of standardized derivatives to control credit risk between parties: Hudson, A., *Supra* note 21, p. 354.

would need sufficient capital, hold collateral from participants and monitor their exposure. Maintaining the credibility and the solvency of the clearing house is an important object of derivatives industry regulation.[68]

Counterparty risk is being identified as one of the causes of the global financial crisis of 2007–2009, and, following analysis of the causes, there are increasing calls for a clearing house for OTC derivatives. Further recommendations to increase the resilience of markets and institutions can be expected to follow.

For example, the Counterparty Risk Management Policy Group III has recommended the creation of central clearing counterparties (CCPs) for transactions (starting with CDSs) to improve the stability of credit derivatives by creating a "shock absorber" to lessen the impact of default.[69] This would be through initial margin, variation margin and a guarantee fund, designed to mutualize counterparty risk with a reduction in the number of trades to be unwound in the event of default. The Group III Report has acknowledged the challenges in setting up a clearing house, including the importance of participant criteria (that there are sound and reliable counterparties, with adequate resources, operational capacity and appropriate capital requirements as protection from risk of default). Other identified challenges include the availability of daily end-of-day pricing across the entire cleared portfolio, and the establishment of the appropriate margin and guarantee fund structure.

The SEC is working within its current authority with industry participants to reduce counterparty risk on a voluntary basis. The then chair of the SEC had called on Congress to authorize US federal regulators to mandate the use of one or more central counterparties for the CDS market.[70] Pending the final regulatory environment for OTC derivatives, the SEC, the Federal Reserve and the CFTC in the US have authorized until September 2009 temporary CCPs to clear certain credit default swaps.[71]

In Europe, there are calls by the European Commission and the European Central Bank to create a "European solution" by June 2009 for

---

[68]Latimer, P. (1990), "Futures Market Regulation in Australia: What Is It Trying to Achieve?" *University of New South Wales Law Journal* 13:370, 384.

[69]Counterparty Risk Management Policy Group III (2008), *Containing Systemic Risk: The Road to Reform*, 6 August, pp. 125–130, at www.crmpolicygroup.org, accessed 1 September 2010.

[70]Cox, C., *Supra* note 43.

[71]Aguilar, L.A. (2009), "Speech by SEC Commissioner: Empowering the Markets Watchdog to Effect Real Results," North American Securities Administrators Association's Winter Enforcement Conference, San Diego, California, 10 January, at http://www.sec.gov/news/speech/2009/spch011009laa.htm, accessed 25 February 2011.

the clearing of OTC CDSs in the form of a temporary CDS clearing house. One current issue to be resolved concerns extraterritoriality uncertainties due to the EU's lack of regulatory and supervisory offshore jurisdiction and access to information, for example, in the case of a clearing house subject to US jurisdiction.[72]

Market Misconduct

As OTC contracts are privately negotiated contracts on a public regulated market with no mandatory disclosure, there is a potential for an OTC market to provide a cover for institutions to sell OTC at an unfair or non-transparent price. If so, there are many provisions in Australia regulating the market conduct of parties to OTC contracts, such as legislation dealing with misleading or deceptive conduct.[73]

Common Law

OTC transactions are of course subject to common law remedies including the liabilities of principal/agent, breach of contract and negligence.[74]

Prudential Regulation: Capital Requirements and Risk Management

APRA Prudential Standard APS *Capital Adequacy: Market Risk* "aims to ensure that all deposit-taking institutions engaged in activities giving rise to risks associated with potential movements in market prices adopt

---

[72] Grant, J. and Tait, N. (2009), "European CDS Clearing Hits Hurdle," *Financial Times* (Asia ed.), 13 January, p. 23.

[73] For instance, *Australian Securities and Investments Commission Act 2001* (Cth) s 12DA; Corporations Act 2001 (Cth) s 1041H; Baxt, R. *et al.*, *Supra* note 64, para 8.79–8.93.

> CASAC Report, *Supra* note 19, Recommendation 45: ASIC should have a power to control undesirable derivatives advertising by prohibiting a person from publishing or broadcasting statements concerning on-exchange or OTC derivatives.

[74] Baxt, R. *et al.*, *Supra* note 64, para 15.11.

management practices and meet regulatory capital requirements that are commensurate with the risks involved".[75]

In the case of OTC derivatives like credit default swaps, total rate of return swaps, credit-linked notes, first-to-default baskets, institutions must report to APRA their effect on transparency on credit portfolios, and they must give information to APRA as required by its Large Exposures Return.

Under APRA's reporting requirements, authorised deposit-taking institutions (ADIs) must provide APRA with details of credit derivative transactions that give rise to large exposures as required by APRA.

7. OTCs IN AUSTRALIA DURING THE GLOBAL FINANCIAL CRISIS

Australian financial markets are part of the global financial integration that has occurred with financial deregulation and the cross-border capital flows of the last 30 years. They are open to world trends, with no foreign exchange controls and no controls over the cross-border transfer of funds. Data from APRA, the Australian Treasury and the Reserve Bank of Australia demonstrates that Australian financial markets, financial institutions and financial products including OTCs are well-regulated under Australia's three peaks — ASIC, APRA and ACCC. In terms of regulatory changes, the Australian regulators are currently watching the actions of overseas regulators.

There is evidence that Australia's financial institutions are strong, and, for example, of the 11 banks around the world that are rated AA and above, four are Australian.[76] One reason Australian financial institutions

---

[75] Made under the *Banking Act 1959* (Cth).

> CASAC Report, *Supra* note 19, Recommendation 26: OTC market-makers (other than RBA-regulated entities and other exempt OTC market-makers) should be required to satisfy (ASIC) that they have a minimum satisfactory risk system for their derivatives transactions.

Recommendation 27: OTC market-makers (other than RBA-regulated entities and other exempt OTC market-makers) should be required to satisfy ASIC that they meet minimum capital standards.

APRA, Guidance Notes AGN 113.4: Treatment of Credit Derivatives in the Trading Book; AGN 113.1: The Trading Book and the Trading Book Policy Statement.

[76] Gillard, J., Then Deputy Prime Minister (2009), Address to the Australian Reception, World Economic Forum, Davos, Switzerland, 29 January, at http://www.deewr.gov.au/ Ministers/Gillard/Media/Speeches/Pages/Article_090130_100921.aspx, accessed 1 September 2010.

are less affected than many other countries by the global financial crisis of 2007–2009 may be that they are of lesser global significance. Another reason is that most trades of credit risk derivatives in Australia (and East Asia) are carried out by foreign firms under the ISDA master agreement, which is itself a risk mitigation tool.[77]

The Australian financial system is strong and in the view of the Reserve Bank is reported to be coping well with the global financial crisis:[78]

> In this difficult environment, Australia has benefited from having strong and profitable financial institutions with few problem assets on their balance sheets, and a sound regulatory regime. While the Australian financial system has not been completely insulated from developments abroad, it is weathering the current difficulties much better than many other financial systems.

---

[77]In Australia the most affected firm appears to have been the ANZ Bank, which seems to have lost AUD$530 million in the US CDS market but which has also indicated that part of that loss may be recouped as the crisis in the market passes. See, e.g. Murdoch, S. (2008), "ANZ Warns of More Bad Debts," *The Australian*, 19 December, p. 19.

[78]Reserve Bank of Australia (2008), Financial Stability Review — September 2008, Overview, available at www.rba.gov.au, quoted by Dr John Laker, Handsard, Senate, Standing Committee on Estimates, Economics, 23 October, E4, at http://www.aph.gov. au/hansard/senate/committee/S11358.pdf, accessed 1 September 2010.

Chapter 5

CREDIT DERIVATIVES: UNDERSTANDING THEIR CHARACTERISTICS AND RISK POTENTIAL

P.M. Vasudev

[Derivatives] are an increasingly important vehicle for unbundling risks. These instruments enhance the ability to differentiate risk and allocate it to those investors most able and willing to take it.

Alan Greenspan (1999)

1. INTRODUCTION

Credit derivatives played an important role in the financial market events of 2008–2009, usually referred to as the "credit crisis". Collateralized debt obligations (CDOs)[1] and credit default swaps (CDSs) are among the major credit derivatives developed by the financial industry in the recent decades. This chapter examines the characteristics of these financial instruments, to understand their risk potential. To do so, it traces the process by which CDOs and CDSs were transformed from their original conception — as devices for improving the returns from debt securities and diffusing the credit risk in them — into instruments of financial speculation and agents of systemic instability. Tracing the developments is helpful in gaining a better understanding of the risks became embedded in CDOs and CDSs.

"Synthetic" collateralized debt obligations, which are built around "reference" portfolios of debt securities, offer a good illustration of risk

---

[1] Here I have used "CDOs" as a composite term to include all securitized debts, including mortgage-backed and asset-backed securities.

potential. In this variety of CDO, the underlying debt securities do not change hands; in other words there is no transfer, or diffusion, of the credit risk — which was the original justification for the derivatives. Despite the fact that synthetic CDOs did not involve any transfer of risk from the lenders, credit default swaps were (and are) sold for them. The default swaps entitle the "counterparties" to payment from the sellers of swaps in the event of default in the securities included in the reference portfolio or a fall in the market value of the CDO. These market practices made a significant contribution to systemic risk and the credit crisis. Their consequences were exemplified, quite dramatically, by the meltdown at American International Group (AIG), which was a leading seller of CDSs.

In the US, the *Dodd–Frank Wall Street Reform and Consumer Protection Act* has just been enacted,to regulate the trade in derivatives. It is apparent that the underlying approach is inadequate, viewed from the perspective of risk and the experience from the credit crisis. The legislation does not concern itself with the substantive character of the derivative instruments. It merely addresses the mechanics of trade in them, and the legislative measures provide for a transition from unregulated, over-the-counter (OTC) markets to a more orderly framework for trade in derivatives.

The goals are, obviously, to promote transparency in price discovery and develop procedures for clearing and settlement of trade transactions. These *are* improvements over the present situation, but they do not address an important cause of the problem — namely, the risk potential that is inherent in the credit derivatives as they have been engineered. This is an issue with the regulatory reforms just introduced. They do not substantially address the systemic risks in credit derivatives which contributed to, and exacerbated, the credit crisis of 2008–2009. This emphasizes the need for vigilance, on the part of investors and investment experts, about the risks in credit derivatives.

The chapter is divided into five parts. Sections 2 and 3 discuss, respectively, the characteristics of CDOs and CDSs. Synthetic CDOs and default swaps for this variety of CDO are the subject of Section 4. Section 5 concludes with a brief discussion of some practical aspects — namely, the issue of whether credit derivatives are "securities" for trade on stock exchanges, the documentation used for credit derivatives transactions and the trend in some recent legal cases on disputes related to them. A list of reference materials is appended at the end.

2. COLLATERALIZED DEBT OBLIGATIONS: IMPROVING THE YIELD FROM DEBT SECURITIES

A common complaint against credit derivatives is about their complexity. The features and characteristics of credit derivatives are described as being so complicated that they defy understanding — even by expert investors. In 1994, George Soros referred to this in a testimony before the Banking Committee of the US House of Representatives. The recent credit crisis generated considerable interest in these instruments, and they have been subject to more rigorous analysis. Now there is greater clarity about the nature and characteristics of credit derivatives. This section outlines the characteristics of CDOs and their features.

Collateralized debt obligations are, in essence, pools of debt securities. A broad range of debt securities, ranging from corporate bonds and residential and commercial mortgages to credit card debt and student loans, are bundled together and the resulting package is labelled a "CDO". Drexel Burnham Lambert, a financial firm which is now defunct, is credited with having devised CDOs in the 1980s. The theory underpinning CDOs is that by combining debt that is relatively safe but yielding low returns (e.g. corporate bonds with good credit rating) with less safe debt which carries higher returns (e.g. credit card balances and subprime residential mortgages), it is possible to develop a portfolio that finely balances risk and return. The process will, according to market theory, result in a portfolio that yields a better return with no significant increase in the average credit risk.

The discussion in this section deals with "balance-sheet CDO", in which the debt securities actually change hands from the originating lender to the special purpose vehicles (SPVs), or special-purpose entities (SPEs), which manage the CDO. Upon transfer, the debt portfolio is removed from the balance sheet of the lender, hence the name. Balance-sheet CDOs must be distinguished from synthetic CDOs in which the debt portfolio remains with the originating lender. The latter are discussed in Section 4.

Balance-Sheet CDO: An Outline

In a balance-sheet CDO, the consolidated securities or debt portfolios designated "CDO" are transferred by the originating lender to the SPV created for the purpose. The SPV then issues "notes" to the investors who purchase tranches or slices of the CDO. In this variety of CDO, the SPVs are fully funded to the extent of the nominal value of the debt securities pooled in them. Along with the debt portfolio, the credit risk in them is also transferred by the original lender to the SPVs. The SPVs, being fully funded, have the capacity to absorb any defaults by the borrowers and consequent losses in the CDO. Such losses will not trigger fresh liability for any party to make a payment. Balance-sheet CDOs, therefore, do not add to the risk overall. Credit risk continues at the pre-existing level and there is no increase or multiplication of the risk. It is merely transferred from the original lender to the SPVs, which would have the capability to handle any losses.

The CDO device has been used on a significant scale by banks and other lending institutions to transfer their loan portfolios to bond investors (see, e.g. Duffie, 2008). By doing so, the banks were able to comply with regulatory rules on capital; see, e.g. the statements of AIG in its annual report for 2007. They could also release the funds tied in the loans and recycle the funds. These were the advantages of CDOs for the lenders who sold them. For the buyers, the incentive was improving the yield from debt securities without a significant increase in the credit risk. These were, by and large, the commercial rationale for the purchasers of CDOs.

Incidentally, the ability of banks and other lenders to transfer debt portfolios and credit risk through CDOs also contributed to the so-called "moral hazard" problem. The lenders no longer had to be as sure of the creditworthiness of the borrowers, because they would transfer the credit risk soon after making the loan. There is evidence that this new-found method led to a fall in lending standards in recent years (see, e.g. Instefjord, 2005).

A CDO is about arriving at an optimum combination of diverse debt securities which provides a higher return without significantly increasing the average credit risk in the portfolio. A CDO, in other words, aims at averaging out the credit risk through a combination of high-risk/high-yield and low-risk/low-yield debt securities. The resulting combination would, according to market theory, achieve the twin goals of increasing the average yield of the portfolio without a significant increase in the average credit risk — indeed it would reduce the average risk. The theory underlying CDOs is shown in Fig. 1.

The logic of CDOs is plausible, perhaps even reasonable. However, the difficulty would be in striking the right blend or combination of securities — one that can achieve the twin goals of improving the return without

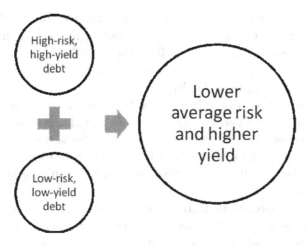

Fig. 1 The Theory of Collateralized Debt Obligations: Balancing Risk and Return.

increasing the risk. There would be immense challenges in assessing the risk in individual securities comprised in a CDO consisting of a large number of loans, grading the combination as a whole and defining the quality of the aggregate debt. In developing and marketing CDOs, the financial industry had to tackle the transition from theory to practice.

To build a low-risk/high-yield debt portfolio of the kind conceived in CDOs, the financial industry developed a number of techniques — which have added to the complexity of the instrument. These include the composite return models and the slicing, or "tranching", of the debt portfolios in CDOs. In addition, the risk is assessed by credit-rating agencies. Credit-rating and use of the by-now familiar labels — "AAA" or "AA" — are meant to interpret the risk in CDOs to the investors in simple terms and facilitate decision making.

Yet another device developed to protect the investors in CDOs is credit default swaps (CDSs), which are similar to credit insurance. In their original conception, CDSs were developed to eliminate the risk in CDOs. They are, however, a story unto themselves, and are the subject of Sections 3 and 4. Let us now look at some of the key features of CDOs — namely, the pricing and return models, tranching, and credit rating.

Return Model and Pricing

The return model for collateralized debt obligations is rather unconventional. Usually in debt securities, the return for the holder would be the interest paid by the issuer and, finally, repayment of the nominal value of the security. In CDOs, however, the principal and the return are not treated separately. The cash flows from the portfolio — interest receipts and principal repayments — are aggregated, and the focus is on the total cash flows emanating from the debt securities.

This approach is inherently complex. CDOs consist of a number of debt securities, each with a different tenor, level of risk and rate of interest. Again for some instruments, such as variable-rate mortgages, the rate of interest could vary during the term of the debt. To price a CDO and to measure the return from it, all the cash flows from such a disparate pool of debt securities are totaled.

Understandably, mathematical models had to be developed for the purpose. Andersen and Sidenius (2005) have provided a survey of the models, such as copula and random factor load (RFL), which are commonly used for pricing CDOs. The models are complex, which is hardly surprising considering the diverse nature of the debt securities pooled in a CDO and the need to present the risk and return in relatively simple terms that the investors can understand. Yet their complexity, as George Soros pointed out in 1994, was real and forbidding. Experience suggests that the reservations expressed about the derivatives were not without justification.

An important issue is about the efficacy of the mathematical models and techniques in serving the purposes for which they have been developed — namely, assessing the risk in CDOs and measuring the return from them. A related question is whether the mathematical models were not sophisticated enough, or whether the exercise itself was so complex that it defied practical and accurate solutions. These issues are crucial for the credibility of CDOs and their sustainability as investment instruments.

To be clear, in a CDO we deal with a large number of securities which are wide-ranging in the nature or character of the debt (e.g. corporate bonds and credit card balances) and the type of borrower (business corporations and personal credit card holders). Diversity, again, rules the individual borrowers and their characteristics. For example, in considering corporate bonds it would be necessary to distinguish between issuers who are healthy and profitable and those less so. Similarly, among credit card holders, those with good financial discipline and track records must be separated from those with less perfect records.

Another vital fact is that the borrowers operate in a dynamic environment which is itself subject to constant change. This affects the borrowers' position. To illustrate this, the oversupply in housing in the US in the early

2000s, clearly a factor exogenous to individual borrowers, contributed to the recent decline in house prices after several years of steep rises. This development — namely, a fall in house prices — would affect the quality of the mortgage debt, for no reason attributable to individual borrowers. To interpret the dynamics of such diverse situations faced by a large group of debtors and present them in simple measures of risk or rates of return are daunting tasks. These are the challenges the financial industry assumed — and the results are rather mixed.[2]

It is debatable how accurately we can (i) assess the combined average risk in large and complex pools of debt securities and (ii) measure the return from them by clubbing interest receipts and principal repayments. For the former — namely, assessment of risk — the financial industry developed a number of techniques including credit rating by professional agencies. These are discussed in the next subsection.

The other question about the efficacy of the mathematical models used for computing the return from CDOs and determining the price for them remains, more or less, open. The equations presented by Baz and Chacko (2004) provide a glimpse into the complexities of the exercise of pricing financial derivatives. Such models were put to the acid test during the credit crisis.

Major factors in the crisis were falling investor interest in CDOs and the difficulty in finding buyers for them. These were compounded by the fact that CDOs were traded, at the time, in unregulated OTC markets which are considered less transparent and less efficient in price discovery. The inability to find buyers for CDOs resulted in a downward spiral in their prices.

The whole point about mathematical models is their ability to provide results that are verifiable and logical. In other words, it should have been possible to demonstrate that the prices determined for the CDOs were scientific and that they made commercial sense. If the mathematical models had indeed been successful in determining accurate prices for the

---

[2]Actuarial techniques, which are the standard in the insurance industry, attempt to forecast future risks by referring to past records. However, actuarial tools do not appear to have been used, on a significant scale, in the mathematical models developed for CDOs for pricing and computing the return. See, e.g. the discussion on pricing and valuation of credit derivatives by Choudhry (2004) which is mostly about events in the financial markets, rather than issues with the borrowers or the larger economy in which they operate. Actuarial methods, however, found greater application in risk-modelling for CDOs which is discussed a little later.

CDOs, *a fortiori*, it should have been possible for sellers to find investors willing to buy at such prices. Alternatively, prospective sellers would retain the CDOs if the returns from them made commercial sense. The sellers might not have persisted with their attempts to sell the CDOs, which led to a rush to sell and the consequent loss of confidence among market players.

The reality in the credit crisis was, however, different. CDO sellers were unable to find buyers and the chain of events led to a freeze not merely in the CDO market, but in the entire financial market. These point to the deficiencies in the prevailing CDO theory and the models applied for determining their price and measuring the return from them.

Credit Risk Assessment, "Tranching" and Credit Rating

Credit risk is another crucial issue. To understand and interpret the risk in CDOs, the financial industry has developed a number of techniques, and they include

- "tranching", or splitting the CDO into different segments classified by the gravity of risk;
- use of credit risk models; and
- rating by professional credit-rating agencies.

These techniques, presented in Fig. 2, are supported by a broad theory which is quite logical. But they failed to stand up to the test of the events in the run-up to the credit crisis.

As we have seen, there would necessarily be differences among the nature of the debt securities included in CDOs and the characteristics of

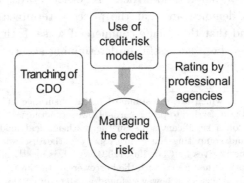

Fig. 2 Managing the Credit Risk in CDOs: Techniques Used.

the contracting borrowers for individual debts. To assess the risk, therefore, it makes sense to identify similarly placed debt securities within the larger consolidated CDO pools and form them into groups. This is accomplished by dividing the CDOs into different segments, termed "tranches", and classifying them according to the level of risk perceived in each segment. Each of the segments consists of a group of debt securities which are considered to possess a similar level of risk (see Cuchra and Jenkinson, 2005). In the terminology of credit-rating agencies, the groups classified by their level of risk would range from "AAA", which denotes the highest security and lowest risk, to "CCC", used for indicating the lowest security and highest level of risk.

The financial industry applied tranching as a technique in developing CDOs into marketable investment products. An obvious commercial rationale for tranching is that it facilitates the sale of tranches among different investors, depending on their risk appetite. The low-risk tranches could be sold to conservative investors, while more venturesome ones might be willing to take tranches that provided better yields but carried a higher level of risk.

"Toxic waste", another term in the credit derivatives lexicon, refers to the tranche carrying the highest rate of risk. It would be at the bottom of the scale in terms of investment safety. This high-risk tranche is, in many cases, retained by the originating lender, and this has been used as a promotional tool in marketing the other tranches. Investors purchasing CDOs have the reassurance that the seller has retained the securities carrying the greatest risk.

The next issue is about risk modelling. The task is to interpret the probability of default by the borrowers and the consequences of default — in simple and easy-to-understand terms. Credit risk modelling is about understanding the risk and interpreting it to the investors.

To begin with, the financial industry adopted the readily available and well-oiled techniques from actuarial science which are, in turn, based on statistical tools and methods. The idea, broadly stated, is that a survey of the sample (in this case, a set of borrowers) and an analysis of the patterns of defaults seen in the past can help in making reasonably accurate forecasts of the trend of events in the future. Actuarial Credit Risk Accounting (ACRA), as the name suggests, is based on this principle. RiskMetrics, CreditMetrics and CreditRisk+ are some other major models used for assessing the credit risk in CDOs (on this, see Chorafas, 2000). Standard & Poor's has developed the CDO Evaluator Engine as an analytical tool for examining a portfolio's credit quality, predicting default rates and other related purposes.

The credit crisis was a testing ground for the risk models applied to CDOs and the efficacy of the models. During the crisis the CDO market, as pointed out earlier, dried up, triggering a fall in CDO prices. Quite obviously, defaults in the underlying portfolios were an important trigger in these events. Questions linger about the potential inaccuracies in the risk models and the role such errors played. Detailed empirical research can help in better understanding how the risk models applied to CDOs worked in reality.

The third element is the credit rating of CDOs by professional agencies. From the commercial standpoint, independent credit rating of CDOs by professional agencies such as Standard & Poor's and Moody's makes marketing sense. This would make it easier for sellers to market the CDOs if the risk in them has been assessed by independent experts. In this sense, credit rating is a logical extension of the idea underlying the CDO device — namely, pooling of debt securities, managing the risk and encouraging trade in them. CDOs were presented as securities whose price, risk and return had been determined scientifically. Assessment of credit risk by professional agencies further added to their credibility. Brennan, Hein and Poon (2009) have discussed the widespread trend among CDO investors to rely on credit rating.

In discussing default forecasting models, Chorafas (2000, pp. 245–246) has presented the tables used by Standard & Poor's, which indicates the statistical or quantitative part of the exercise. It is not clear what, if any, qualitative inputs are considered by the rating agencies in assessing risk. Qualitative inputs and information about credit records and changes in circumstances would be relevant for individual borrowers, at the micro level, and the larger economic environment, at the macro level. Here, again, the complexity with CDOs is that each represents a large number of debt securities — not just one. The rating exercise must pay attention to numerous contracting borrowers, their individual positions and the dynamic environment in which they operate. The task is, quite obviously, a challenge.

The role of credit-rating agencies has come under scrutiny, and there are complaints about the ratings given by them (see, e.g. Partnoy, 2006). Brennan, Hein and Poon (2009, p. 893) have made a distinction between "systematic" risk and "total" risk, and have offered the omission of the rating agencies to consider systematic risk (defined as "taking account of the states of the world in which the losses occur") as an explanation for the failure of the credit-rating device in the recent debacle.

There can be little doubt that the rating procedures need refinement. It is, however, possible to rationalize, if not justify, the work of the agencies albeit in a simplistic fashion. The credit ratings they gave, in particular for subprime mortgages which later experienced significant defaults, were against the backdrop of the constant increases seen in real estate prices in the US in the last couple of decades. The upward trend lasted until recently. In a world of rising house prices, in the absence of fraud such as lending vastly in excess of property value, it could be assumed that residential mortgages would always be sound, regardless of the credentials of individual borrowers. In the event of default, the property could be sold and recovery of the amounts outstanding would be assured. A rating model based on this principle would necessarily falter when house prices started falling, due to oversupply and a host of other factors. These developments and the recent experience underscore the importance of considering the "big picture" and tempering financial innovation with greater realism about the complexities of the world in which we live.

3. CREDIT DEFAULT SWAPS: "BULLETPROOFING" CDO

Balance-sheet CDOs, as I have just explained, make sense both to lenders who can transfer their loan portfolios and credit risk and recapitalize themselves, and to investors who wish to improve the yield from debt securities without incurring higher risk. The features that have been built into CDO — namely, tranching and credit rating — were meant to make the product more easily understandable and improve its marketability. With these add-ons, investors had assurance from the credit-rating agencies about the quality of the debt securities included in CDOs.

If, in addition, they could be protected against possible default by the borrowers, it would make CDOs a near-perfect product. With the availability of protection against credit risk, investors could get higher returns from CDOs without having to worry about possible default by the borrowers. This is, apparently, the thinking that inspired the development of credit default swaps. This section examines CDSs and their characteristics.

CDSs are similar, in principle, to credit insurance which has existed for a long time. There is evidence of awareness in the financial industry about the similarities between the two. "Credit default swaps" is the name coined for the default protection instrument designed for CDOs, and the new name has apparently been quite useful. It has served a number of purposes, such as providing a "branding" effect and a marketing flair to the product, keeping the product out of the net of the cumbersome regulation applicable to insurance, and offering scope for more financial innovation.

In substance, credit default swaps provide their buyers with protection against default in the debt portfolios covered by the swaps. This is clearly protection against credit risk, and is in the nature of insurance. The principle of CDSs has been stated, in the following terms, by PIMCO, a leading bond investment company with assets of over US$1 trillion under its management as of March 2010:

> In its most basic terms, a credit default swap is similar to an insurance contract, providing the buyer with protection against specific risks... CDS contracts can mitigate risks in bond investing by transferring a given risk from one party to another without transferring the underlying bond or other credit asset...

In a CDS, one party "sells" risk and the counterparty "buys" that risk. The seller of credit risk — who also tends to own the underlying credit asset — pays a periodic fee to the risk buyer. In return, the risk buyer agrees to pay the seller a set amount if there is a default (technically, a credit event) (PIMCO, 2006).

For a periodic payment, a CDS seller agrees to pay the buyer a specified amount which is usually the nominal value of the underlying debt security. The periodic payment to be made by the CDS purchaser is determined by the level of risk assessed for the debt issuer. Credit events, or events of default, are specified in the CDS agreement, and they normally cover default by the issuer, or major restructuring undertaken by the issuer. Restructuring is understood as affecting the creditors, and is accordingly treated as a trigger for CDSs. The credit events are defined in the Master Agreement prepared by the International Swaps and Derivatives Association (ISDA). These are normally used for derivatives transactions.

When a defined credit event occurs, the CDS seller must pay the agreed amount. On receiving the payment, the CDS purchaser assigns or hands over the debt security to the CDS seller. This is similar to subrogation in insurance, when the insurer-provider steps into the shoes of the insured person on making payment following the occurrence of the event covered by the insurance contract. In a similar fashion, the CDS seller acquires all the available remedies with respect to the debt security which is the subject of default.

The element of insurance is vital in CDSs. It protects CDO buyers against the credit risk in the debt securities included in CDOs. This is true of balance-sheet CDOs in which the CDO buyers actually acquire the debt securities from the lender and there is transfer of the economic interest in the debt from the originating lender to the SPV managing the CDO. This is quite legitimate, and there can be little argument about the purchasers of balance-sheet CDO getting risk protection for their investment. The case is different with synthetic CDOs which present more potential for speculation. There can be issues about the legitimacy of default swaps for synthetic CDOs, which are discussed in the next section.

In any case, CDSs issued for balance-sheet CDOs do not also add to systemic risk. They merely transfer the risk from the CDOs to the seller of the default swaps. The overall quantum of systemic risk remains the same, except that the cost of default must now be borne by the CDS seller rather than the originating lender or the CDO buyer. This stresses the importance of appropriate risk modelling by the swap seller who must ensure that it can meet its obligations. The consequences of not doing so were seen in what happened at AIG.

4. SYNTHETIC CDOs AND RISK COVER UNDER CDSs

Synthetic or arbitrage CDOs were the next frontier in financial innovation. These instruments, which further develop the principle of CDOs, offer greater scope for financial speculation. They do not involve any transfer of debt securities or the underlying credit risk. Synthetic CDOs acquired an outsized presence in the recent years. Out of the total $550 billion of CDOs issued in 2006, roughly $471 billion, or over 85%, were of the synthetic or arbitrage variety. The credit crisis presented evidence of the potential of synthetic CDOs to encourage financial speculation and the consequent systemic risk. Their scale was truly impressive. This section is divided into three parts which deal, respectively, with synthetic CDOs, the features of CDSs applied to this variety of CDO, and the concept of credit events in CDS contracts.

Synthetic CDOs: A Critical Analysis

The tale of credit derivatives narrated here, until now, has been quite straightforward. The theory of CDOs, the techniques of tranching and credit rating, and default swaps for protection against credit risk were all driven by generally legitimate considerations. The CDO investors fully funded the SPVs and acquired the debt portfolios from the originating lenders and attempted to protect themselves against credit risk. In the process, as we have seen, credit risk merely changed hands. There was no addition to systemic risk. However, it is apparently not in human nature to leave well enough alone.

The next step in financial innovation was synthetic CDOs, which share the principle of balance-sheet CDOs in that they are also based on a portfolio of debt securities. However the similarity ends here, more or less. In synthetic CDOs, there is no transfer of the debt securities or the credit risk in them to the SPVs unlike in balance-sheet CDOs; hence the name "synthetic". Logically, the SPV is thinly capitalized and not fully funded to the value of the debt securities. The debt portfolio in synthetic CDOs is designated as the "reference" portfolio, reflecting its referential character and the fact that there is no transfer of the debt securities.

If the debt portfolio is not transferred to the SPV that manages the synthetic CDO, then obviously the cash flows from the so-called reference portfolio would not accrue to the SPV. This is an important feature of synthetic CDOs. There would be no revenue to the SPV managing the CDO — either from interest payments or principal repayments in the reference portfolio. The commercial rationale for synthetic CDOs must, therefore, lie elsewhere. From the available material, it is difficult to construct a crystal-clear framework for synthetic CDOs. The following discussion, based on *The JP Morgan Guide to Credit Derivatives* (Section 7: Synthetic Securitisation), reveals some of the complexities in synthetic CDOs. The difficulties reinforce the complaints heard often about credit derivatives and their opacity.

JP Morgan, a pioneer in synthetic CDOs, launched its Broad Index Secured Trust Offering (BISTRO) in 1997. According to JP Morgan, important arguments against balance-sheet CDOs are high transaction costs and the difficulties in effecting transfer of the debt securities in the portfolios (for example, the condition in some cases that the borrowers must agree to the transfer). Synthetic CDOs are presented as a cost-effective alternative for banks to achieve the same object — namely, transfer of credit risk. This is to be accomplished through the procurement of credit default swaps by the synthetic CDO vehicles for the reference portfolios. The *JP Morgan Guide* has the following description of the advantages of synthetic CDOs:

> As alternatives to traditional securitisation, transactions have
> been and are being developed that make use of credit derivatives
> to transfer the economic risk but not the legal ownership
> of the underlying assets. Credit derivatives can be used to
> achieve the same or similar regulatory capital benefits of a
> traditional securitisation by transferring the credit risk on the
> underlying portfolio. However, as privately negotiated confi-
> dential transactions, credit derivatives afford the originating
> bank the ability to avoid the legal and structural risks of
> assignments or participations and maintain both market and
> customer confidentiality (p. 73).

The passage points out that the synthetic CDO mechanism enables banks
to be in the background. The banks can accomplish their goal of obtaining
protection against credit risk without having to disclose the fact to the
market. This is among the incentives for lenders to embrace synthetic
CDOs. The incentive for investors in synthetic CDOs is more complex,
which I will discuss a little later.

As pointed out, synthetic CDOs typically have very low capitalization
in comparison to the "notional value" of the reference portfolio for which
they procure default swaps. In JP Morgan's BISTRO, for instance, the SPV
which managed the synthetic CDO had a capital of $700 million as against
the notional value of $10 billion for the reference portfolio. In other words,
the SPV's capital was just 7% of the reference portfolio's value. Therefore,
to begin with, the investment in the SPV was rather marginal; it bore no
relation to the value of the portfolio. The *JP Morgan Guide* (p. 75) explains
the synthetic transaction structure in the Fig. 3.

The figure makes it clear that the crux of the transaction is the
credit default swaps covering the reference portfolio. The synthetic CDO
mechanism would not make sense without the CDSs — and hereby hangs
a tale. The SPV pays for the CDSs, and it would receive payments from
the seller of the swaps for the first $700 million in losses in the reference
portfolio. This amount of $700 million represents the highest-risk debt, or
the so-called toxic waste referred to earlier. For this tranche, the lending
bank retains the risk and it would not receive any compensation. For losses
in excess of $700 million, the swap seller must make the payment to the
originating bank.

Apparently, the SPV uses a part of its capital of $700 million to make
the periodic premium payment to the swaps seller and invests the rest

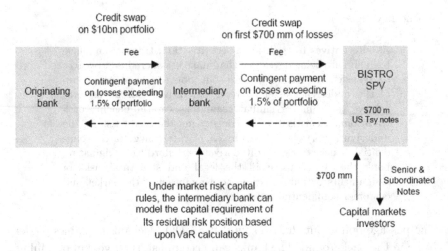

Fig. 3 Structure of the BISTRO Synthetic CDO.

in Treasury notes. This is a reasonable interpretation of the structure of synthetic CDOs, as presented in the *JP Morgan Guide*. The premium paid for the swaps is an expense for the SPV, and any recovery from the swaps seller on the occurrence of the credit events would, hopefully, produce a profit for the SPV. Thus, the SPV acquires a vested interest in default and is really betting on defaults in the reference portfolio. Fewer defaults mean less recovery for the SPV under the CDSs. To this extent, the premium it paid the swaps seller would be a loss. The SPV would, therefore, be pleased with substantial defaults in the portfolio.

Up to this stage, it is still possible to locate in the CDO mechanism — even in its synthetic version — a commercial rationale and a degree of legitimacy. The bank, which has substantive economic interest in the debt portfolio, obtains protection against risk cover through a third party — investors in the synthetic CDO. It is a different matter that it provides a perverse incentive to the investors — namely, reward — if there are defaults in the reference portfolio. This would naturally tempt the investors to look forward to defaults. To this extent, the synthetic CDO mechanism contributes to systemic risk.

In the synthetic CDO structure explained above, risk cover under the default swaps is available partly to the originating lender and partly to the SPV which paid for the cover. The credit risk in the portfolio thus shifts from the originating lender to the seller of swaps, but in the end there would only be one cover for the credit risk in the debt securities included in the portfolio. Assuming a face value of $10 million for a reference portfolio, the CDS cover for it would be the same amount. Therefore, the synthetic CDO transaction does not add to the overall risk. Like with balance-sheet CDOs, it merely shifts the risk from the originating lender to the CDS seller, although the considerations are different in the synthetic version.

Things change, arguably for the worse, when we get to multiple synthetic CDOs for a single debt portfolio and multiple default swaps for the portfolio. After all, if there can be one reference portfolio which never actually changed hands, there can also be more than one such portfolio. In the run-up to the credit crisis the availability of default swaps, apparently, facilitated the unhealthy practice of multiple CDOs and default swaps. There *were* investors willing to pay for default swaps. Their only interest in the transaction was the money they could collect if the specified credit events occurred. In truth, these investors had no substantive economic interest in the debt security. The advent of multiple synthetic CDOs and many CDSs for a single debt portfolio marked their transition into purely speculative devices.

By the late 2000s, it was common for an issuer to have multiple default swaps outstanding for its debt securities. Gibson (2007, p. 39) pointed out:

> [A]s the credit derivative market has grown, it has become common for the notional amount of CDS outstanding referencing a particular issuer to be larger than the face value of the issuer's bonds outstanding.

Default swaps were, thus, available in multiples of the value of the bonds covered by them. Apparently, sellers were willing to issue swaps without paying serious attention to the factual position and the underlying risk. The market reality of multiple swaps explains the phenomenal value of the outstanding default swaps, which was estimated at US$62.2 trillion in 2007 (*Economist*, 2008). Detailed empirical research can reveal the extent to which there were multiple synthetic CDOs and CDSs, and the identity of the investors.

As pointed out a little earlier, the investors in synthetic CDOs procured swaps for reference portfolios in return for the right to collect money from the swaps seller for the first specified part of losses (e.g. the first $700 million in the case of BISTRO, as discussed above). In the multiple synthetic CDO/CDS scenario, there will be a number of swap holders demanding payment for a default in the reference portfolio. Assuming that a portfolio has 10 sets of swaps outstanding, a default of $1,000 could trigger a liability of $10,000 for the swap sellers. The multiple swaps were bets, pure and simple, designed to benefit from defaults or losses in the reference portfolios.

In the market meltdown experienced in the credit crisis, the practices just described played an important part. They led to a huge increase in the total quantum of *financial* risk, even though there was no matching expansion in the underlying economic risk — namely, the debt securities on which the bets were made. Regrettably, the legislation just enacted in the US — the *Dodd–Frank Wall Street Reform and Consumer Protection Act* — is not likely to have any direct effect on such tendencies recently seen in the financial markets.

Credit Default Swaps: Their Application to Synthetic CDOs

To be clear, insurance is an important element in CDSs — indeed, the defining feature. Speculation is inherent in insurance, as pointed out by Lord Mansfield as early as 1766 in *Carter* v. *Boehm*. A number of rules have been developed in the law of insurance to undermine the speculative element and to promote the integrity of insurance contracts. These rules emphasize the character of insurance as a tool for legitimate protection against genuine risks. They are designed to check speculation and betting on future events which are uncertain.

An important principle in the law of insurance is the requirement of insurable interest. The rule requires a person seeking protection against risk to have a relationship, labelled "insurable interest", in the subject matter of the insurance contract. The relationship must be such that it exposes that person to loss or injury as a result of the event against which insurance is sought. A simple example is the proprietary interest the owner of a house property has in it. It would be legitimate for the owner, who has invested in the property, to take an insurance policy against the risks of fire, flood, vandalism, etc. The owner has a substantive economic interest in the property, and by taking insurance cover, s/he seeks to protect this interest.

The law has a strong concern for the legitimacy of insurance contracts, and the rule on insurable interest is an expression of this concern. It prevents persons who do not have substantive economic interest in an asset or a transaction from betting on the future with the hope of benefiting from the occurrence of uncertain events. The concept of insurable interest, therefore, promotes the integrity of insurance contracts.

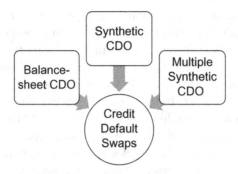

Fig. 4 CDOs in Three Versions and CDSs.

For CDSs, the principle of insurable interest is a handy tool to assess their legitimacy. As we have seen, the market has developed three varieties of CDO: (i) balance-sheet CDO, (ii) a single synthetic CDO for a reference portfolio, and (iii) multiple synthetic CDOs for a single reference portfolio. Default swaps were sold for all three varieties, as shown in Fig. 4.

The question of insurable interest must be analysed separately for each of them because they have distinctive characteristics and the implications are different in each case. There is little difficulty with balance-sheet CDOs. In their case, the SPV managing the CDO acquires the portfolio and has substantive economic interest in the debt securities included in it. Therefore, the existence of insurable interest is undeniable. There can be little complaint about the sale of default swaps for the debt securities included in balance-sheet CDOs.

When we move on to single synthetic CDOs, the relationship becomes somewhat tenuous. In a synthetic CDO, as noted, the SPV does not acquire the debt securities in the reference portfolio and has no real economic interest in them. Yet it pays for the CDS because it will receive payment in the event of defaults in a portion of the reference portfolio. For defaults in the remaining parts, payment will be made to the originating bank or lender. The picture is hazy, and it is difficult to identify clear insurable interest for the SPV that manages the synthetic CDO in any part of the reference portfolio. Payment by the swaps seller to the originating lender for the remaining part of the portfolio is also rather ambiguous because the lender has not paid for the CDS. Obviously, there is *some* relationship between the three — the SPV managing the synthetic CDO, the original lender and the swaps seller — but the question is whether this is adequate for the SPV to procure risk cover for the reference portfolio, viewed from the lens of insurable interest? This important question must be deliberated and answered if the goal is to promote market stability and check speculation.

The picture gets even murkier for the third variety — default swaps for multiple synthetic CDOs for a given reference portfolio. To begin with, it is not clear whether the synthetic CDOs had any relationship with the originating bank or lender. In the absence of better information about the existence of such a relationship and its nature, it is difficult to come to a definitive conclusion on insurable interest. In any event, multiple swaps for a single portfolio of debt securities clearly lack legitimacy. A default in the portfolio will give rise to payment obligation in multiples of the face value of the security. This is clearly speculative, and was a major factor in the credit crisis. From the perspective of insurable interest, it is apparent that the SPVs managing the multiple synthetic CDOs had no genuine economic interest in the reference portfolio. Lacking insurable interest, it would not be legitimate for them to seek cover or protection against the credit risk in the portfolio.

There have been efforts to deny the insurance character of credit default swaps. ISDA, a private agency that promotes swaps and derivatives, has argued that CDS transactions are not in the nature of insurance contracts, and the argument was accepted by the US Court of Appeal for the Second Circuit. In *Aon Financial Products, Inc.* v. *Société Générale*, (2007), ISDA intervened in the action as *amicus curiae*, and referring to its submissions, the court observed approvingly:

> CDS agreements are thus significantly different from insurance contracts. As amicus correctly points out, they "do not, and are not meant to, indemnify the buyer of protection against loss. Rather, CDS contracts allow parties to 'hedge' risk by buying and selling risks at different prices and with varying degrees of correlation."

ISDA emphasized that CDSs lack the element of indemnity, or compensation against loss, which is crucial in insurance. But the second part of ISDA's submission is less than clear, which is typical of industry statements about credit derivatives. ISDA is, after all, a promoter of derivatives and has an interest in increasing the trade in them. Its denial of the insurance element in CDSs is understandable. It is anxious to keep default swaps out of the stringent regulation applicable to insurance, and *Aon Financial Products* enables this. This case was decided by the court in 2007 — before the onset of the credit crisis and the meltdown at AIG. It is an open question how the courts might view the issue in the aftermath of these developments.

The issue of whether CDSs share the principle of insurance is hardly academic. It defines how CDS contracts are sold in the market and this, in turn, determines their availability. The proliferation in CDSs, seen in the run-up to the credit crisis, is not likely to have happened if CDSs had been recognized as insurance contracts and subjected to the rules on risk modelling and reserves applicable to the insurance industry. The fact that they were not recognized as such has, as I have argued elsewhere, contributed significantly to the large-scale issue of CDSs by AIG and the meltdown that followed (Vasudev, 2010). AIG's default swaps business was handled in its Financial Products division, rather than the Insurance arm, and as a result, inadequate attention was paid to the underlying risk and the ability of the company to meet its obligations.[3]

Another important issue, from the insurance perspective, is about risk modelling. If CDSs are recognized as insurance contracts, their providers are likely to have applied more traditional and conservative methods in determining the risk in the debt portfolios in CDOs. If appropriate models did not exist for assessing the risk, it is likely that either insurance cover would not have been sold, or the premium fixed at very high levels. High premiums would have acted as a dampener on the CDS market. This, in turn, could have brought back a sense of sobriety to the market. It is, however, apparent that the conventional risk models used in insurance were not applied to CDSs.

CDS: Understanding Credit Events

In CDS transactions, triggers for the liability of the swaps seller are more complex, indeed nebulous, when compared with regular insurance. They lack the clarity and stability which characterize the regime governing payments by insurers. In CDSs, the liability of the swaps seller is normally dependent on the occurrence of credit events, which ISDA defines as follows:

> An event linked to the deteriorating credit worthiness of an underlying reference entity in a credit derivative. The occurrence of a credit event usually triggers full or partial termination

---

[3]Eric Dinallo, Superintendent of The New York State Insurance Department, pointed out that AIG conducted its CDS business in its Financial Products arm and this prevented the Insurance Department from regulating it (Dinallo, 2009). Significantly, Dinallo had earlier referred to the brief of the Insurance Department to "provid[e] an appropriate way for those with an insurable interest to protect themselves" (Dinallo, 2008).

of the transaction and a payment from protection seller to
protection buyer. Credit events include bankruptcy, failure to
pay, restructuring, obligation acceleration, obligation default
and repudiation/moratorium (ISDA, 2010).

Quite clearly, the swaps seller's liability is broader than the liability of
an insurer in a typical insurance contract. In the description of credit
events, extracted above, the phrases "deteriorating credit worthiness...
of [a] reference entity" and "obligation acceleration" are significant. They
make it clear that actual default is not necessary; a lowering of the credit
rating for an issuer is adequate to trigger the liability of the swaps seller to
pay under the CDS. To use the analogy of health insurance, this provision
would place the insurance company under an obligation to make payment if
there is any deterioration in the general health of the insured person — not
actual illness requiring treatment.

Again, decline in the market value of the CDO is a ground for
demanding payment from the CDS provider. Recent events showed the
gravity of this condition, especially when markets go into a bear phase
and prices fall. In the credit crisis, the drying up of the market for CDOs
was compounded by the fact that they were traded in OTC markets where
price discovery procedures are not quite transparent.[4] AIG explained the
seriousness of the consequences in its annual report for 2007 — a few months
before its meltdown and bailout by the US government.

AIG's Liquidity May Be Adversely Affected by Requirements to Post Collateral

Certain of the credit default swaps written by AIG Financial Products
contain collateral posting requirements. The amount of collateral required
to be posted for most of these transactions is determined based on the
value of the security or loan referenced in the documentation for the credit
default swap. Continued declines in the values of these referenced securities
or loans will increase the amount of collateral AIGFP must post, which
could impair AIG's liquidity (AIG, 2007, p. 17).

During the credit crisis, the set of circumstances were almost completely
against CDS sellers, given the engineering of the swaps described here. On
one hand, there were defaults in subprime mortgages. On the other, lack of

---

[4]The financial regulatory reforms just introduced in the US address this specific issue
through a clearing house mechanism for trade in derivatives.

liquidity in the market and loss of confidence led to a fall in CDO prices. The irony was that, often, CDS sellers had to make payments to persons who had little economic interest in the underlying debt securities.

5. CREDIT DERIVATIVES: SOME PRACTICAL ISSUES

This concluding section provides a brief overview of some practical issues connected with credit derivatives. These are the questions of whether credit derivatives are "securities" governed by general securities regulation, the documentation used for derivatives transactions and lessons from the trends seen in some recent legal cases involving CDOs and CDSs.

Credit Derivatives: Are They "Securities"?

The answer to the question of whether derivatives are "securities" depends, essentially, on the securities legislation in force in a jurisdiction. Some countries (e.g. India[5]) have specifically included derivatives in the definition of securities. This could potentially attract a number of other rules such as registration, filing of prospectus, trading on recognized stock exchanges, and so on. These issues are essentially jurisdiction-specific and the regulations of individual countries must be examined for their applicability and impact.

Documentation for Transactions

As pointed out earlier, ISDA, which is headquartered in New York, has developed a set of documentation for derivatives transactions. These have become, more or less, the standard in the financial markets. However, recent legal cases, which discussed are next, point to potential issues in the standard agreements, for example, the disclaimers included for the sellers of CDOs and the consequent risk for CDO purchasers. This suggests the need either for having individual agreements for transactions, or alternatively, an overriding set of special terms signed by the parties. A related issue is about the impact that special agreements or clauses may have on the tradability of the instruments. When documentation deviates from the industry standard, there could be issues about how they are received in the markets.

---

[5] *Securities Contracts (Regulation) Act, 1956*, Section 2, Clauses (ac) and (h).

Credit Derivatives Litigation: Recent Trends

In general, courts in the US and UK have not been receptive to complaints by the buyers of CDOs and allegations of oral representations about the quality of the underlying debt (see, e.g. *Banco Espirito Santo de Investimento* v. *Citibank* [2004]). However, recently in *HSH Nordbank* v. *UBS*, the New York State Supreme Court allowed the plaintiff to pursue its claim for compensation for alleged breach of contract, fraud, negligent misrepresentation, and breach of fiduciary duty by UBS. Clarke and Lamberton (2010), who have provided an overview of litigation on the subject, have argued that purchasers of CDOs do not warrant any special consideration. The legal cases offer valuable lessons to investors, in particular about some issues in the documentation currently used for transactions and their inconsistency with other representations made by the sellers, verbal or documentary, as pointed out earlier. The emerging body of case law will facilitate better decision making and provide guidance on developing appropriate safeguards.

REFERENCES

American International Group (AIG). Annual Report (Form 10-K). Available at http://www.sec.gov/Archives/edgar/data/5272/000095012308002-280/0000950123-08-002280-index.htm, accessed 22 July 2010.

Andersen, L. and Sidenius, J. (2005). "CDO Pricing with Factor Models: Survey and Comments." *Journal of Credit Risk*, 1(3):71–88.

Baz, J. and Chacko, G. (2004). *Financial Derivatives: Pricing, Applications, and Mathematics*, Cambridge, UK: Cambridge University Press.

Brennan, M., Hein, J. and Poon, S. (2009). "Tranching and Rating." *European Financial Management*, 15(5):891–922.

Chancellor, E. (1999). *Devil Take the Hindmost: A History of Financial Speculation*, New York: Farrar Strauss Giroux.

Chaplin, G. (2005). *Credit Derivatives: Risk Management, Trading & Investing*, Chichester, UK: John Wiley.

Chorafas, D. (2000). *Credit Derivatives & the Management of Risk, Including Models for Credit Risk*, New York: New York Institute of Finance.

Choudhry, M. (2004). *Structured Credit Products: Credit Derivatives & Synthetic Securitisation*, Singapore: Wiley-Finance.

Clarke, S. and Lamberton, E. (2010). "Collateral Damage: A Reference Pool of CDO Claims." *Journal of International Banking Law and Regulation*, 25(7):315–329.

Cuchra, M. and Jenkinson, T. (2005). "Security Design in the Real World: Why are Securitization Issues Tranched?" EFA 2005 Moscow Meeting. Available at http://papers.ssrn.com/sol3/papers.cfm?abstract_id=676730, accessed 22 July, 2010.

Dinallo, E. (2008). Testimony to the US Senate, 14 October. Available at http://www.ins.state.ny.us/speeches/pdf/sp0810141.pdf, accessed 22 July 2010.

Dinallo, E. (2009). Testimony to the US Senate, 5 March. Available at http://readme.readmedia.com/Testimony-by-N-Y-Insurance-Superintendent-Eric-Dinallo-on-AIG-to-the-United-States-Senate/418527, accessed 22 July 2010.

Duffie, D. (2008). "Innovations in Credit Risk Transfer: Implications for Financial Stability." Working Paper 255, Bank for International Settlements, Basel, Switzerland.

Economist (2008). "Credit Derivatives: The Great Untangling." 6 November.

Gibson, M. (2007). "Credit Derivatives and Risk Management." *Federal Reserve Bank of Atlanta Economic Review*, 4:25–41.

Instefjord, N. (2005). "Risk and Hedging: Do Credit Derivatives Increase Bank Risk?" *Journal of Banking and Finance*, 29(2):333–345.

ISDA (2010). International Swaps and Derivatives Association, Derivatives Consulting Group Glossary. Available at www.isda.org, accessed 22 July.

JP Morgan Guide to Credit Derivatives (date not provided). Available at http://www.investinginbonds.com/assets/files/Intro_to_Credit_Derivatives.pdf, accessed 22 July 2010.

Partnoy, F. (2006). "How and Why Credit Rating Agencies are Not Like Other Gatekeepers." In Fuchita, Y. and Litan, R (eds.), *Financial Gatekeepers: Can They Protect Investors?* Washington, DC: Brookings Institution Press.

Partnoy, F. and Skeel, D. (2007). "The Promise and Perils of Credit Derivatives." *University of Cincinnati Law Review*, 75(3):1019–1052.

PIMCO (2006). "Bond Basics" (June, 2006). Available at http://www.pimco.com/LeftNav/Bond+Basics/2006/Credit+Default+Swaps+06-01-2006.htm, accessed 13 October 2009.

Rajan, R. (2005). *Has Financial Development Made the World Riskier?* Address at Federal Reserve Bank of Kansas Symposium. Available at http://www.kansascityfed.org/PUBLICAT/SYMPOS/2005/PDF/Rajan2005.pdf.

Tavakoli, J. (2008). *Structured Finance & Collateralized Debt Obligations: New Developments in Cash & Synthetic Securitization*, Hoboken, NJ: Wiley Finance.

Vasudev, P.M. (2010). "Default Swaps and Director Oversight: Lessons from AIG." *Journal of Corporation Law*, 35(2):101–142.

Jurisprudence

Aon Financial Products, Inc. v. *Société Générale*, 476 F.3d 90 (2d Cir. 2007).

Banco Espirito Santo de Investimento v. *Citibank*, 2004 US App. LEXIS 20885, 110 Fed. Appx. 191.

Carter v. *Boehm* (1766), 97 Eng. Rep. 1162.

HSH N Nordbank v. *UBS*, File no. 600562/2008, New York Supreme Court (Manhattan).

Chapter 6

A NEW FRAMEWORK FOR ASSET-BACKED
SECURITIES (ABSs)

Mingyuan Zhang and Clark Abrahams

Man's mind stretched to a new idea never goes back to its
original dimensions.

Oliver Wendell Holmes

1. INTRODUCTION

This is a time of historic importance in terms of new regulations and
stakeholder[1] attempts to restore trust and liquidity to the ABS market
in the wake of the financial crisis.[2] The outcome of current legislative
initiatives and rule making in the US will have a profound impact on how
those markets will operate in the years, and decades, to come. In the spirit
of making a contribution to this subject at such a critical juncture, we offer
some insights from our recent research into a new lending system that has
significant implications for loan securitization. We refer to this new system
as a comprehensive credit assessment framework (or CCAF, pronounced
"see-caf").[3] The CCAF better serves loan originators, securitizers, and

---

[1] E.g. ABS issuers, lenders, rating agencies, and professional accounting and investment
organizations, such as the Financial Standards Accounting Board (FASB), CFA Institute,
and so on.

[2] One such effort by the Federal Reserve to revive the ABS market was the introduction
of the Term Asset-Backed Securities Loan Facility (TALF) on 25 November 2008. See the
Federal Reserve System 2008 Monetary Policy Releases: http://www.federalreserve.gov/
newsevents/press/monetary/monetary20081125a1.pdf.

[3] For detailed descriptions of the CCAF, please see Abrahams, C. and Zhang, M.
(2009), *Credit Risk Assessment: The New Lending System for Borrowers, Lenders, and
Investors*, John Wiley & Sons, Inc.

investors in securities backed by loans by providing more accurate risk assessment and greater consistency and transparency to all stakeholders. In addition, it promotes standardization of the asset-pooling process and definitions. It also enhances stakeholders' ability to compare, rank, monitor and report loan pool performance across securities in terms that are easily understood. As a result, cash flows associated with even the most complex ABS can be better classified, and their associated uncertainties can be better quantified.

The topic of ABSs is a regulatory focus and is both timely and important for the following key reasons:

(i) *Shortcomings in the credit rating methodology for ratings on securities*: It is anticipated that new broader powers will be granted to the SEC to regulate NRSROs.[4] The new SEC rule states that

> A new Office of Credit Ratings ("Office") is required to examine NRSROs at least once a year and make key findings public. The Office will write new rules, including requiring NRSROs to set up internal controls over the process for determining credit ratings.[5]

The rule also requires NRSROs to set up an independent board of directors and to disclose more to the public and investors. In addition, it requires them to come up with a broad set of ratings that span asset classes and types of issuer. NRSROs that give inaccurate ratings over time can be deregistered, and there are new professional standards and formal examinations that will force ratings analysts to maintain and improve their competency. The new law will include provisions dealing with conflicts of interest, and it will take measures to reduce reliance on ratings, including replacing references to credit ratings, credit rating agencies, and NRSROs with an appropriate standard of creditworthiness that the federal agencies must set forth.

---

[4] A Nationally Recognized Statistical Rating Organization (NRSRO) is a credit rating agency which issues credit ratings permitted by the US Securities and Exchange Commission (SEC) for other financial firms to use for certain regulatory purposes.
[5] See Joint Explanatory Statement of the Committee of the Conference on the amendment of the Senate to the bill H.R. 4173 (*The Wall Street Reform and Consumer Protection Act of 2009*), Title IX (Investor Protections and Improvements to the Regulation of Securities), Subtitle D (Improvements to Asset-Backed Securitization Process). See http://docs.house.gov/rules/finserv/111_hr4173_finsrvcr629stmntofmgrs.pdf.

(ii) *Disconnection between securitizers and investors*: New US federal regulations require that securitizers must

> retain an economic interest in a material portion of the credit risk for any asset that securitizers transfer, sell, or convey to a third party. Risk retention requirements and exemptions will be determined by regulators, which will vary for different asset classes and also for securitizers versus originators.[6]

Furthermore, the soon to be enacted federal law provides regulators with discretion to require that issuers of more complex ABSs retain a degree of risk that is most appropriate to the structure of the security (e.g. issuers of collateralized debt obligations, commonly referred to as CDOs, would be required to maintain a greater stake than issuers of straight mortgage pass-through securities). Subtitle D also requires that issuers disclose the data associated with the underlying loans. We agree that it is important for ABS issuers to make loan-level information available and transparent to regulators, investors and ratings agencies to enable them to accurately evaluate asset performance and associated credit risk.[7]

(iii) *The need for greater information, as reflected in the recent SEC Proposed Rules to Increase Investor Protections in Asset-Backed Securities*:[8] The SEC's intention is to require that ABS investors get information that is more timely and granular and that they be afforded additional time to determine whether or not the ABS they are considering is a good investment for them. ABS valuation may be complicated. Clearly there is a need to make them more visible and comprehensible to potential investors, who must possess the means to easily monitor and evaluate the performance of the underlying assets, and readily connect security prices with their underlying asset credit quality. Going forward, ABS valuation needs to better reflect the business reality and economic dynamics of the security market as well as the performance of the underlying assets. At present, there is a significant gap between the business reality and the modelling process. Our new framework is designed to close that gap.

---

[6] *Ibid.*

[7] See Association of Mortgage Investors (2010), "Reforming the Asset-Backed Securities Market," AMI White Paper, March.

[8] SEC (2010), "SEC Proposes Rules to Increase Investor Protections in Asset-Backed Securities," 7 April, http://www.sec.gov/news/press/2010/2010-54.htm.

We begin our discussion with a description of the basic asset securitization process and the associated issues, and challenges. We briefly examine ABSs in the context of the financial crisis, and note some securitization-related risks. Next, we introduce our new approach, which we describe in some detail. We illustrate it with an example using mortgages and credit card receivables to create and value an ABS. Finally, we highlight current efforts surrounding market regulation, and we discuss some important policy implications for issuers, regulators, and investors.

2. ABS AND THE ASSET SECURITIZATION PROCESS

Asset-backed securities (ABSs) are bonds, or notes, backed by the cash flow of pooled loans or receivables. Types of loans include mortgage loans, home equity loans, manufactured housing contracts, student loans, credit card receivables, and business loans and receivables. ABSs can also be classified according to the type of payment made: amortizing and non-amortizing. Amortized payments are applied to loans made for a specific amount (e.g. installment contracts), whereas non-amortizing payments are applied to open-ended loans (e.g. revolving credit lines). Mortgages and auto loans are familiar examples of amortizing loans, whereas credit cards represent the most common type of revolving account.[9]

Asset securitization provided an important funding, capital and risk management tool for financial institutions since its inception in the 1980s. Since then, the ABS market enjoyed steady growth until August 2007 when the US ABS market began to shrink, followed by the collapse of credit and ABS markets due to the financial crisis. By the second quarter of 2007, there was about $6.39 trillion in total US residential mortgage-related securities,[10] of which 34% was related to non-conforming mortgages, which did not meet conventional underwriting standards.[11] Figure 1 shows the new ABS volume by non-mortgage loan types from the period 2005–2009

---

[9]ABSs based on amortizing payments pay both principal and interest to investors in each payment, whereas ABSs based on revolving loans pay only interest for a specified amount of time, then pay only principal during the final phase before the final maturity date.

[10]See Goodman, L. *et al.* (2008), *Subprime Mortgage Credit Derivatives*, John Wiley & Sons, pp. 3–4.

[11]*Ibid.*

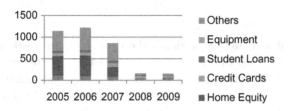

Fig. 1 ABS Volume Trend (US).

Source: Thomson Financial (2010), 10 May.

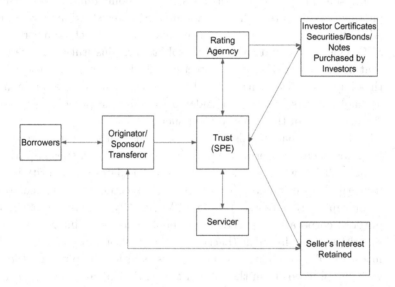

Fig. 2 Basic ABS Securitization Process.

(excluding mortgage-associated securities). It shows that ABS issuance volume reached its peak during 2006–2007.[12]

An ABS is created when loan originators turn their loans into liquid securities through a process known as securitization using financial engineering techniques. The basic setup of asset securitization is shown in Fig. 2. At a high level, the process consists of the following key steps

---

[12]Thomson Financial (2010), 10 May. See also Agarwal, S. *et al.* (2010), "Rescuing Asset-Backed Securities Markets," Chicago Fed Letter, Federal Reserve Bank of Chicago, January, Number 270.

and players:

   (i) Financial institutions originate the loans that are used to create the ABS. The originators usually include banks, credit card providers, auto finance companies, mortgage companies, and consumer finance companies. Often, a bundle of loans is divided into separate securities with different levels of risk and returns. Payments on the loans are distributed to the holders of the lower-risk securities, i.e. to lower-interest securities first, and then to the holders of the higher-risk securities. Most public offerings of ABSs are commonly referred to as "shelf offerings", which are made via expedited SEC registration procedures. ABS offerings also are sold as private placements, which do not require SEC registration, and are typically sold to large institutional investors that do not require the same protection afforded general investors when they buy and sell securities.[13] If the transactions pass certain legal and accounting tests, they are considered to be a true sale of assets from the originator of the loans to the issuer.

  (ii) The loan originator sells a pool of loans with minimal recourse (e.g. documentation errors may be an exception) to a special-purpose vehicle (SPV), which is a legal entity that insulates the security issuer from the loan originator (this protection is commonly referred to as "bankruptcy remoteness"). The SPV (usually a trust or a single-purpose corporation) packages the pool of loans as interest-bearing securities and sells them (backed by the pool of loans purchased) to investors. The originator of the loans is paid for the purchased loans with the proceeds from the sales of the ABS. The loan originator may retain the right to service the loans for the SPV for a fee.

 (iii) The cash flows generated from the underlying assets (mortgage or loans) consist of interest payments and principal payments made by the borrowers of the loans. These cash flows are allocated to the investors according to the terms of the securitization trust agreement, which specifies the priorities assigned to various classes of investors. In the case of revolving credit, a revolving trust is used for assets that have a high turnover, such as credit card, trade, and dealer floorplan receivables. A revolving trust issues ABSs with a revolving period (when investors are paid interest) and an accumulation,

---

[13]These institutional investors are known as qualified institutional buyers (QIBs) as defined in SEC Rule 144A under the *Securities Act of 1933*.

or controlled-amortization period (when the principal is repaid as monthly payments over a specified time).[14]

(iv) The servicers manage the cash flow of asset-backed securities, and they collect and process the payments from the loan pool, pay the investors, and also attempt to collect from delinquent borrowers. Servicers are usually paid a fixed fee from the pool's remaining collateral balance. Near the end of the ABS term, when the remaining pool balance falls below about 10% of the original pool balance, the cost to service the pool becomes greater than the servicing fee.

3. ABSs AND THE FINANCIAL CRISIS

During the financial crisis, ABS holders suffered huge losses.[15] The fallout stemming from severe difficulties in subprime lending and ABS markets reached epic proportions, with such notable failures and bailouts as Lehman Brothers, Bear Stearns, Washington Mutual, IndyMac, Wachovia, and AIG. The impact was also felt globally, most notably in Europe. The systems, procedures, and regulations surrounding the ABS value chain, indeed the entire lending value chain, were undeniably inadequate. Many ABS investors were completely caught off-guard. This was due to both their lack of awareness of the true risk in the underlying loans within the securitized asset pools, and their almost total reliance on the credit grading assigned by the rating agencies, which proved in many cases to be way off the mark. Even today, the securitization market remains inactive for the most part.

The role of ABSs in the financial crisis has attracted extensive discussions.[16] The current securitization process created the following disconnections as shown in Fig. 3:

(i) *Disconnection between the borrower and the lender*: The prevailing lending system that the lender uses does not reflect the true

---

[14]See FDIC (2007), *Risk Management Credit Card Securitization Manual*, March.

[15]For example, from 2000 to 2007, Moody's rated $4.7 trillion in RMBSs and $736 billion in CDOs. The sharp rise in mortgage defaults that began in 2006 ultimately led to the mass downgrading of RMBSs and CDOs, and resulted in significant impairments. The huge losses to investors and write-downs on these securities were attributed to the resulting financial crisis. See Financial Crisis Inquiry Commission (2010), "Credit Ratings and the Financial Crisis," 2 June http://www.scribd.com/doc/32651377/Financial-Crisis-Inquiry-Commission-Report-on-Credit-Ratings.

[16]See Abrahams, C. and Zhang, M. (2009) *Credit Risk Assessment: The New Lending System for Borrowers, Lenders, and Investors*, John Wiley & Sons, Inc. pp. 5–11.

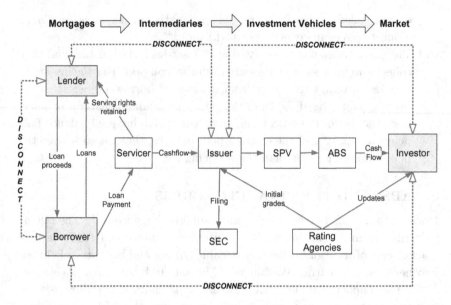

Fig. 3   Securitization Silos.

affordability of the loan. As a result, the traditional pooling methods
have a tendency to overestimate or underestimate the credit risk
associated with the transaction.

(ii) *Disconnection between the securities issuer and the lender*: The issuer
does not have the underlying information to put performance into the
broader context for risk assessment regarding the individual loans in
the pools.

(iii) *Disconnection between the issuer and the investor*: The investor has
limited information regarding how the securities are valued and no
loan-level cash flow information. Investors do not have the ability
to understand the valuation process, given the sophisticated loan
securitization process.[17] As a result, they have to rely on a rating
agency's ratings. The investor is unable to monitor and evaluate the
performance of underlying assets.

(iv) *Disconnection between the investor and the borrower*: The investor
has limited information regarding the underlying loan performance

---

[17]Whereas the credit rating of bonds depends on the creditworthiness of the issuer, the
credit rating of ABSs is derived primarily from the structure of the ABS. Compared with
other securities, an ABS has less chance of an event-triggered credit rating downgrade (e.g.
downgrades due to corporate buyouts, mergers, restructurings, and recapitalizations).

as a whole, or by borrower segment (handle), and no information at the individual loan level. This includes information sourced at the time of loan underwriting and also information periodically refreshed on payment behavior, credit utilization, and the borrower's financial status.

The root causes of these disconnections are the flawed credit risk assessment systems that failed to capture the hidden risks in a transparent, accurate and forward-looking manner.[18] The meltdown of the credit and investment markets during the financial crisis still affects investors' confidence in the ABS market today. Because loan securitizations are an important funding source and risk management tool, the ABS markets will eventually recover. The key is to restore the investors' confidence with a more transparent and effective system. The rebirth of securitization will focus on quantifying the hidden risks associated with the underlying asset pools, making the pool creation process more transparent, and enhancing modelling accuracy.[19] Before we describe how our new framework can restore the connections among those stakeholders and effectively monitor risks, we first discuss the types of risk associated with ABSs and the associated securitization process.

4. SECURITIZATION-RELATED RISKS

One of the main risks is associated with credit quality and the underlying pool asset performance. Poor credit quality may require higher credit enhancements, which can increase funding costs. In the early stages of the financial crisis, interest rate spreads on three-year AAA-rated ABSs backed by credit card receivables were as high as 7.09%. Large increases in interest rate spreads can significantly reduce lenders' funding ability and lessen their appetite to issue new ABSs.[20]

Asset-backed securities are diverse, with different yields, maturities, collateral, and credit ratings. Asset-backed securities can pay either a fixed rate of interest or a floating rate (floaters). The actual yield earned by the investor will depend on the purchase price of the ABS and the actual term length of the security. The interest rates on floaters are tied to a designated

---

[18]See Abrahams, C. and Zhang, M. (2009), *Credit Risk Assessment: The New Lending System for Borrowers, Lenders, and Investors*, John Wiley & Sons, Inc., pp. 215–221.
[19]See Koegel, D. (2009), "Securitization Reborn: Transfer of Credit, Insurance, and other Risks," *The RMA Journal*, 91: 30–35.
[20]See Agarwal, S. *et al.* (2010), "Rescuing Asset-Backed Securities Markets," Chicago Fed Letter, the Federal Reserve Bank of Chicago, January, Number 270.

index, such as the LIBOR, or Treasuries of comparable maturity. When the underlying portfolio consists of floating-rate loans, such as credit card loans, then income and payments for the issuer are matched. If the underlying portfolio pays a fixed rate of interest, it can be converted to a floating-rate ABS by the use of interest rate swaps, where the issuer swaps the fixed rate of the portfolio with a floating rate from a third party, such as a bank. The reverse is also true. The use of interest rate swaps presents an additional non-trivial challenge for cash flow modelling and forecasting.

When the pool is formed, the issuer simply adds a sufficient number of loans to ensure that all scheduled principal and interest cash flows to investors will be exceeded. At the time of issuance, there must be sufficient cash flow projected from the loan pool to make the scheduled principal and interest payments on both the senior and junior certificates. Over time, holders of the subordinated certificates are paid, provided there is sufficient cash flow exceeding the amount needed to pay the senior certificate investors. The key is to make sure that the excess cash flows due to the inclusion of additional loans in the pool will be sufficient to cover the actual losses that might occur. To shield the investors from credit risk, various risk mitigation facilities reinforce the cash flow structure, including the following:

(i) *Excess spread*:[21] This is typically one of the first defenses against loss. Even if some of the underlying loan payments are late or default, the coupon payment can still be made. In some extreme cases, excess spread is applied to outstanding classes as principal.

(ii) *Seller's interest*: The seller's interest is designed to absorb minor receivable fluctuations. Any factors that decrease the pool of receivables, beyond the maximum amount that can be absorbed by the seller's interest, require the credit card-issuing bank to provide additional accounts to the trust. In general, the seller's interest can be specified as a percentage of the total value of securitization pools.

(iii) *Credit tranching*: According to tranche seniority. According to tranche seniority, credit losses are charged to the most junior class of bondholders so long as the principal value of their investment exceeds zero, after which the next class of bonds absorbs credit losses. This process continues and

---

[21]Typically, excess spread can be defined as yield − base rate (investor coupon and serving fee) − (charge-off rate). For definitions in the case of securities backed by credit card receivables, see FDIC (2007), *Risk Management Credit Card Securitization Manual*, March.

in extreme cases may impact the most senior class of bondholders. It is customary in this "class structure" for the issuer to purchase the junior subordinated certificates, while the more senior ones are sold to investors. Hence, the senior certificate holders are only at risk (not to get paid) in the event that the actual losses in the loan pool are greater than the scheduled payments on the subordinated certificates.

(iv) *Overcollateralization*: This means that the face value of the underlying pools is larger than the security it backs. As a result, even if some of the payments from the loan borrowers are late or default, principal and interest payments on ABSs can still be made.

(v) *Reserve account*: This is created to reimburse the issuing trust for losses up to the amount allocated for the reserve. The reserve account will often be non-declining throughout the life of the security, meaning that the account will increase proportionally up to some specified level as the outstanding debt is paid off.

(vi) *Letter of credit (LC)*: The letter of credit is one form of extra protection that is purchased from a third-party financial institution (not the loan originator) such as a bank or insurance company. Credit enhancement most often takes care of a specified percentage of the pool losses, where the percentage is based on a historical benchmark, plus a margin. The credit enhancer receives a fee for providing this loss protection. In case of mortgages, a similar process is followed. For instance, mortgage loans are purchased from banks, mortgage companies, and other originators and they are assembled into pools. The issuer may be a private entity, a government agency or a government-sponsored enterprise. Public issuers offer some governmental backing to mitigate the risk of default associated with the mortgages.

From the issuer's perspective, attrition is another main source of risk. This is mainly caused by competitive forces (better offers) or changes in terms by servicers (lower limit, high minimum payment requirement, high nuisance fees, e.g. late fee, over-limit fee, etc.) which cause faster or early payment and a lower pool size. This will shorten the lifetime of the ABS if there is any danger that the investors will not be fully paid. These payouts based on triggers are generally required by the credit rating agencies for an investment-grade rating. Early amortization triggers include insufficient excess spread, insufficient payments by the underlying borrowers, increase in default rate above a specified level, or bankruptcy of sponsor or servicer. Once triggered, the revolving or accumulation period ends, and all money received from the underlying assets is used to repay the principal to the ABS investors. This process is irrevocable — everyone is paid regardless of the expected maturity date.

From the investor's perspective, ABSs also have a higher market risk in the secondary market, since the secondary market price depends on the fluctuating credit spread between ABSs and other types of fixed-income securities, and also on how many new issues of ABSs are being brought to market.[22] Sector risk can affect the price of ABSs. For example, the huge spike in subprime defaults sent mortgage-backed security prices spiralling downward, and also adversely affected prices on home equity loan-based ABSs. Another example would be a securitization of auto loans where a particular manufacturer makes up a significant share of the pool and has huge recalls of its models due to serious manufacturing defects that make the cars lose their value. Along the same lines, if the price of oil increases significantly for a prolonged period, the value of non-hybrid vehicles (that likely make up 90% of the collateral for the loans in the pool) may drop, causing a higher loan-to-value ratio in the pool, which is associated with higher risk and a potential performance decline.

In the next section we will describe how the new ABS framework can effectively identify and quantify those risks in a dynamic and transparent manner.

5. PROPOSED FRAMEWORK AND COMPONENTS

To reconnect borrowers, lenders, issuers and investors, we propose an enhanced framework that effectively creates asset pools that not only exhibit similar historically based behavioral characteristics, but also possess identical borrowers, collateral (in the case of secured loans), and product characteristics.

The CCAF considers all relevant factors simultaneously to come up with a pool segment at the account level and its associated risk assessment, or rating. The rating agencies use a process that is incomplete and fragmented. The component risk factors they measure are based on partial information that results in an overstatement, or understatement, of the true risk. Those risk factors are not independent and cannot be accurately

---

[22]The yields of asset-backed securities are generally higher than that of corporate bonds of comparable maturity and credit rating. The main reason for this is that the maturity is variable. Because cash flows resulting from loans and revolving lines of credit are highly variable, the maturity of an ABS is estimated by using pre-payment models based on projections. If the projections are wrong, then the yield will be different than expected.

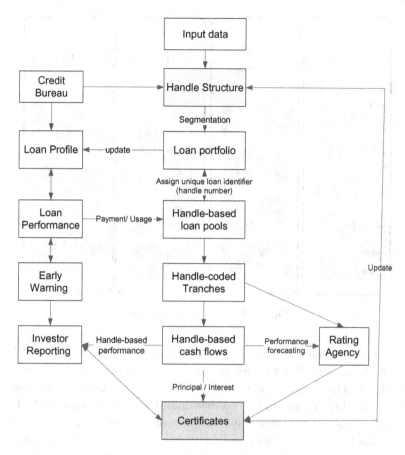

Fig. 4 The Proposed Framework.

viewed separately and then jointly summarized. That process is flawed and needs to be replaced with a holistic approach.

The CCAF process for valuing ABSs is shown in Fig. 4. All relevant information concerning historical account performance; the borrower's character, capacity, and capital; the terms of the credit account; and external market and economic historical data are sourced, validated, and stored in a form that is amenable to subsequent analysis. Construction of the CCAF handles occurs here. The handle distribution is determined overall, and the financial performance is estimated for each handle, including line utilization, payments of principal and interest (including pre-payment of the entire outstanding loan balance), non-performing percentage, incidence and amount by loan grade, credit bureau score distribution, loan default incidence and amount of credit losses.

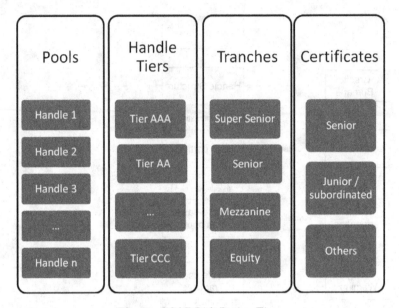

Fig. 5 CCAF Risk Rating Tiers.

Next, the handles are mapped to standard risk rating tiers (e.g. AAA, AA, A, BBB, BB, B, CCC, where the granularity of grading may vary); see Fig. 5. The securitization pools are then created from the estimated account-level cash flows using non-deterministic simulation methods. Part of that simulation exercise involves assignment of accounts from designated risk rating tiers to each pool based on quotas. Those quotes are determined by the sampling method to be necessary and sufficient in order to meet the performance characteristics of the loan pools. In the following step, cash payments from borrowers are forecast for every handle, and the likelihood and amount of any losses are also predicted at the handle level. Now, it is possible to estimate handle-based profitability. In effect one can construct a profit and loss statement in every handle. Hence, securities can be priced within the handle context using a net present value approach with various discount factors that reflect the probability of default (PD) for each specific handle. This technique greatly reduces the variability of the estimates. In our experience, with an effective segmentation of the pool, 90% of the losses fall into fewer than 12% of the handles. With the handle-based pools constructed, it is a purely mechanical exercise to proportionately allocate cash flows, along with necessary identifiers and parameters, from the securitization pools to the ABS tranches.

With the handle-based structure, it is easy to measure and monitor the performance of the underlying assets by simply measuring the population distribution shift across the handle cells. This can be done in terms of changes in percentage of loans in a handle cell or changes in handle cell frequency rankings. Any changes in risk are captured by measuring changes in default odds in a handle cell, or changes in handle cell risk rankings. Risk rankings can be readily validated with either statistical or logical analysis.[23] Figure 6 shows that for the same pool of loans, more loans or accounts have shifted from lower-risk handle cells to higher-risk handle cells, assuming the handles are ranked from the lowest risk (handle 1) to the highest risk (handle 11) based on the PD.

To help illustrate these concepts, consider the following simplified example. In practice, we seek to narrow down the number of primary factor categories for the framework to no greater than half a dozen. The resulting number of handles ranges anywhere from 50 to 500, depending on the type of loan, the degree of heterogeneity of the portfolio that is being securitized (in whole or in part), and the pooling requirements.[24] Once the primary

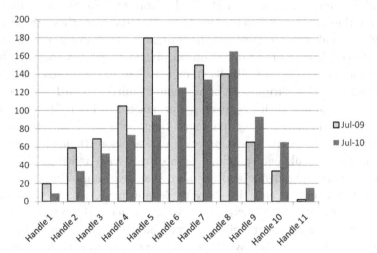

Fig. 6 Risk Migration Identification.

---

[23]For example, some simple statistical tests can be used to measure if the population shift is statistically significant, for instance the Kolmogorov–Smirnov test, chi-square test, or Spearman's rank-order correlation, etc. See Corder, G.W. and Foreman, D.I. (2009), *Nonparametric Statistics for Non-Statisticians: A Step-by-Step Approach*, Wiley.

[24]Sometimes it is necessary to develop more than one CCAF where there are stark performance differences for subsets of accounts or sizeable concentrations by account source channel, product terms, specific programes, geography, and so on.

factor categories are defined, the next step is to identify key metrics that "cover" each category.

The primary factor categories for our example are defined to be character, capacity, capital, and credit usage. Now we proceed to specify the key metrics by category, beginning with character.

Borrower Character Rating Criteria

There are typically a number of considerations when rating borrower character (willingness on the part of the borrower to meet their obligations). These include such things as past credit payment history, job stability, frequency of moving residence, educational level, record of meeting non-credit obligations (e.g. rent, utilities, phone) and so on. For simplicity, we focus our example solely on payment history and only three related considerations for the CCAF character component. First, we rate the borrower on whether they are established in making payments over time for a minimum number of obligations (e.g. three or four) over a minimum period of time (e.g. two years). If the borrower meets the minimum criteria, they are deemed to be "established". Otherwise, they are rated as "new". Second, we determine whether or not the borrower is a "defaulter" (e.g. if they have ever defaulted on an obligation with a balance above some minimum threshold, like $500, or have had any repossessions, liens, foreclosures, or bankruptcies) or a "non-defaulter". Third, we seek to determine whether their payment performance has been (i) "perfect or just mild delinquency", e.g. no more than once 30 days late on any tradeline, (ii) "moderate delinquency", e.g. no more than once 30 days late on any installment tradeline, or no more than twice 30 days late on any revolving tradeline and no more than five times 30 days late on all credit tradelines, and (iii) "severe delinquency", e.g. no more than once 30 days late on a mortgage tradeline or once 60 days late on any revolving or installment tradeline, or twice 30 days late on any installment tradeline, or four times 30 days late on any revolving tradeline, and no more than seven times 30 days late on all credit tradelines. The corresponding ratings for combinations of these three sub-components would be (i) "poor" for all defaulters, unless they are established and have perfect or only mild delinquency; for non-defaulters who are established and have severe payment delinquency; (ii) "fair" for defaulters who are established and have perfect or only mild delinquency; non-defaulters who are new and have moderate payment delinquency; and (iii) "good" for non-defaulters who either have only mild payment delinquency, or who have moderate payment delinquency, but are established.

Capacity Rating Criteria

Capacity is a function of borrower income, obligations, standard of living, discretionary spending, retirement plan contributions and savings. Income is a function of base wages, commission, bonus, investments, gifts, financial support, business interest, and other factors. Obligations depend upon such things as credit, taxes, insurance, rent, utilities, telecom, and other periodic non-credit payments. In this simple example, we measure borrower capacity using two financial ratios, namely debt-to-income (DTI) and savings-to-income (STI, which is defined as the average monthly savings rate for the last 12 months divided by the average monthly income over the same period).

The reason for these choices is that DTI is a gauge for how much credit financing is prudent relative to income, while STI is a measure of consumer financial discipline and ability to live within their means. A strong STI may safely offset a higher than customary DTI. We need to get a bit more granular on the definitions of DTI and STI for programming the classification of loans according to the CCAF handle. We adopt the following rules for them: DTI = max(current DTI, average DTI previous 12 months) and STI = min(current STI, average STI previous 12 months). Next, we must determine what the thresholds are for DTI and STI ratings and we map them to just two summary capacity ratings of low and high. In this example, we chose the savings ratio categories to be none, low (less than 4%), moderate (4–8%), and high (9% or more). The debt ratio is categorized as low (for values 25% and under), moderate (for values 26–38%), and high (for values greater than 38%).

Capital Rating Criteria

Capital refers to borrower assets that can be converted to cash. Some types of capital are more liquid (i.e. easy to sell) than others. Examples of liquid capital assets are bank checking and savings accounts, certificates of deposit, brokerage money market accounts, US Treasury securities, cash value of one's whole life insurance policy, and so on. An example of illiquid capital would be equity in a home, because real estate may be difficult to value or sell on a moment's notice.

Rather than key on the absolute amount of liquid capital available, we can look at capital relative to cash inflows (i.e. monthly income) and lifestyle (i.e. obligations plus discretionary spending). A candidate metric for capital might be months of reserves (MOR), defined as liquid assets divided by the difference between current monthly income and monthly savings. In practical application, we might further require that MOR equal the minimum of the current MOR and the average MOR over the previous 12 months. The rating categories for capital are "low" if reserves cover less than six months, and "high" otherwise.

Credit Usage Rating Criteria

Credit usage can be characterized in a number of different ways as shown in Table 1. For this example, we consider the degree to which accounts utilize their credit line and also the way in which they tend to pay down their current balance. We consider the following candidate metrics for usage: payment behavior and credit utilization. We define the values for these metrics, and their associated thresholds, in the following manner:

(i) Payment behavior defined for each account as follows:

   (a) *Minimum payers*: Accounts with a balance and finance charge at least once during the last three months. In addition, the last payment on the account must be less than 125% of the minimum payment due.

   (b) *Revolvers*: Accounts with a balance and finance charge at least once during the last three months. In addition, the last payment

Table 1   CCAF Ratings for Credit Usage.

Case	Payment Pattern	Utilization Rate	Usage Rating
1	Min payer	Low/Mod	Low
2	Min payer	Low/Mod	High
3	Min payer	High	High
4	Min payer	High	High
5	Revolver	Low/Mod	Low
6	Revolver	Low/Mod	Low
7	Revolver	High	High
8	Revolver	High	High
9	Transactor	Low/Mod	Low
10	Transactor	Low/Mod	Low
11	Transactor	High	Low
12	Transactor	High	High

on the account must be equal to or greater than 125% of the minimum payment due.

(c) *Transactors*: Accounts with a balance, but no finance charges, during the last three months.

(ii) Utilization rate is defined for each account as the current cycle balance divided by the current credit limit. There are three possible values, namely low (below than 25%), moderate (25–79%), and high (80% or more).

We note that in instances where credit usage is calculated over all credit trade lines, it still ignores capital and capacity positions of the borrower. When utilization is a component of the FICO score, it is taken completely out of context and given improper weight. The holistic CCAF score and its companion handle represent a comprehensive, concise, and a far better gauge of the borrower's creditworthiness than other measures. The popular FICO score fails to simultaneously consider borrower capital and capacity positions when it weighs credit utilization in the derivation of the loan default probabilities.

Table 2 lists all possible handles for a credit card securitization, and their associated component ratings. The primary factors include character, capacity, capital, and credit usage.

Now that we have a specified handle structure, we can demonstrate how it would be used to construct a loan pool. Further suppose that the issuer wanted to create a pool with an average holistic CCAF-based risk score of 710, with no loans having a "poor" character rating. Table 3 illustrates a selection scheme for accomplishing the issuer's objective by using the holistic risk score in combination with the handle structure (and its transparent component sub-ratings) to develop a sampling plan.

In addition to the 5 Cs of credit and associated variables, other factors also come into play, such as

(i) breadth and depth of borrower relationship with the institution originating and servicing the loan;

(ii) geographic location (e.g. borrower residence, business footprint);

(iii) industry economic strength and outlook (relative to either the business obligor or borrower's employer);

(iv) insurance coverage (e.g. health, accident, income continuation, term/whole life, cash value of annuities);

Table 2 CCAF Handle Structure for Simple Credit Card ABS.

Handle	Character	Capacity	Capital	Credit Usage
1	Poor	Low	Low	High
2	Poor	Low	Low	Low
3	Poor	Low	High	High
4	Poor	Low	High	Low
5	Poor	High	Low	High
6	Poor	High	Low	Low
7	Poor	High	High	High
8	Poor	High	High	Low
9	Fair	Low	Low	High
10	Fair	Low	Low	Low
11	Fair	Low	High	High
12	Fair	Low	High	Low
13	Fair	High	Low	High
14	Fair	High	Low	Low
15	Fair	High	High	High
16	Fair	High	High	Low
17	Good	Low	Low	High
18	Good	Low	Low	Low
19	Good	Low	High	High
20	Good	Low	High	Low
21	Good	High	Low	High
22	Good	High	Low	Low
23	Good	High	High	High
24	Good	High	High	Low

(v) alternative data that includes payment performance on non-credit
    obligations, such as rent, utilities, phone, cable, etc.;

(vi) borrower vulnerability to rising market interest rates and significant
    collateral/personal asset depreciation.

These secondary factors are of practical importance and they are typically
included by adding a final primary factor, which we term "secondary
factors", that takes on one of two possible values (namely, no or yes)
depending on whether or not any of the specified "sufficient" conditions are
satisfied. The effect of adding this primary factor is to double the number
of handles in our example to 48, which is at the lower bound of the 50–500
handle range for most applications.

In the next sections we use a credit card ABS example to illustrate how
the CCAF plays into each of the above steps to afford greater accuracy and
transparency.

Table 3 Credit Card Loan Pool Creation via Handle-Based Selection.

Sampling Tier	Sampling Quota	Avg. Holistic Score	Handle	Character	Capacity	Capital	Credit Usage
0	0%	575	1–8	Poor	Low/ High	Low/ High	Low/ High
1	10%	600	9	Fair	Low	Low	High
			10	Fair	Low	Low	Low
2	20%	650	11	Fair	Low	High	High
			12	Fair	Low	High	Low
			13	Fair	High	Low	High
			14	Fair	High	Low	Low
			17	Good	Low	Low	High
			18	Good	Low	Low	Low
3	50%	725	15	Fair	High	High	High
			16	Fair	High	High	Low
			19	Good	Low	High	High
			20	Good	Low	High	Low
4	20%	790	21	Good	High	Low	High
			22	Good	High	Low	Low
			23	Good	High	High	High
			24	Good	High	High	Low

6. TYPICAL FRAMEWORK EXAMPLE: POOLING CREDIT CARD RECEIVABLES

We now describe how to apply the handle structure discussed in the previous section to pool credit card receivables. There are several advantages to pooling using the handle. These include greater accuracy due to the holistic nature of the handle classification, greater transparency afforded by the ability to decompose the handle readily into its component factors, an adaptive risk estimation model that gets more predictive over time, and the ability to select loans based on perceived future vulnerability in addition to quantified risk based on historical data. For example, on the last point, borrowers having a high FICO score but low capacity, low liquid capital (i.e. highly leveraged and living paycheck-to-paycheck with no savings), and a loan with variable pricing pose greater risk logically than their individual risk metrics may indicate. Through the handle, the pool can be constructed so as to limit, or eliminate, loans that appear, based on well-established credit expert reasoning, to have more risk, despite

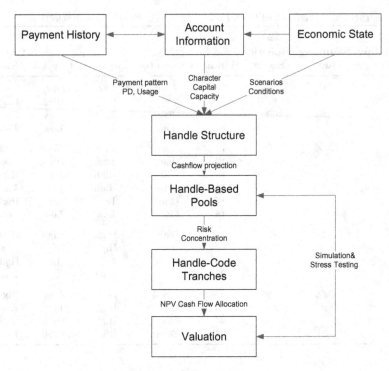

Fig. 7 Loan Pooling Method.

quantitative risk estimates to the contrary. This basic process is shown in Fig. 7.[25]

Required Input Data

Mainly, the input data should contain loan-level granularity of information which can be used to construct the pools. Each pool would be made up of segments of loans with homogenous attributes in terms of credit risk and cash flows. Typically, the input data for credit card ABS valuation includes the following data sources:

(i) *Credit card payment history*: Usually 3–5 years of monthly credit card payment history are required. Key variables include outstanding balance, principal payment and finance charges, credit limit, payment

---

[25] For a detailed description of the credit card securitization process, see FDIC (2007), *Risk Management Credit Card Securitization Manual*, March.

date, fees, frequency and severity of delinquency, early payment, credit
utilization rate, number and age of trade lines, types of credit in use,
or any other public derogatory records (e.g. bankruptcy).

(ii) *Borrower information*: Includes the card holder's account information,
bank relationship, breadth and depth, geographic location, profession,
education, industry, etc.

(iii) *Macro economic data (if applicable)*: For instance, CPI, unemployment
rate, market indices, etc.

Handle-based Pool Creation

Asset-backed securities having credit card receivables as their underlying
assets may have millions of accounts in the pool. According to current SEC rules, those offerings are exempt from loan-level information
requirements. However, the proposed new rules would require issuers to
disclose more granular information regarding the underlying credit card
accounts in tagged, computer-readable and standardized groupings. Under
the proposed rules, issuers of ABSs backed by credit cards would need to
present statistical data about accounts with similar characteristics grouped
by credit score range, age of account, payment status, and geographic
location.

Pool structuring is usually based on start date, number of issues/series,
receivable values and coupons, and distribution of cash inflows. Payments,
principal balances, and interest rates from individual accounts are typically
aggregated using a weighted average approach. In contrast, we exploit
the handle structure to divide the pools into homogenous performance
segments.[26] For example, the handle structure can be used to structure
pools exhibiting homogenous credit quality. Credit quality including charge-
offs and delinquency can have a significant impact on the value of cash flows.
Charge-off amounts are uncollected credit card balances removed from a
bank's books and charged against its loss reserve. The charge-off rate is
the amount of charge-offs divided by the average outstanding credit card
balances owed to the issuer. Since, in most cases, there are insufficient
charge-off data to perform meaningful forecasting, the PDs are usually
estimated by calculating the charge-off rate. Once the PDs are predicted at
the account level, key performance indicators such as the charge-off rate,

---

[26]See Abrahams, C. and Zhang, M. (2008), *Fair Lending Compliance: Intelligence and
Implications for Credit Risk Management*, John Wiley & Sons, Inc., pp. 289–297.

excess spread, and pool stability can be calculated naturally within the handle structure.[27]

Cash Flow Forecasting and Allocation

Cash flows from credit receivables mainly consist of two sources: finance charges and principal payment. Finance charges include interest charged to the card holder, and various types of fees such as an annual membership charge, servicing fees, over-limit fees, late payment fees, and so on. Principal payments can be those required (included in the monthly minimum payment) or excess payments (early paydown of the credit line to a zero balance). Fluctuations in cash flows can be caused by many factors as described in a previous section.

Typically, the cash flow allocations for each master trust are specified in the pooling and servicing agreement. Simulation techniques (e.g. historical, Monte Carlo, or the scenario-based approach) are used to create various market states to show how values of pool receivables are affected by changes in related market risk factors. In this step, cash from one or more handle-based pools will be allocated to the tranches based on seniority (waterfall) and pre-specified rules (maturity, payment frequency, coupon rate and principal).

Stress Testing and Validation

Traditionally, more than 80% of stress tests have been conducted at pool level by considering variables such as a sudden and significant change in interest rates, pool size, delinquency rates, or other factors. The main focus of historical-based stress testing has been to determine the sensitivity relative to various inputs of the model's prediction of the distribution of outcomes. What is missing here is a holistic scenario-based stress testing that includes more relevant risk factors and scenarios at the loan level plus the borrower's credit behavior levels (such as borrower's risk profile and loan affordability) all viewed in a proper context.

The key to effective stress testing is to design a testing scheme that incorporates a set of more complete and relevant risk factors and all possible thresholds. Using the CCAF's holistic approach, the handle-based segmentation process can readily help identify which factors, and their

---

[27]For example, estimated charge-off rate = PD*LGD*EAD. Pool stability = beginning outstanding balance − principal payment − credit losses/beginning outstanding balance.

associated scenarios, have the most impact on cash flows. For example, scenarios can be created based on a number of factors, such as charge-off rate, principal payment rate, credit usage, borrower's debt ratio, etc. Those scenarios can be used to evaluate both the individual and combined impact of these factors on the cash flows.[28] Stress testing is also performed in order to validate the tranche pricing using pre-determined scenarios to gauge the impact of scenario assumptions on both security prices and the credit enhancement piece. The effective discount rate[29] can be obtained based on the valuation of each scenario to validate and qualify the joint effects of various factors associated with simulated results.

Policy Implications for the ABS Market

There are four main stakeholders who care about policies that deal with the ongoing support and management of individual asset-backed securities. They are the originators of loans that back those securities, the issuers of those securities, the agencies that assign ratings to ABSs, and the ABS market at large. In this section, we review the current regulatory proposal and describe how it is addressed by our new framework. We then discuss the policy implications for selected areas from the perspectives of ABS issuers, regulators, and investors. We underscore how the CCAF provides superior capabilities to (i) validate conformance with existing policies (audit capability); (ii) maintain, enhance, or sunset current policies; or (iii) develop additional policies.

7. CURRENT PROPOSAL OF REGULATORY REFORM

On 7 April 2010 the Securities and Exchange Commission put out rules for comment on ABSs. SEC Chairman Mary L. Schapiro said, "The rules we are proposing stem from lessons learned during the financial crisis. These rules if adopted would revise the regulatory regime for asset-backed securities

---

[28] For some typical credit card securitization variables used in stress testing, see Furletti, M. (2002), "An Overview of Credit Card Asset-Backed Securities," Discussion Paper, Federal Reserve Bank of Philadelphia, December.

[29] This also can be viewed as an adjusted or implied PD, which reflects credit quality and interest rate spread. See Di Giambattista, J. (2007), "Fitch Equity Implied Ratings and Probability of Default Model," Quantitative Research Special Report, July 13.

in order to better protect investors". The CCAF would greatly improve several of these proposed rules[30] as follows:

(i) *"Require the Filing of Tagged Computer-Readable, Standardized Loan-Level Information"*: The CCAF would provide investors access to critical loan-level data in a simplified and easy-to-interpret form, sufficient for them to carry out independent and accurate analysis of all ABS instruments. The CCAF would promote greater data definition consistency, which is vital to enabling comparability and standardization of ABS instruments across issuers. The CCAF can, and should, be updated on a monthly basis. Furthermore, a chronology of past classifications and risk estimates at the individual loan level should be maintained in order to construct and view trends in CCAF-based risk-homogeneous loan segments to more accurately estimate the timing of future cash flows. The CCAF segment classification (referred to throughout as a "handle") and its associated holistic risk score constitute additional critical attributes needed for an ABS loan-level analysis, and most certainly for ABS investor reporting.[31] One option would be to embed the handle (either at the time of loan origination, or at the time of pool inclusion) into the loan identification number. This would enable the loan and its performance to be tracked throughout the life of the associated asset-backed security.

(ii) *"Require the Filing of a Computer Program that Gives Effect to the Waterfall"*: CCAF-based pre-payment, general valuation, risk, and stress-testing models would be a valuable supplement to the standardized models in use today, which the SEC can, and should, promote in relation to the analysis of ABS securities. This would be especially valuable for smaller investors and asset managers who face the challenge of putting in place the technology infrastructure that is needed to effectively manage a significant amount of loan-level data and to implement waterfall models. The CCAF could help reduce the complexity, obscurity, and difficulties in interpretability

---

[30] Securities and Exchange Commission, 17 CFR parts 200, 229, 230, 232, 239, 240, 243 and 249; Release Nos. 33-9117; 34-61858; File No. S7-08-10 RIN 3235-ak37; Asset-Backed Securities, http://www.sec.gov/rules/proposed/2010/33-9117.pdf.

[31] At present, the proposed rules treat credit card receivables as an exception relative to loan-level requirements. This information is routinely used by lenders to manage their card holder accounts, so there is, in fact, no technical barrier that precludes them from furnishing this level of data granularity to the investment community.

that are typically associated with mathematical models used in the analysis of ABS instruments. As a result, the CCAF could be of considerable help to investors, if adopted as part of an industry ABS information technology blueprint (endorsed by the regulators) that specifies standard valuation models along with loan-level data.

(iii) *"Repeal the Investment Grade Ratings Criterion for ABS Shelf-Eligibility"*: There can be no question that the credibility and accuracy of the current ABS ratings system has been undermined. Hence, elimination of the requirement for a rating from an NRSRO makes sense, provided investors can readily take on their own ratings analysis either independently, or with the assistance of a qualified independent third party that has no ties to the issuer of the ABS. The rule requires that

> the ABS issuer provide a mechanism whereby the investors will be able to confirm that the assets comply with the issuer's representations and warranties, such as representations and warranties that the loans in the ABS pool were underwritten in a manner consistent with the lenders' underwriting standards.[32]

The CCAF would make it very easy to verify that the pool assets "were underwritten in a manner consistent with the lenders' underwriting standards".[33] This is because the collections of CCAF handles, and their associated risk and operating metrics and parameters, would embody all criteria, and enumerate all possible cases encountered during loan underwriting. The CCAF provides precisely the level of transparency and information that lawmakers are attempting to put in place in order to restore confidence in ABS ratings and valuations.

(iv) *"Increase Transparency in the Private Structured Finance Market"*: We assert that ABS instruments currently in the exempt private structured finance market can, and should, meet the transparency requirements applied to non-exempt instruments. Our reasoning is that this would further promote consistent, safe and sound practices and would be advantageous to both issuers and investors alike. Furthermore, the CCAF would facilitate compliance for any pass-through vehicles, as we illustrate later in this chapter.

---

[32] *Ibid.*
[33] *Ibid.*

Issuers

Two concerns for investors revolve around loan performance relative to specific loan originators, and pool concentration risk. For example, if the Government National Mortgage Association (Ginnie Mae) experiences higher delinquencies than dictated by policy in Veterans Affairs/Federal Housing Administration mortgage pools for loans originated by a particular bank, it will notify the bank in question. The CCAF would help significantly to further pinpoint those loans where higher delinquencies were occurring, based on the handle. The case may be that the bank in question has a higher percentage of loans in certain handles that are experiencing higher delinquencies in general, so that it is more of an issue of segment risk, rather than issuer risk. On the other hand, it may be the case that the loan originator in question has a handle frequency distribution that mirrors the pool at large. In this case, there would be a problem with that specific originating bank.

Relative to pool concentration risk, current practices may consider segments by credit bureau (FICO) score bands and/or loan-to-value ranges, geographic boundaries, standard industry groupings, seasoning (account age with different breaks by type of loan), and so on. The CCAF handle provides a singular identifier and associated holistic risk measure that can be used to measure, monitor, and regulate pool concentrations at the time of pool construction, and also over time. By providing a total picture that is drillable to the loan level of detail, the CCAF takes the guesswork and speculation out of analysis that is aimed at providing explanations of observed period-to-period variances in pool performance and ABS valuations. For issuers, enhanced risk management capability is key. Through its handle-based segmentation, the CCAF can capture business and market reality by effectively incorporating cash allocation rules, credit enhancements, and market dynamics.

Regulators

The main concerns for regulators are overall market liquidity and the stability of markets having direct bearing on the collateral of the underlying loans, provided the loans are secured. For example, in the case of mortgage-backed securities, regulators would be concerned with the stability of the housing market because of the impact that would have on loan default and pool reserve adequacy.

The CCAF can help on these fronts in two main ways. First, by including vulnerability as a primary factor, the CCAF can immediately zero in on the pool exposures to highly vulnerable handle combinations (i.e. loan segments), which affords greater transparency. This is especially relevant for regulatory early warning systems, which too often are based upon elevation in delinquency severity or adverse patterns and trends in either past due performance or loan default. With the CCAF, increasing exposures in risky segments can be identified and dealt with in advance of any decline in pool performance. Second, pool stress testing can examine the range of expected loan defaults at the handle level, as opposed to the total pool level. Here, the CCAF approach affords greater accuracy.[34]

By adopting standard handle definitions, those handle tables would be additive across institutions, geographies, institutions, and so on. Because regulators have access to as much data as they wish, they could develop benchmarks for handle percentages in the typical loan pool for each type of loan product, e.g. mortgages, credit cards, and so on. This would afford regulators a wide array of different views into loan pools, and they could also combine everything to produce a systemic view for the global market, or any sub-market. Furthermore, summary rating tiers could also be defined according to the CCAF handles, in addition to the CCAF holistic score. In this way, supervision could extend to assessing safety and soundness at any/all levels, and could span institutions, countries, regions, industries, and so on as illustrated in Table 4.

Table 4 CCAF-Based Early Warning System.

CCAF Tier	A	B	C	D	E	F
1	2	2	3	4	1	2
2	3	4	5	6	7	5
3	5	7	9	10	8	6
4	9	7	11	13	10	11
5	14	10	13	13	11	12
6	16	18	15	14	15	13
7	18	23	19	20	18	19
<7	33	29	25	20	30	32
Average default rate	6.2	6.6	5.6	5.3	5.7	5.8
Average CCAF score	699	696	708	712	707	705

---

[34]For a detailed discussion of how the CCAF can be used to build an effective early warning system, see Abrahams, C. and Zhang, M. (2009), *Credit Risk Assessment: The New Lending System for Borrowers, Lenders, and Investors*, John Wiley & Sons, Inc., pp. 286–289.

If in Table 4 we had an institutional view, then lending institution B has the lowest average CCAF score and the highest default rate. The rating tier frequency distribution confirms that lender B has the highest concentration of tier 6 and 7 rated loans. Essentially, the handle structure can be deployed and aggregated at any level. Column B could also be defined as a collection of lenders that meet certain criteria, such as high quartile return on equity (ROE) for institutions falling into a given range of asset size. Similarly, this same report could represent a country analysis, or regional analysis, provided consistent handle definitions are adopted and applied. A composite benchmark could be created for countries falling into different groupings, according to market size, population, economic activity, or other criteria.

If regulators had possessed this type of loan pool monitoring, trouble could have been spotted years in advance of its growth to the massive proportions that triggered the financial system crisis in September 2008.

Investors

ABS ratings and performance reporting for specific securities are created to help investors understand the risk associated with the securities they invest in. Historically, investors have heavily relied on security ratings from the rating agencies, but that confidence has been seriously shaken. In addition to questions about the adequacy of the rating methodologies, there are also moral hazard issues stemming from the fact that rating agencies are paid by the security issuers. As a result, investors desire to have greater transparency and information that will allow them to independently form conclusions based on analysis either they, or their designated independent agent, may perform.

Performance reporting requirements are mandated by the regulatory agencies, such as the Securities and Exchange Commission.[35] These should be viewed, however, as a minimum threshold. We assert that the performance of the underlying pool of loans needs to be taken to the next level. More specifically, the CCAF handles can be mapped to rating tiers, as shown in Table 4. In this example, there are eight such tiers. A key difference between the CCAF bucketing by rating tier involves risk ranking driven not only by the more holistic score, but also by the common sense ordering of the handles themselves.

---

[35]For more information concerning the role of the SEC, please refer to the *Securities Exchange Act of 1934*, http://www.sec.gov/about/laws/sea34.pdf.

Referring back to Table 2, handle 1 is the highest-risk segment, while handle 24 is the lowest-risk segment of accounts. Their holistic scores would validate that fact. The easy interpretation afforded by the handles provides investors with a transparency not previously seen. For example, handles 1, 9, and 17 represent accounts having high credit usage and little capital or capacity. These are people living paycheck-to-paycheck, with no savings and a high reliance on credit. Although handle 17 has accounts with a good credit history, perhaps even a high FICO score in the 800s, they would still be viewed as vulnerable and higher-risk by the CCAF. Investors should know whether the loan pool backing their security has a significant number of borrowers living paycheck-to-paycheck with no savings. Keying only on the FICO score range and/or the LTV range is an incomplete and misleading way to construct or monitor a loan pool.

Investors would be well-served to have trend reports, produced quarterly, that show the percentage breakdown of handle-based risk tiers, both in terms of dollars and loans (accounts). If there is a shift in the handle mix of the loan pool, then the investor should automatically receive an additional series of reports that pinpoint the flow of loans from less risky to more risky handles, and vice versa. This detailed reporting should also be triggered when the percentage of accounts in the riskier tiers exceeds pre-specified policy thresholds. Better informing the investor community will go a long way towards rebuilding trust and restoring ABS market liquidity.

For investors, improving transparency is paramount. The use of the new framework described above can promote the standardization of the asset-pooling process so it will be easy to compare and rank asset performance and securities across pools. This will enhance the investors' ability to make investment decisions among various deals and issuers, and effectively monitor and evaluate the performance of the underlying assets, and readily connect security values with their underlying asset credit quality.

8. CONCLUSION

The recent financial crisis exposed systematic flaws that undermined the credit markets. Throughout the loan value chain, the ability to effectively measure and monitor key risk elements in the proper context is challenging, but critical to all stakeholders. In particular, loan securitization hinges on accurate risk classification and calibration to portray realistic investment risk and returns associated with ABSs. Connecting the underlying loan performance with the valuation of any ABS should be a primary concern for both investors and rating agencies. Assurances provided to investors (e.g. credit enhancements, pool overcollateralization, portfolio insurance, etc.) have proven insufficient.

The framework we have described in this chapter supports and connects the interests of all stakeholders through the use of a standardized and consistent view afforded by a unique loan-pooling process that captures the risk dynamic and more closely reflects the business realities. The key advantages of this framework are its comprehensive, forward-looking, transparent, and adaptive properties. If adopted, it will provide investors with the ability to validate both ABS rating and valuation and serve to restore their confidence in the ABS market. The net result will be greater ABS market liquidity, which will help spur a stronger and faster economic recovery.

REFERENCES

Abrahams, C. and Zhang, M. (2008). *Fair Lending Compliance: Intelligence and Implications for Credit Risk Management.* New Jersey: John Wiley & Sons, Inc.

Abrahams, C. and Zhang, M. (2009). *Credit Risk Assessment: The New Lending System for Borrowers, Lenders, and Investors.* New Jersey: John Wiley & Sons, Inc.

Agarwal, S., Cun, C. and De Nardi, M. (2010) "Rescuing Asset-Backed Securities Markets." Chicago Fed Letter, Federal Reserve Bank of Chicago, January, Number 270.

Association of Mortgage Investors (2010). "Reforming the Asset-Backed Securities Market." March.

Di Giambattista, J. (2007). "Fitch Equity Implied Ratings and Probability of Default Model." Quantitative Research Special Report, 13 July.

FDIC (2007). *Risk Management Credit Card Securitization Manual,* March.

Financial Crisis Inquiry Commission (2010). "Credit Ratings and the Financial Crisis." 2 June, http://www.scribd.com/doc/32651377/Financial-Crisis-Inquiry-Commission-Report-on-Credit-Ratings.

Furletti, M. (2002). "An Overview of Credit Card Asset-Backed Securities." Discussion Paper, Federal Reserve Bank of Philadelphia, December.

Goodman, L., Li, S., Lucas, D.J., Zimmerman, T.A. and Fabozzi, F.J. (2008). *Subprime Mortgage Credit Derivatives.* New Jersey: John Wiley & Sons, Inc., pp. 3–4.

Koegel, D. (2009). "Securitization Reborn: Transfer of Credit, Insurance, and other Risks." *The RMA Journal,* 91: 30–35.

SEC, 17 CFR parts 200, 229, 230, 232, 239, 240, 243 and 249; Release Nos. 33-9117; 34-61858; File No. S7-08-10 RIN 3235-ak37; Asset-Backed Securities, http://www.sec.gov/rules/proposed/2010/33-9117.pdf.

SEC. *Securities Exchange Act of 1934*, http://www.sec.gov/about/laws/sea34.pdf.

SEC (2010). "SEC Proposes Rules to Increase Investor Protections in Asset-Backed Securities." 7 April http://www.sec.gov/news/press/2010/2010-54.htm.

Joint Explanatory Statement of the Committee of the Conference on the amendment of the Senate to the bill H.R. 4173 (*The Wall Street Reform and Consumer Protection Act of 2009*), Title IX (Investor Protections and Improvements to the Regulation of Securities), Subtitle D (Improvements to Asset-Backed Securitization Process), http://docs.house.gov/rules/finserv/111_hr4173_finsrvcr629stmntofmgrs.pdf.

SIFMA (2010). US Research Quarterly, 2010 Q1, http://www.sifma.org/uploaded Files/Research/ResearchReports/2010/CapitalMarkets_ResearchQuarterly_20100518_SIFMA.pdf.

Chapter 7

RISK MANAGEMENT OF COLLATERALIZED DEBT OBLIGATIONS

Shwn Meei Lee

1. INTRODUCTION

The term collateralized debt obligation (CDO) refers to a wide variety of structured investment products. The products are normally maintained by a broad range of essential securities such as bonds, credit default swaps, loans and asset-backed securities as well as more unusual collateral such as equity default swaps and CDO tranches from external sources. A CDO raises money by offering debt and equity to investors. The money raised is then used to invest in a pool of financial assets, either corporate or structured. In theory, an investment decision is made through a highly rational process (Shleifer and Vishny, 1997; Thaler, 1999). With no exception, if there are other opinions or suggestions during the process of decision making, investors will feel a need to conform to the others' expectations because of such irrational factors as conflict avoidance and the pressure of social norms (Camerer, 1998; Daniel and Titman, 1999). The proceeds from the assets are then distributed to the investors according to the level of liabilities and the associated risks (Lucas, Goodman and Fabozzi, 2007) as shown in Fig. 1.

The makeup of any CDO depicts the volume and amount of tranches and the policies that govern the distribution of the security profits to the tranches. These policies and the makeup differ widely from one collateral deal to another. For instance, interest payments to the tranches are made in accordance with the position of the tranche on the tranche ladder. As Morokoff (2003) states, "the structures may be simple pass-throughs,

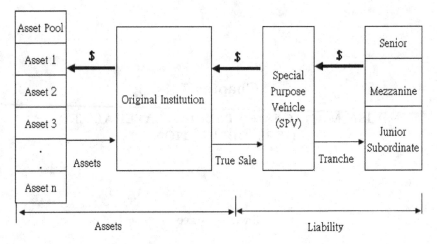

Fig. 1   Assets Pool of CDO.

Source: Lucas, Goodman and Fabozzi (2007).

whereby interest payments are made in order of tranche seniority". In other cases, there are rules which require that interest payments be made based on the value and performance of the principal securities. In short, each CDO deal has an exceptional makeup made to suit the current market situation, the features of the underlying securities and the demand of the investors at the time the CDO deal is made. Despite these variations, majority of the CDOs are structured in a manner that will guarantee that the highest ranking tranche is given the highest rating by the debt rating agencies as far as credit worth is concerned. CDO deals are officially instituted as special-purpose entities (SPEs).

An SPE acts as an autonomous company. To this end, any CDO deal has four major attributes which enable it to run as a company. These attributes include assets, liabilities, purposes and credit structures. The assets of a CDO are financial in nature and vary widely from corporate loans to mortgage-backed collateral. As an independent company, a CDO deal has liabilities which include preferred dividends and AAA-rated senior liabilities. Besides assets and liabilities, CDO deals are characterized by credit structures which fall into either of two groups: cash flow and market value protections. Lastly, CDO deals are created to fulfil certain purposes which include reducing their balance sheet, reducing the requisite regulatory and financial capital, reducing funding costs, obtaining assets under management and management costs, and increasing equity capital (Lucas, Goodman and Fabozzi, 2007).

The capital makeup of CDO deals is very basic in nature: the assets owned are the pool of securities, whereas the liabilities are the tranches offered to the public or private entities. Individuals or companies interested in CDO deals buy the tranches, and the proceeds from the sale of the tranches are then used to buy the assets. After every three or six months, the interest earned on the assets together with the principals are gathered and deposited into accounts. The cash flows are then used to make payments to the tranches. According to Morokoff (2003), "the set of rules for how the funds are distributed at a given payment date is known as the cash flow waterfall for the CDO". In a normal waterfall, the rules stipulate that taxes and management costs should be compensated for first, followed by the interest accruing to the most senior tranche. The senior-most tranche is the one that invests the highest amount of principal (75–90%) but receives the lowest interest. The reason behind this is that the possibilities of risk and losses reduce as one moves up the tranche ladder because the most senior tranches get paid first.

The lowest-ranking tranche at the foot of the waterfall is referred to as the equity tranche. This tranche normally does not get a prearranged interest like the more senior tranches. Rather, the junior tranche gets the remaining interest after the CDO has paid the senior tranche. Because of this, junior tranches bear the highest possibilities of incurring losses. On the other hand, the equity tranche can also perform well especially in situations involving significant excess spread (that is, the sum of interest earned by the security pool above what is payable to the tranches). However, as more and more defaults transpire in the collateral pool, the sum of excess spread reduces. In such situations, the equity tranches become the first lot to suffer a loss from the investment. Many CDO deals avert proceeds away from the junior tranche when the performance of the collateral falls consistently. As Morokoff (2003) states, "many deals have collateral quality triggers that divert all cash flows away from the equity if the collateral quality deteriorates too much".

The collateral supervisor of a CDO deal is accountable for supervising the security assets as their credit quality is revolutionized. This entails purchasing and trading assets, in addition to investing back the money that has been obtained from defaulting or budding names. The ability and the approach of the manager to manage the security pool can have a significant impact on the functioning of the collateral deal. As far as risk management is concerned, the most crucial aspect that affects the functioning of a CDO deal is the sum of the loss in security pool value over the existence of the deal as a result of associated defaults within the pool. Every tranche can endure a certain amount of loss in the security pool before it fails to earn its expected interest and principal. The performance of a CDO deal is also highly affected by the instance of defaults, especially for the junior tranche. Other risk factors that affect the performance of a CDO deal include the rates of interest, the rates of maturing and prepayment of the securities, and the rates of recovery on the defaulted security. Most importantly, the price risk, that is, the variation of the worth of the collateral as a result of the quality of the credit or the rates of interest, as well as reinvestment risk, also affects the performance of any CDO deal (Morokoff, 2003).

2.   INTRODUCTION OF CDOs INTO THE FINANCIAL MARKET

CDOs were first launched in the financial market in 1987. CDOs make use of the securitization expertise which was initially employed to create housing mortgage-backed collateral. With time, CDOs became popular among the investment elite and in 1998 alone almost $100 billion worth of CDOs were issued (Fig. 2). Indeed, CDOs "were the fastest growing investment

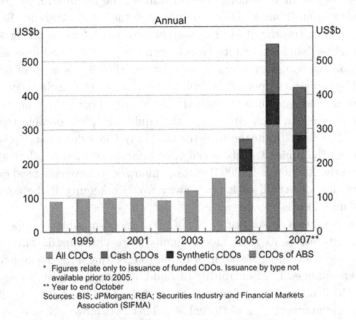

Fig. 2   Global CDO Issuance.

Source: http://www.rba.gov.au.

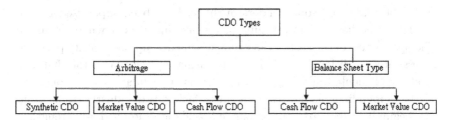

Fig. 3 Types of CDO.
Source: Lucas, Goodman and Fabozzi (2007).

vehicles of the last decade" (Goodman, Lucas and Fabozzi, 2007). There are different types of CDOs, which include collateralized loan obligations, balance-sheet CDOs and arbitrage CDOs (Fig. 3). A collateralized loan obligation (CLO) is a CDO whose portfolio includes corporate loans. These CLOs were initially used by financial institutions to shift the risk involved in a collateral pool of commercial banks. A balance-sheet CDO, on the other hand, is mainly used for risk management dealings. Lastly, arbitrage CDO is a CDO that is used to capture the difference between the security portfolio and the cost of the loan offer. Since its inception, the CDO market has expanded to the extent that it leads in the underlying security markets, especially high-yield loans, mezzanine mortgage asset-backed collateral, and trust-preferred debt (Goodman, Lucas and Fabozzi, 2007). High-yield loans, mezzanine mortgage asset-backed securities and trust-preferred debt are the backbone of the American CDO market and comprise 35%, 20% and 5% of the underlying securities, respectively. The issuance of CDOs that are supported by these three collaterals has consistently risen, thereby leading to a rise in collateral issuance and a reduction in collateral distribution.

CDOs and the Real Estate Market

The housing market has suffered numerous recessions in the past. However, unlike the previous recessions, the current housing recession has caused the greatest destruction in the financial market due to write-offs on collaterals associated with subprime mortgages. The write-downs approached $400 billion by the end of last year with the cost of the housing slump nearing $1 trillion (Kim, 2008). All the parties of the collateral and the housing markets, including the investors, lenders, borrowers, federal regulators and the rating agencies, have been held accountable for the slump. The risk involved was speculated at two points: the level of the mortgage agreement and the level of the mortgage portfolio tools. The risk levels speculated by some lenders ought to have been supervised by the regulatory bodies and intervening strategies undertaken where required. The opaqueness of the security instruments making up the security portfolio necessitated additional caution by the rating agencies, a factor that was rarely implemented. The American government regulators were conscious of the impending challenges that were facing the industry right from the beginning. In 2001, an "expanded guidance intended to strengthen the examination and supervision of institutions with significant subprime lending programs" was issued by the Federal Reserve System, the Federal Deposit Insurance Corporation, the Office of the Comptroller of the Currency, and the Office of Thrift Supervision (Johnson and Neave, 2008). The instructions provided standards and principles that were to be followed for loan and lease losses, loan assessment and categorization, recovery programs and unethical lending. Unfortunately, the four federal banking agencies had no authority over the rate of conformity and assessment, hence the majority of the concerned parties failed to adhere strictly to the guidelines. The purpose of the rating agencies also needs to be mentioned. Lenders as well as borrowers need to be aware of the risk and profit features of their prospective ventures. Adequate risk analysis and rating is especially important when dealing with opaque collaterals that bear a number of underlying tools. The reduction in the worth and real default of a number of these tools which initially had high ratings, as well as the high incomes earned by the rating agencies, raises concern about the thoroughness of the rating agencies in assessing and supervising the collaterals. However, the heaviest blame seems to rest on the models that were used by the rating agencies to rate CDOs.

3. CDO RATING MODELS AND THE CURRENT FINANCIAL CRISIS

Collateralized Debt Obligation is a form of structured financing and typically generates a fixed cash flow (Liou and Shiue, 2009). It has been the fastest-growing investment vehicle of the last decade (Lin, 2009).

There are a number of rating agencies such as Standard & Poor's, Fitch and Moody's. The major interest of all these agencies is the potential risk that any CDO investor is faced with. The agencies therefore provide investors with information and opinions about the likelihood of incurring risk from a particular collateral. This is normally done using different model-based computations which differ from one rating agency to another.

However, of importance to each computation is an evaluation of the probability that a tranche will face certain losses during the lifetime of a CDO deal. In the past, losses were defined based on a buy-and-hold approach and were therefore restricted to losses as a result of defaults. This has changed in the recent past in which losses also include those that result from mark-to-market risks (Hwa, 2009). The rating models used by rating agencies had several weaknesses which rendered them incapable of evaluating the credit risks involved in the subprime mortgages. Kim (2008) states that "given the size of the market failure, it's fair to question the methodology that the rating agencies used to assign credit ratings to subprime collateralized debt obligation tranches".

Between the year 2005 and the third quarter of 2007, close to four-fifths of all subprime mortgages were transformed into AAA portfolios. A tool supported by subprime mortgages could obtain four-fifths of the estimated sum at AAA rates. This raised concerns about the possibility of converting B-rated paper into AAA-rated vehicles. The underlying explanation for this mysterious conversion is that there are numerous junior-class notes ranked lower than AAA. In actuality, there exists at least one class of paper, referred to as the equity note, that has not been ranked. Proceeds from mortgages are rewarded according to the seniority of the tranches on the tranche ladder; that is, from the most senior tranche to the most junior tranche. As a result, if defaults occur, the most junior tranche suffers the loss first, followed by the next and so forth. However, the interest rate paid to the most junior tranche is higher than that paid to the tranches above on the ladder due to the substantial risk the most junior tranche bears (Kim, 2008), as shown in Fig. 4.

CDO Rating Models

The rating agencies depended on the CDO rating models in evaluating and appraising the potential financial risks of CDO tranches. Traditionally, CDO rating models were mainly employed for assessing CDOs for companies' debt. The first rating model, the binomial expansion technique (BET), was first developed by Moody's. The model became widely used to rate CDO portfolios, including those associated with subprime mortgages. The model produces the sum of defaulted loans in a portfolio with the rate of recurrence if loans of the security portfolio are more or less identical in probability of default (PD) and disclosure, and if defaults of loans are self-determining incidents. For instance, for a portfolio of 100 loans, the likelihood of only one loan default over the lifetime of the portfolio is very

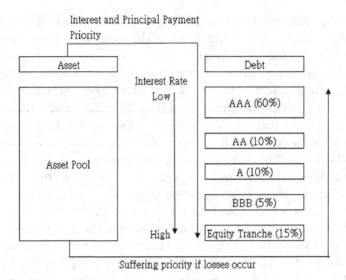

Fig. 4   Interest, Principal, and Losses Priority.

Source: Kim (2008).

small. Likewise, the likelihood that 99 loans will default is very low. In actuality, since the portfolios are heterogeneous in nature, the probability that many loans will default is quite high (Kim, 2008).

The principal notion of BET is to plot the actual pool into a theoretical identical pool by computing the average probability of default of the disclosures and the diversity score. The diversity score summarizes the degree to which the actual portfolio is identical. More significantly, it mirrors the default link between loans by restoring the sum of the loans in the portfolio. Using the above example, if the diversity score is 70, the rate of recurrence of the amount of defaulted loans is computed as if there are just 70 loans in the portfolio. The major requirements of the model to do the computation are the ratings or probabilities of default of the loans. The rating models that were used for corporate credits proved to be efficient due to the fact that the credit value of companies is normally well studied and documented. However, when it comes to the subprime market, questions linger as to whether these rating models can be adequately used to assess the default risks of the tranches.

Ratings of Subprime CDO Tranches in CDO Rating Models

The mathematical nature of the rating models makes it difficult for actual and potential investors to evaluate the credit value of CDO deals. However, the models are useful as they enable the investors to make a point of reference to their investments. There are a number of reasons behind the ratings borne by CDO products. First, the three major rating agencies — Moody's, Fitch and Standard & Poor's — are Nationally Recognized Statistical Rating Organizations (NRSROs). As such, the agencies are permitted by federal and state laws to float their collateral portfolios in financial market funds and insurers, among others. Subprime mortgages, unlike corporate bonds, lack secondary markets. To worsen the situation, rating agencies have very little expertise in the housing sector. Despite this and the anticipation that the housing market boom would explode, rating agencies continued to employ CDO rating models to assess subprime mortgages using consumer credit scores (FICO) as the key. This strategy became problematic for two reasons.

First, a rating model for subprime mortgages depends heavily on consumer credit scores at the time of inauguration. Single FICO scores are charted according to credit history and some unique monetary characteristics. Hence, they hardly ever vary until real defaults take place. The FICO scores are then plotted to the real rate of occurrence of defaults of subprime mortgages. Because these were predicted during the expansion of the housing market, the likelihoods of defaults and default links among subprime mortgages were much lower than what would be anticipated during a slump in the housing market. This indicates 80% of enormous AAA portfolio of subprime mortgages (4/5).

The second reason is that the majority of credit risk models fail to effectively function during a traumatic time. To worsen the situation, even pool diversification fails to improve the situation during such times since the new relationships lead to an unforeseen concentration of risk. This event is referred to as correlation breakdown, which is common in many investment markets. The lack of active sales of existing CDOs in secondary markets makes the problem of subprime mortgages more severe. Even if a market slump had been anticipated by the rating agencies, the CDO rating models used would produce almost identical ratings for subprime CDO deals. Devoid of a pricing mechanism, the subprime market cannot regulate itself until it collapses (Kim, 2008).

Monoline Insurers and Residential Mortgage CDO Products

Monoline insurance companies play a vital role in the structuring of CDO products associated with housing mortgages. These companies offer credit security to the senior-class tranches of CDOs. Because they do not provide credit security to tranches of lower classes, they attract investors to this class, thereby increasing its percentage. This adjustment can be achieved in two ways. First, notes of all tranches of a CDO deal can be reduced when a substantial credit risk for housing mortgages is anticipated. Second, the percentage of senior tranche notes in the CDO deal is increased in comparison to the remaining estimated sum of security because the majority of the defaults are taken up by the junior tranches. Additionally, the rating is done according to the standard risk of the senior notes. To minimize the probability of incurring losses, monoline insurance companies divided the senior class into two groups: a senior class and a first-loss class. Despite this, the monoline companies have failed to avoid selling insurance to the latter group (Kim, 2008).

A Structural Model of Subprime Mortgages Based on Housing Market Risk

A perfect CDO model for subprime mortgages should incorporate the following two features: an overt inherent price risk of single-family units and a method of showing that a fall in the housing price index increases both the likelihood of default for sole subprime borrowers and the default relationship between subprime borrowers. Given the housing market price risk, the likelihood of default by subprime borrowers over the maturity period of their mortgages is equivalent to the likelihood of distance-to-default stabilized by housing market price instability. It is important to note that consumer credit scores are not used by the structural model to analyse the likelihood of defaults of mortgages (Kim, 2008). To compute the financial risk of subprime CDO tranches, it is necessary to compute the probability of portfolio loss. Of most convenience is the need to pinpoint one factor that can influence the prices in the housing market. This factor could be variations in the rates of mortgages. According to Kim (2008), "housing market prices tend to move in the opposite direction of mortgage rate changes, and the severity of portfolio loss in general depends on the size of mortgage rate changes".

Portfolio Loss Rate Distribution

The pool of subprime mortgages is coarse, a feature characteristic of consumer goods. This means that single mortgages are minute in comparison to the volume of the pool, which may contain hundreds of mortgages. This means that the real pool loss can be directly estimated from the anticipated portfolio loss. The provisional portfolio loss relies heavily on the general factor which is variations in the rates of mortgage. As a result, the distribution of the pool loss rate can be described as a growing normal distribution dependent on the variations in mortgage rates. Subprime mortgages can be divided into CDO classes that can be ranked without using the Monte Carlo simulations. CDO class ratings obtained from this approach are essentially dissimilar from the conventional rating models in two ways. First, the risks of the housing prices are overtly inherent in the model. Second, every CDO class is ranked according to the rigorousness of general feature movements. Consequently, if the volume of defaults within subprime mortgages increased, it would be due to the universal decline in housing prices rather than correlation breakdown.

4. COMMON CDO RISK MEASURES

Tranche default probability: This measure forms the foundation for rating agencies to allot a rating to a CDO class for a probability-based model.

Expected tranche loss: This measure is not only concerned with whether or not an individual tranche is faced with a loss, but also with the volume of the potential losses. This measure is especially used by Moody's to assign ratings to CDO tranches.

Tranche loss-given-default: This measure is calculated by dividing the expected tranche loss by the tranche default probability given that the expected tranche loss and the tranche default probability are not correlated. The ideal assessment made by rating agencies is done using a probabilistic notion of tranche losses and as a result, it is highly influenced by the postulations made in the internal credit pool model. Such postulations are ideally approximated from past ratings and default information, and the likelihood and the anticipations taken into account are thereby taken as the real or past measure (Hwa, 2009).

Market Risk

The inception of any market vehicle is always accompanied by the concern that members of the market will fail to comprehend the related risks. For instance, there is proof in the interest rates swap market of companies supposedly failing to comprehend these risks. The same can be said about the CDO market. These tools have been crucial credit inventions, but there have been cases in which investors suffered from difficult financial challenges due to the fact that the product was invented and introduced into the market before the public could be educated about it. As Lucas, Goodman and Fabozzi (2007) state, "these instruments have been important financial innovations, but there were investors who experienced financial fiascos because product innovations may have run far ahead of product education". In situations where a financial establishment wants to enter into the new credit risk transfer vehicles' market, the sale of more complicated goods, such as synthetic CDOs, may increase the establishment's risk of incurring losses and losing its position in the market. Additionally, there is also the risk of modelling. For instance, in reference to single-tranche CDOs, the investor may obtain an unfair position in the market and thus try to improve this position through delta hedging (Lucas, Goodman and Fabozzi, 2007). The risk in such a case occurs if the investor fails to hedge accurately. As a result, there is a need for market investors to keep on enhancing their risk management skills and for managers and regulators to keep on enhancing their understanding of the related concerns (Jobst, 2006). Risk management, exposure and assessment are the three most important issues that investors in the market need to take into account.

5. SENSITIVITY MEASURES

Sensitivity measures of a CDO deal can be divided into four types: tranche sensitivity to variations in correlation, tranche sensitivity to wide variations in credit spreads, the subordination effect, and the standard deviation of losses.

Correlation Sensitivity

Correlation sensitivity measures the changes of the tranches as the correlation is adjusted. The most junior tranche (equity tranche) has the longest correlation because its value rises as the correlation increases. On the other hand, the distribution declines with higher correlations. The explanation for this trend lies in the fact that "higher correlation increases the probability of fewer defaults as well as the probability of more defaults" (Hussain, 2007). Equity tranches are very sensitive to defaults because in case of any default, they are the first to suffer losses. As a result, equity tranches favor higher likelihoods of less and default and therefore greater correlation. Contrary to the junior-class investors, Class A investors are short correlation. A greater correlation for this class translates into a reduction in the creditworthiness of the tranche and an increase in its distribution.

The tranches that fall in the middle of the CDO capital makeup behave in a similar manner as either the equity tranche or the senior-most tranches, depending on their sensitivity to the correlation postulations. For instance, Class C (6–9% tranche) demonstrates rigid sensitivity to variations in correlations outside the initial 25% correlation. On the other hand, the higher classes on the tranche ladder are vulnerable only to severe market disruptions that lead to higher market correlations and numerous defaults (Hussain, 2007). These observations demonstrate two essential characteristics of CDO deals. First, market participants having dissimilar correlation postulations will place different rates on an individual tranche. This generates a model risk and a chance for correlation or model arbitrage. The measurement of correlation is difficult to compute because it is vulnerable to prediction errors, personal bias and correlation collapse. Second, mezzanine tranches are the least susceptible to variations in the correlation measurement and to modelling errors. For instance, Class C investors record very few variations in the creditworthiness of their tranche even when correlation multiplies. Investors who desire to reduce parameter risk will for that reason have a preference for the middle tranches of a CDO deal.

Sensitivity to Broad Spread Changes

In order to illustrate the impact of changes in broad spreads on CDO tranches, the tranche fair spreads are computed after increasing the credit distributions. The decline in the tranche's mark-to-market (MtM) value is also computed. The results of these computations show that the spread on the most junior tranche is the least vulnerable to a great variation in credit spreads. On the other hand, the equity tranche records the greatest hypothetical MtM variations as a fraction of the tranche.

The spread on the topmost tranche is the most vulnerable to wide variations in credit spreads, but its MtM is least affected. These trends are anticipated because an increase in credit spreads puts an upward pressure on the possibility of a greater volume of credit defaults to which the topmost classes are more vulnerable. What this implies is that in a market situation where the value of credit is constantly falling, the likelihood of numerous credit defaults rises, which in turn reduces the credit subordination for the topmost tranches and raises the likelihood of credit losses affecting the topmost tranches. It is worth noting that it is impossible to tell apart the impact of a wide increase in default likelihoods across credits from the impact of a rise in the default correlation across the same (Hussain, 2007).

The Subordination Effect

The anticipated loss of a tranche is affected mainly by the credit spreads of the underlying assets as well as the credit improvement offered to the tranche. The subordination changes with variations in the average spread on the underlying portfolio. As the quality of the underlying portfolio is reduced, greater rates of subordination are required to preserve the anticipated loss of junior classes at a level that is comparable to its base level. This assessment demonstrates another feature of CDO structure: Virtually any sought-after rating can be achieved for a tranche if the accurate level of credit improvement can be made available to that tranche. Hussain (2007) argues that "the lower the credit quality of the reference portfolio, the more subordination the tranche will require to achieve the same rating". A higher subordination also has a great impact on the leverage of any tranche. Leverage in this circumstance is used to refer to the anticipated loss of the tranche divided by the anticipated loss of the underlying pool. Higher subordination creates lower leverage and vice versa. In short, the credit quality of the underlying pool is directly related to the leverage required by a tranche to attain its desired rating.

Standard Deviation and Unexpected Losses

In CDO deals, standard deviation is used to describe computations for unforeseen losses and requisite financial capital to cushion against severe losses. In this case, the unforeseen loss of a tranche is defined as "the loss level at one standard deviation above the expected loss of the tranche" (Hussain, 2007).

6. ASSET-BACKED SECURITIZATION

One strategy of releasing regulatory capital is to offer CDOs for project finance loans. As discussed earlier, CDOs entail collecting a pool of loans and securitizing the repayment duties. The ranked notes are then floated to investors. The principal goal of such transactions is to minimize the regulatory capital prerequisite of the related loans. Also influencing the current reputation of structured finance CDOs is improved investor desire for disclosure to infrastructural sectors through issuance of bonds, and the reality that CDOs provide investors with a variety of credit exposures and a competent diversification of risk. A second common characteristic of such transactions is to offer the instigating bank the capability of acquiring the credit risk for the loans again after the expiry of an agreed-upon time frame (Bliss and Harud, 2007).

As far as the rating process is concerned, the whole pool, as well as single instruments, is rated. The ranking of the underlying portfolio involves an analysis of incidents that are related to a credit assessment. The rating also takes into consideration the risk of default correlations; that is, the likelihood that one loan default will influence the default of other loans as a result of loan congestion in the market. To this day, rating agencies have stuck to the belief that portfolios of PFI/PPP loans are to a certain degree cushioned against correlations because every loan in the portfolio is strictly structured on a single project-specific foundation and therefore insulated from the effect of broader financial activity (Bliss and Harud, 2007).

7. THE ROLE OF TECHNOLOGY
IN THE CDO MARKET

Like in the majority of sectors in any economy, technology has an important role to play in the CDO market. Indeed, one of the questions that still linger in the minds of many following the current financial crisis is the prospect of CDOs and other suchlike markets. The CDO market is presently seen to be on the verge of dying. The number of losses and write-downs that continue to be recorded are a clear indicator of the fragility of the CDO market. The only opportunities remaining for players in the market are to hold on to profit chances and to adopt effective risk management mechanisms (Davenport, 2008). Unlike in the past, however, players in this market will invest in a different manner. They will tread more cautiously in the market and will want a better comprehension of what exactly it is they are investing in than was the case in the past.

This can only be achieved if more information delivered through advanced technological devices is offered to investors prior to making any investment. The potential of implementing technology in the CDO market is however riddled with numerous challenges. The ability of potential and actual investors to completely comprehend the makeup, constituents and risks involved in the CDO deals requires an overhaul of the structure and proper documentation of information and data that can be distributed to investors. These data and information can then be used by investors to make informed choices about their investments (DeBenedictus, 2008). Second, new rules need to be developed about the payments made in any given CDO deal. Addressing all these challenges and restoring the CDO market will necessitate the use of advanced technology both by the mortgage investors and the providers of the secondary market. It will also require cooperation among the interested parties. As DeBenedictus states, "originators, secondary market issuers, industry groups and rating agencies will see value in cooperative development of best practices and standards for what data elements are appropriate" (Bliss and Harud, 2007). These policies will assist market participants in obtaining the much-needed data and making the data available to investors.

8. CONCLUSION

CDOs became part of the financial market in 1987 but their popularity grew tremendously particularly in the past decade. These vehicles refer to pools of loans, some of which are homogenous while others are heterogeneous in nature. The CDO market was hit hard by the current financial crisis as a result of the risks involved in the portfolios and the ignorance of CDO managers in addressing such risks. All participants of the market, including lenders, borrowers, investors, federal regulators and rating agencies, bore a part of the blame of the collapsing market. However, the inefficient rating models used by the rating agencies bore the biggest share of the blame because they provided investors with inaccurate information regarding the performance of the collaterals. Today, risk management is seen to be one of the important aspects of the CDO market. Various risk management tools are used to assess the credit risks of the underlying collateral portfolios. The CDO market can indeed pick up from where it fell but only if advanced technology is used to collect, manage and distribute accurate and timely information to all the players involved in the market. Only then will investors be able to make sound decisions concerning their actual and potential investments.

REFERENCES

Bliss, N. and Harud, V. (2007). "The Mother of Invention." *International Financial Law Review*, 26:38.

Camerer, C.F. (1998). "Can Asset Markets Be Manipulated? A Field Experiment with Racetrack Betting." *Journal of Political Economy*, 106:457–482.

Daniel, K. and Titman, S. (1999). "Market Efficiency in an Irrational World." *Financial Analysts Journal*, 55(6):28–40.

Davenport, T. (2008). "The Crisis So Far: A Market Restructured." *American Banker*, 173(8):1–3.

DeBenedictus, M. (2008). "Technology's Role in Restoring the CDO Market." *Mortgage Banking*, 69(3):91–95.

Goodman, L.S., Lucas, D.J. and Fabozzi, F.J. (2007). "Financial Innovations and the Shaping of Capital Markets: The Case of CDOs." *The Journal of Alternative Investments*, 10(1):62–71.

Hussain, J. (2007). "Pricing and Risk Management of Synthetic CDOs." *Journal of Structured Finance*, 12(4):17–28.

Hwa, M.S. (2009). *International Financial Management*, Taipei: Shinlou.

Jobst, A.A. (2006). "European Securitization: A GARCH Model of Secondary Market Spreads." *Journal of Structured Finance*, 12(1):55–82.

Johnson, L.D. and Neave, E.H. (2008). "The Subprime Mortgage Market: Familiar Lessons in a New Context." *Management Research News*, 31(1):12–18.

Kim, Y. (2008). "Subprime CDO Ratings and the Current Financial Crisis: A Modeling Perspective." *The RMA Journal*, 91(2):48–53.

Lin, C.F. (2009). *Multinational Corporation Financial Management: Global Vision and Applied Strategies*, Taipei: Princeton University Press.

Liou, Y.C. and Shiue, C. (2009). *International Financial Management*, Taipei: Tunghua.

Lucas, D.J., Goodman, L.S. and Fabozzi, F.J. (2007). "Collateralized Debt Obligations and Credit Risk Transfer." Yale ICF Working Paper No. 07–06.

Morokoff, W.J. (2003). "Simulation Methods for Risk Analysis of Collateralized Debt Obligations." *Proceedings of the 2003 Winter Simulation Conference*.

Shleifer, A. and Vishny, R. (1997). "The Limits to Arbitrage." *Journal of Finance*, 52:35–55.

Thaler, R.H. (1999). "The End of Behavioral Finance." *Financial Analysts Journal*, 55:12–17.

Chapter 8

FINANCIAL LEVERAGE RISK: NEW DEFINITION AND EMPIRICAL ILLUSTRATION

Tomasz S. Berent

1. INTRODUCTION

The roots of the current financial crisis has been a hot topic for both practitioners and academics for some time now. Many causes have been proposed with varying weight assigned to them. Incorrect pricing of risk, usually associated with new, complex and difficult-to-understand financial products, is universally agreed to be one of them. This risk is typically magnified (geared up) by leverage.[1] High debt positions featured in the portfolios of virtually all market participants from financial institutions, with sky-high debt-to-equity ratios — in the case of Lehman Brothers, of more than 50 — to households with the debt position at an all-time high. Undoubtedly, such a level of leverage makes the whole system more vulnerable to any financial shock. In this chapter I focus on that part of the risk, which arises from leverage only and therefore is referred to as financial leverage risk.

To say that the current crisis is finance-driven, with leverage playing a prominent role, is not a controversial view. However, to claim that it is leverage itself, with its inborn capacity to lead to a bankruptcy spiral, that has caused the trouble is no longer that obvious. The debate over the role of financial leverage risk in the current financial crisis resembles that

---

[1]I use "leverage" and "gearing" as well as "to lever" and "to gear (up)" interchangeably. Similarly, I use "levered" or "geared (up)" or an incorrect, yet popular (see Miller, 1991) form, "leveraged", to indicate the presence of debt and/or financial costs.

surrounding leveraged buyouts in the late 1980s. The high rate of defaults of so-called junk bonds at that time was widely argued to be a clear proof of excessive leverage. This claim, however, can be contested on the grounds that leverage as such is a value neutral concept, as we have known for some decades now thanks to the ingenious work of Modigliani and Miller (1958). The MM propositions clearly prove that under some conditions leverage neither creates nor adds to value. In his Nobel Memorial Prize Lecture presented to the Royal Swedish Academy of Sciences, Miller (1991) argued that

> highly visible losses and defaults... do not mean that over-leveraging did in fact occur; second... increased leveraging by corporations does not imply increased risk for the economy as a whole; third... the financial distress being suffered by some highly leveraged firms involves mainly private, not social costs; and finally... capital markets have built-in controls against overleveraging.

Although Miller's statements were issued 20 years ago and were related to the leveraged buyout (LBO) controversy, they seem to be relevant to the current crisis too. Miller claimed that a finance-driven crisis is merely an example of an ordinary downturn, caused by imbalances between supply of and demand for a particular product, be it leveraged equity or a mortgage loan. He then argued that provided timely and adequate steps are made by the central bank to address the liquidity issue, those imbalances are limited and self-regulating.

Miller was well aware that "to point out that the market has powerful endogenous controls against overleveraging does not mean that who holds the highly leveraged securities is never a matter of concern" (Miller, 1991, p. 486). He continued to argue that both savings and loan institutions as well as commercial banks should be prevented from too much leverage due to the very nature of their business — a recommendation not heeded over the last few years.

It may be pointed out that Miller made some implicit assumptions in his argument, mainly that of full information regarding financial products traded — an assumption clearly violated in the current crisis environment characterized by poor understanding of the risks involved, not only on the part of investors but often on the part of product sellers too. The dubious role of rating agencies in the (mis-)pricing of default risk is also symptomatic. In such situations, the in-built controls may indeed be less effective and overleverage may indeed be promoted.

But even in the absence of misinformation and ignorance, one could argue that leverage, with its propensity to increase bankruptcy risk, does indeed lead to a bankruptcy contagion effect, if only indebted parties do not prudently guard themselves against undesirable outcomes in the future. One could additionally argue that in the face of a series of bad outcomes even conservatively managed companies are bound to suffer if levered. Leverage could also magnify any potential damage caused by the appearance of risks classified by advocates of the so-called Black Swan theory as "unknown unknowns", i.e. factors impossible to predict, hence difficult to price in. Modigliani and Miller would probably argue that in most of those cases, it is not actually financial leverage risk that causes crisis but inadequate information, fraud, bad management, and bad luck, etc. All in all, Modigliani and Miller's claim that leverage itself changes little cannot be so easily dismissed.

The aim of this chapter is not to unravel all the complexities of risk inherent in investment products. The aim is more modest — to describe that component of risk that results from leverage either already in-built in a financial product or created as a result of financing the purchase of a financial product with debt. This increase in risk due to leverage will be called financial leverage risk. Understanding the risks inherent in investment products, given the nature of financial innovations, is one thing; understanding the magnifying impact of leverage on the existing risks, given the old tradition of financial leverage literature, is something utterly different. Thus the task seems much easier.

Over the last few decades financial leverage has become a standard topic in any corporate finance and investment course, playing a prominent role in explaining the effect of raising debt on the financial performance of a company. As such, the topic is well represented in all academic textbooks and non-academic professional training materials. It may come therefore as a surprise that this literature does not provide a clear answer to the question of what financial leverage risk actually is and how it should be measured. Quite the opposite: the "terminological confusion" relating to leverage definition and its measurement proclaimed nearly half a century ago (Dilbeck, 1962) has never been clarified. If anything, it has deteriorated to a state of a "peculiar conceptual chaos" (Zwirbla, 2007).

I believe Modigliani and Miller themselves may have inadvertently contributed to this chaos. By showing the irrelevance of a firm's capital structure, their seminal 1958 paper seems to have given a powerful impetus to those searching for new theories and ideas that would adequately explain the role of debt downgraded by the discovery of "risk conservation law". Unfortunately, the study of leverage itself, its nature and impact on a firm's financial performance, as value-neutral, has lost its appeal to academic scholars in the area of finance theory in particular. Little surprise that this has resulted in the "terminological confusion" as the topic was simply taken away from the realm of finance theory to more practical applications of financial analysis and managerial accounting. In Section 2, I introduce some examples of the surprise bordering on disbelief, taken from scholarly journals from the last 50 years, that such an old and seemingly simple concept like leverage may still cause so much trouble.

In Section 3, I introduce the concepts of simple and cost leverage and consequently group leverage effects into two classes: simple leverage effects and cost leverage effects. Failure to distinguish between these two subcomponents of financial leverage is arguably one of the most important reasons behind the terminological chaos surrounding leverage.

To understand the nature of financial leverage risk, one has to accept that risk does not have to materialize to be a legitimate topic for study. Unfortunately, it is all too often that risk occupies centre stage in debates only during bad times, i.e. when the company/investor makes a substantial loss, sees that a substantial part of its equity has evaporated or simply goes bankrupt. However, risk means uncertainty about the future, not the past. It follows that the risk inherent in financial products should be analysed *ex ante* and from the perspective of the whole distribution of outcomes rather than from the perspective of one or two individual negative results *ex post*. In Section 4, I focus on the distributional properties of return on equity (ROE) for ungeared and geared companies.[2] This leads in turn to a new definition of financial leverage risk, presented in Section 5. The new definition emphasizes the role of leverage in increasing the probability of a geared company to produce extreme (both negative and positive) values of ROE. This propensity of leverage to push returns away from the centre of the distribution is argued to be the constituent feature of leverage. Section 6 summarizes the results of the simulation designed to illustrate how financial leverage increases the odds of getting extremely high or low ROE.

---

[2]All the conclusions regarding financial leverage risk reached in the context of a corporate environment are equally applicable to the performance and risk evaluation of an individual investing in financial products.

2. FINANCIAL LEVERAGE IN THE LITERATURE

The opinion that leverage merits more in-depth analysis than generally practised was first expressed in the pre-MM world by Walter in 1955 in his article "The Use of Borrowed Funds". Walter wrote: "In the interpretation of financial data drawn from corporation reports, explicit attention is rarely directed at the impact of borrowed funds upon shareholder return". He then criticized the ad-hoc attitude to the topic: "No ratios have been introduced which specify the influence of debt financing upon shareholder earnings. At best, debt-equity ratios and rates of return on both long-term investment and common equity are derived and shown alongside one another". He concluded with an appeal: "The relation between debt financing, and shareholder return merits undivided, as opposed to piecemeal, consideration" (Walter, 1955, p. 139).

Despite his efforts, Walter failed to clarify all the issues, prompting Hunt (1961) just a few years later to propose a new definition of leverage, as suggested by the title of his paper, "A Proposal for Precise Definitions of 'Trading on the Equity' and 'Leverage'". In this article Hunt wrote: "Despite the long time that the consequences in introducing financial risk into capitalization of a corporation have been known, there has been surprisingly little effort to give precision to the definition or to the analysis of the factors involved" (p. 377). Hunt conceded that the notion of leverage is simply not clear:

> It is also somewhat surprising that very few attempts have been made to express the degree of leverage in any precise way, or to describe with any precision how much any changes in debt-equity proportions will affect the rate of return on the common stock — in the case of trading on the equity — or how much a change in operating earnings will change the earnings on the common stock — in the case of leverage (p. 379).

The impact of debt on the profitability might well have been understood better after Hunt's work, yet surprisingly, the confusion surrounding leverage remained. In his article "On the Measurement of Leverage", Ghandhi (1966) proclaimed that "Despite — perhaps on account of — the widespread use of the concept of gearing or leverage, there appears to be little agreement regarding its specific content" (p. 715). He subsequently provided an extensive list of various leverage ratios, discussed in detail how they are analytically interrelated and provided empirical evidence of the values they assume in real life.

Ghandhi's work must have been inadequate as Shalit (1975) stated in his article "The Mathematics of Financial Leverage":

> The concept of leverage is as fundamental to finance as marginal cost is to economics. Yet,... the analytical relationships between leverage and other determinants of the return on equity, surprisingly, cannot be found either in finance textbooks or in journal articles. The standard textbook's exposition is confined to "proofs by examples" through a series of numerical tables and tedious computations. The treatment is incomplete because it fails to impart a clear concept of the underlying relationships (p. 57).

Keenan and Maldonado (1976) in turn emphasized the internal inconsistencies in the way leverage is explained:

> Not infrequently, one finds that even in a professional discipline classroom lectures do not jibe with practice in the outside world. Much less frequently one finds that one part of a course or textbook does not even jibe with some other part. There seems to be a glaring example of just such an inconsistency in the field of finance.... We have been able to find no text that directly addresses the question of whether or not financial earnings leverage is a useful analytical concept given the modern theory of shareholder wealth maximization (p. 43).

In 1980, Martin and Sloane made a statement which echoes all the surprise so frequently voiced before: "Despite the fact that the composition of the capital structure and the use of financial leverage is fundamental to corporate finance, few attempts have been made to clearly examine the relationship between financial leverage and return on equity". The title of their paper, "Financial Leverage: A Note on a More Precise Approach", refers explicitly to Hunt's article from 20 years earlier. Their objective was equally ambitious: "It is hoped that this paper will provide an additional dimension by formulating an even more precise definition of financial leverage" (p. 585). Needless to say, the definition of leverage proved to be an elusive task once again.

The "terminological confusion" and "conceptual chaos" have continued to reign as evinced by two recent papers. Dudycz (2007) in "The Different Faces of Leverage" (an apt title!) started with the following claim:

> The concept of leverage is very general, in literature it is defined and measured in different ways. In the article we systematize the definitions and the manners of measurement

of the three kinds of leverage, distinguishing two approaches: static and dynamic. We prove that these approaches can send contradictory information and that is why when we use the expression "high leverage" and "low leverage" we should give the manner of its measurement (p. 1).

A similar sentiment was also expressed by Zwirbla (2007): "There is plenty written on financial leverage to date, yet substantial differences in opinion among economists regarding various aspects of this phenomenon can be noted" (p. 195).

I believe part of the reason why leverage definition and measurement have proved so elusive is the lack of distinction between simple and cost leverage — concepts I describe below.

3. SIMPLE VERSUS COST LEVERAGE

The real source of confusion surrounding financial leverage comes, one could argue, from the lack of agreement regarding what should be understood as leverage in the first place. All too often, the notion of financial leverage is introduced by a mere reference to the fact that the company employs debt. Hence, financial leverage is often identified with the capital structure and measured by one of many capital structure ratios. However, focusing on the act of taking debt alone, this approach seems to identify the source of leverage rather than leverage itself, i.e. the consequences of taking debt.

Among those who focus on the effects generated by debt, many tend to associate leverage with risk, hence the popularity of identifying financial leverage simply with financial risk. Once again, it is not obvious what exactly this proposal should mean. Below I give just a few examples from a long list of what could justifiably be regarded as legitimate consequences of debt taking:

- increase in variance of returns,
- increase in beta of returns,
- increase in the probability of making losses,
- increase in earnings (value) at risk,
- increase in the likelihood of bankruptcy,
- increase in the elasticity of earnings per share (EPS) with respect to operating profit, measured by the popular ratio of degree of financial leverage (DFL).

It is by no means clear which of these effects should be regarded as critical to the way financial leverage risk should be defined. Unfortunately, these effects are not the same, they are measured differently, they come from different sources, etc. As a result, in a given leverage situation some of them may be present while others are not; some may indicate high, while others low leverage.

Some scholars and practitioners believe that instead of looking at risk one should focus on "levered" levels of profitability measured by ROE or EPS, for instance, and define financial leverage accordingly. In Berent (2010b) I argue that this approach could easily be merged with the study of leverage understood as risk. This is done by extending the analysis of how debt affects profitability level into an analysis of how debt affects the difference between any two levels of profitability ("the absolute distance"), or how debt affects the ratio of two levels of profitability ("relative distance"), etc. Such an approach helps to show which variables do actually change (and to what extent) when debt is introduced, i.e. it helps to see financial leverage risk in action. As a result, it can be shown that all the changes in profitability measures fall into just one of only two categories and are responsible for only one of two separate leverage effects, which I call simple leverage effect and cost leverage effect. A simple leverage effect results from the act of taking debt and is measured by the debt-to-equity ratio. A cost leverage effect results from the act of paying for this debt and is measured by the DFL. It can be shown that simple leverage is responsible for the increase in the variance and beta of returns, while cost leverage is responsible for more than a proportional change in EPS caused by a 1% change in operating profit as indicated by DFL > 1. Both effects are therefore not identical. It can be argued that the failure to distinguish between the two is one of the most likely reasons behind the terminological confusion surrounding leverage. Interestingly enough, even Miller seemed to have failed to appreciate this difference. In his Nobel Prize lecture, mentioned above, with the help of a simple numerical example (Miller, 1991, p. 482), he illustrated the rationales for the increase in the cost of leveraged equity by pointing to a higher-than-one value of DFL, i.e. linking this increase with the cost leverage effect. However, this increase is a result of what I call simple leverage (see also Hamada, 1972; Rubinstein, 1973). It can be further shown that DFL > 1 is neither a necessary nor a sufficient condition for the cost of leveraged equity to go up (Berent, 2010a). Below, the difference between simple and cost leverage is explored in more detail.

Let IC denote total invested capital financed by debt D and equity E, hence the debt-to-equity ratio is $d = D/E$. Let i be an interest rate calculated as the ratio of financial costs FC to the book value of debt, i.e. $i = FC/D$, and i^* be an interest rate calculated as the ratio of financial costs FC related to the book value of total invested capital, i.e. $i^* = FC/IC$. Assuming for simplicity corporate taxes to be zero, the return on equity for a geared company ROE_G can be expressed as a function of the return on equity for an ungeared company ROE_U, debt-to-equity ratio $d = D/E$ and i^*:

$$ROE_G = (1 + d) \times (ROE_U - i^*) \tag{1}$$

If debt is cost-free, the case referred to as pure simple leverage ($D > 0$, $i* = 0$), Eq. (1) simplifies to

$$ROE_G = (1 + d) \times ROE_U \tag{2}$$

If the company does not take debt but pays financial costs in the form of various charges for stand-by facilities, etc. ($D = 0$ but $i^* > 0$), the case referred to as pure cost leverage, then Eq. (1) becomes

$$ROE_G = ROE_U - i^* \tag{3}$$

It is further assumed that in the case of $d > 0, FC = i^* \times IC = i \times D$ and consequently that

$$i = i^* \times \frac{1 + d}{d} \tag{4}$$

Based on (4), Eq. (1) translates for $d > 0$ into one of the following forms:

$$ROE_G = ROE_U + d \times (ROE_U - i) \tag{5}$$

$$ROE_G = i + (1 + d) \times (ROE_U - i) \tag{6}$$

It may further be argued that in the absence of debt, charging financial costs FC means simply that $i = FC/D = +\infty$. Consequently, Eq. (4) determines i when debt is actually used, while $i = +\infty$ in the world of no debt and positive financial costs. Table 1 describes four separate cases with respect to different values of D and i.

In the absence of both debt and fixed financial charges (case A in Table 1), there is no leverage at all — as correctly indicated by both the variance of ROE and DFL. Case D with non-zero and finite values of both debt and interest rate is a typical leverage situation, as correctly diagnosed by the increase in variance of ROE as well as a higher-than-one

Table 1   Financial Leverage vs. D and i.

		i	D	Variance of ROE	DFL
A	No leverage	$i = 0$	D = 0	No increase	1
B	Pure simple leverage	$i = 0$	D > 0	Increase	1
C	Pure cost leverage	$i = +\infty$	D = 0	No increase	>1
D	Financial leverage	$i < +\infty$	D > 0	Increase	>1

value of DFL. However, the leverage credentials of cases represented by rows B and C are less sound. When the company takes debt, the variance of ROE goes up regardless of whether debt is costly or not (rows B and D). When the company pays financial costs, then DFL > 1 regardless of whether debt is actually taken or not (rows C and D). Those scholars/practitioners who are determined to identify leverage risk with higher variance of returns exclude case C — pure cost leverage — from a definition of leverage, while those who emphasize the role of leverage in increasing the elasticity of EPS with respect to operating profit would exclude case B — pure simple leverage.

In the next section, I introduce a new simple definition of financial leverage risk, which provides a platform to view all three cases — B, C and D — as true financial leverage examples. This is done with the help of the folded cumulative distribution function, a modified version of a typical cumulative distribution function (CDF).

4.   LEVERAGE CUMULATIVE DISTRIBUTION FUNCTION (LCDF)

Let $f(x)$ and $F(x)$ be the probability density and cumulative distribution functions of ROE, respectively. Figure 1 illustrates $f(x)$ for the cases of pure simple (Fig. 1a) and pure cost leverage (Fig. 1b) under the assumption that ROE, for simplicity, is normally distributed. As can be seen in Eq. (2), taking debt without paying financial costs makes both the variance and the expected value of ROE higher (Fig. 1a). Higher variance means higher volatility of returns, hence higher risk. Bearing financial costs without taking debt manifests itself — as seen in Eq. (3) — in the shift of the distribution to the left (Fig. 1b). Return volatility measured by variance may not increase in this case but the likelihood of negative returns does certainly increase. Some would argue this fact alone is sufficient to justify the name of financial (leverage) risk.

In the case where both i^* and d are greater than zero, the simple leverage effect makes the variance grow, while cost leverage shifts such a

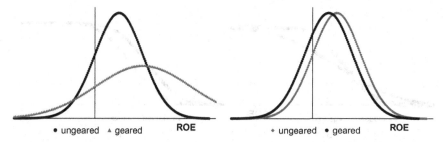

Fig. 1 Probability Distribution Functions for Pure Simple (a) and ROE Cost Leverage (b).

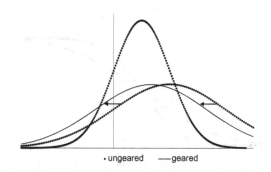

Fig. 2 Probability Distribution Function for an Ungeared and Geared Company.

transformed distribution to the left, so that for ROE > 0 it is somewhat closer to the y-axis than it would have been should the cost leverage effect have been zero (Fig. 2).

Figure 3 illustrates $F(x)$ first for pure simple leverage and then for pure cost leverage. As can be seen in Fig. 3a, taking debt without paying financial costs (pure simple leverage) makes the CDF less "curvy" and pivots it around zero. Paying financial costs without taking debt (pure cost leverage) merely shifts the CDF to the left.

In the standard leverage situation where both debt and its cost are present, the CDF pivots around a non-zero value. It can be easily shown that it is i where the CDF pivots as it is precisely at i that $\text{ROE}_G = \text{ROE}_U$ for $d > 0$ (see Eq. (6)).

In addition, it can be argued that the CDF always pivots around i, even in the cases of pure simple and pure cost leverage. After all, in pure simple leverage the CDF pivots around 0 and $i = 0\%$ in that case, while in pure cost leverage the CDF does not pivot at all, or "pivots" at $i = +\infty$.

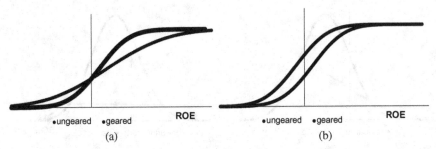

Fig. 3 Cumulative Distribution Functions for Pure Simple (a) and Pure Cost Leverage (b).

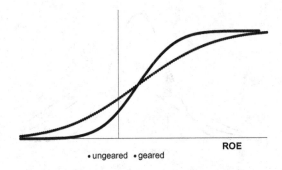

Fig. 4 Cumulative Distribution Function for an Ungeared and a Geared Company.

Both probability density as well as cumulative distribution functions are useful tools to summarize the effect of leverage on the distribution of ROE. However, it is only when viewed from a folded cumulative distribution function perspective that the true meaning of leverage risks can be clearly seen. The folded cumulative distribution function $G(x)$, as its name suggests, is a modified version of the cumulative distribution function $F(x)$. $G(x)$ is identical to $F(x)$ for all values of $x < i$ and is equal to $[1 - F(x)]$ for $x > i$. Figure 5 shows $G(x)$ for two pure leverage cases, while Fig. 6 illustrates a standard case of leverage. The $G(x)$ for pure cost leverage folds at infinity, which in fact means it does not fold at all and therefore is identical to the CDF (see Figs. 3b and 5b).

$G(x)$, hereafter referred to as a folded leverage cumulative distribution function, or simply leverage cumulative distribution function (LCDF), has the following features:

$G(x)$ determines the probability of reaching ROE $\leq x_{\mathrm{L}}$ for the upslope, where x_{L}, called the lower boundary, is any value of $x < i$. This cumulative

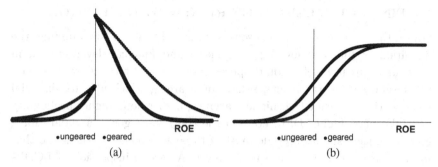

Fig. 5 Folded Cumulative Distribution Functions, or LCDF for Pure Simple (a) and Pure Cost Leverage (b).

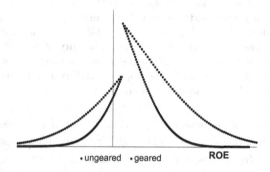

Fig. 6 Folded Cumulative Distribution Function, or LCDF for an Ungeared and a Geared Company.

probability will be referred to as the probability of getting extreme negative values. For the downslope, $G(x)$ determines the probability of reaching ROE $\geq x_H$, where x_H, called the upper boundary, is any value of $x > i$. This cumulative probability will be referred to as the probability of getting extreme positive values.

$G(x)$ is discontinuous at $x = i$, unless the median of the ROE distribution happens to fall at exactly $x = i$.

$G(x)$ for a firm which engages in leverage activities, be it via taking debt or/and via paying financial costs, is always higher than $G(x)$ for an all-equity company. In Figs. 5 and 6 this can be seen in the thicker tails of the LCDF for geared companies. I believe this very characteristic to be the most important feature of financial leverage risk and as such it constitutes the basis for the new definition of financial leverage risk presented below.

5. FINANCIAL LEVERAGE RISK: NEW DEFINITION

Given that there is little consensus in the literature surrounding the definition of financial leverage in general and financial leverage risk in particular, any new definition proposed should not be too narrow. It should not be limited to statements, some would argue, which identify financial leverage rigidly with either higher variance, higher beta, higher probability of bankruptcy, higher DFL, etc. On the contrary, a good candidate for a good definition should precede most of these statements in the sense that most of these should be derivable from it. A careful inspection of LCDFs (Figs. 5 and 6) leads directly to a simple and intuitive definition of financial leverage risk of the following form:

> *Definition*: Financial leverage risk is the increase in the probability of getting extreme negative and/or positive values of ROE after taking debt. By "the probability of getting extreme values" one should understand the probability of getting ROE that is lower than or equal to the lower boundary x_L or that is higher than or equal to the upper boundary x_H, where x_L is any value of $x < i$, while x_H is any value of $x > i$.

The definition of financial leverage risk presented above does emphasize the role of the interest rate i charged for debt. The reasons for ROE spreading away from i as a result of taking debt can easily be seen in Eq. (6). If ROE_U is greater than i, its distance from i increases from $|ROE_U - i| > 0$ to $|ROE_G - i| = (1 + d)|ROE_U - i| > 0$ after taking debt, i.e. towards more positive values of ROE. Similarly, if ROE_U is lower than i, its distance from i increases again from $|ROE_U - i| > 0$ to $|ROE_G - i| = (1 + d)|ROE_U - i| > 0$ after taking debt, i.e. ROE moves to the left towards negative values.

The process of ROE spreading away from i gains momentum with a higher d. As shown in Eq. (6), a higher d catapults ROE away from i with a force proportional to $(1 + d)$. This in turn inflates the probability of getting extreme values of ROE. The increasing force of leverage with a higher d can be seen in Figs. 5 and 6 in the growing distance between the LCDF for an ungeared company and the LCDF for a geared one.

It should be noticed that all the above can naturally be extended to the case of pure simple leverage where $i = 0\%$. Here, as seen in Fig. 5a, leverage means that negative rates of return become more negative, while positive rates of return become more positive. Consequently, the probability of recording losses greater than any predetermined level of ROE < 0 becomes higher, just like the probability of registering profit greater than any given level of ROE > 0. It is evident that the variance of ROE becomes higher as a result.

Interestingly, the case of pure cost leverage can also be discussed in the context of the definition provided. As $i = +\infty$, in order to create the LCDF, the cumulative distribution function must fold at plus infinity. The probability of getting extreme values, which in this case means all the values lower than or equal to $x_L < i = +\infty$, does indeed increase just as the definition suggests. Pure cost leverage therefore generates financial leverage risk in line with the definition above.

The definition provided is not only very general in the sense that it covers most of the risks usually associated with debt. It is also quite flexible as it can be interpreted by its user to suit his individual preferences. This flexibility is available through both the role of the lower and upper boundaries (x_L and x_H) in the definition and the fact that the user can determine himself which values of i are allowed.

For example, a vast body of the literature links financial leverage risk with the increased volatility of returns measured by variance. This consequently implies a higher accounting beta and in the world of market values, a higher equity beta and higher cost of equity. An advocate of this approach would argue that leverage is increasing the chances of making "good" results better at the cost of a higher probability of depressing "bad" results even more. He would use the definition with only one qualification that both the lower and upper boundaries must exist, or — to put it differently, from the perspective of the interest rate — that $i < +\infty$. It should be noted that with such an interpretation, unlike pure simple leverage, pure cost leverage would not be classified as financial leverage at all.

In contrast, those who look to the increased elasticity of EPS with respect to operating profit do regard the act of paying financial costs, regardless of whether debt is taken or not, as constituent to financial leverage risk. The attractiveness of this approach is caused by its elasticity interpretation and the analogy to operating leverage, measured by the degree of operating leverage (DOL). The advocates of this approach would also use the definition with a different qualification that $i > 0$, regardless of whether it is finite or infinite. It should be noted that with such an interpretation, unlike pure cost leverage, pure simple leverage would not be classified as financial leverage anymore.

Those who accept that leverage exists when return volatility is increased, regardless of whether evidenced by the increase in variance (beta) or/and DFL > 1, seem to support the view that financial leverage risk does exist regardless of whether it is due to debt taken or interest charged. In short, it is sufficient for them that either $D > 0$ or/and $i > 0$ (finite or infinite). They would use the definition every time the lower or/and upper boundaries do exist. With such an interpretation, neither the increase in variance nor DFL > 1 is necessary but they are both sufficient conditions for the existence of financial leverage risk.

6. FINANCIAL LEVERAGE RISK: SIMULATION RESULTS

Financial leverage increases the probability of getting extreme values of ROE. This section quantifies this effect by simulating distributions of ROE. To capture the size of financial leverage risk, both graphical and numerical evidence is provided. In graphs, the risk can be seen, as introduced in Section 4, in the distance between the tails of ungeared and geared LCDFs. Additionally, the increase in the probability of getting some extreme values of ROE for predetermined lower and upper boundaries is also quantified. These boundaries are

- $x_L = -100\%$, the level of ROE which implies the loss of all the equity in one year and hence corporate bankruptcy;
- $x_L = -50\%$, the arbitrarily chosen level of loss which may indicate the company is on the verge of bankruptcy;
- $x_L = 0\%$, the threshold beyond which the company makes losses;
- $x_H = 40\%$, the arbitrarily chosen level of ROE which if repeated would double the book value of equity in just two years;
- $x_H = 100\%$, the level of ROE which doubles the book value of equity in just one year.

The simulation is performed in two stages. First, the impact of debt on real ROE (excluding inflation) is studied. Debt-to-equity ratios range from 0.0 ("no debt"), to 0.5 ("low"), 1.0 ("average") and 2.0 ("high") while real interest rates range from 0.0% to 5.0%.[3] Extreme and untypical levels of debt-to-equity of 10.0 ("excessive debt") and of real interest rate of 10% are also analysed. Then the financial leverage risk is studied with inflation included.

---

[3]The annual average of D/E for S&P500 companies has been between 0.6 and 1.0 in 14 of the last 20 years, with three years below and three years above this range, according to Bloomberg. At the same time more than 20% and 7% of S&P500 companies, on average, has had a value of D/E higher than 1.0 and 2.0, respectively.

Financial Leverage Risk Without Inflation

Real ROE_U distribution tends to be different for different companies as it is supposed to capture different operating risk levels. However, even if only one company is analysed and its operating risk is assumed to be constant throughout, the real ROE_U distribution may still vary for this company from one year to another. The real ROE_U may well — by definition — be immune to current inflation but it is certainly not independent of past inflation at all. Past inflation affects both the level of invested capital as well as the level of current earnings. It follows that one company may have different real ROE_U distributions in different years. To analyse companies with both different operating levels as well as changing ROE_U distribution, I study a spectrum of hypothetical firms characterized by different distributions of real ROE_U.

The reported and widely available values of ROEs are nominal, with the inflation effect incorporated in them, and it is by no means trivial to strip these returns of the inflation. This requires detailed knowledge of the cost and revenue structure of the firm, i.e. the way the revenue and costs, be it fixed or variable, change with inflation. Different accounting practices of firms in general and their depreciation policy in particular make the task even harder. All this makes matching any given firm to a specific form of ROE distribution difficult and hence justifies the use of a wide spectrum of input parameters.

Although the LCDF analysis may be performed using any functional form of probability density function, it is assumed for simplicity that ROE is normally distributed. The four ROE_U distributions differ therefore in the first two moments only: mean μ, set arbitrarily at two levels of 4% and 8%, and standard deviation σ equal to a low of 5% and a high of 20%.[4] As shown in Tables 2–5, two general conclusions can be reached from the simulation:

- At any given level of interest rate, more debt means more financial leverage risk as defined above. This can be seen in the higher probability of getting extreme values of ROE (on both the negative and positive sides of the LCDF) after increasing debt. This conclusion is also valid even for cost-free debt — pure simple leverage — as shown in the first row of each panel in the tables.

---

[4]The values for μ and σ are derived from the operating profitability of S&P500 companies as reported by Bloomberg.

Table 2 Cumulative Probabilities of Getting Extreme Value of Real ROE ($\mu = 8\%, \sigma = 20\%$).

		Debt-to-equity				
		0.0	0.5	1.0	2.0	10.0
	Interest rate					
$x_L = -100\%$	0.0%	0.0%	0.0%	0.2%	1.9%	19.6%
	2.0%	0.0%	0.0%	0.2%	2.3%	22.3%
	5.0%	0.0%	0.0%	0.3%	2.9%	26.5%
	10.0%	0.0%	0.0%	0.4%	4.2%	34.5%
$x_L = -50\%$	0.0%	0.2%	1.9%	4.9%	10.9%	26.5%
	2.0%	0.2%	2.1%	5.5%	12.2%	29.6%
	5.0%	0.2%	2.4%	6.4%	14.3%	34.5%
	10.0%	0.2%	2.9%	8.1%	18.4%	43.1%
$x_L = 0\%$	0.0%	34.5%	34.5%	34.5%	34.5%	34.5%
	2.0%	34.5%	35.7%	36.3%	36.9%	37.9%
	5.0%	34.5%	37.6%	39.2%	40.8%	43.1%
	10.0%	34.5%	40.8%	44.0%	47.3%	52.2%
$x_H = 40\%$	0.0%	5.5%	17.5%	27.4%	39.5%	58.6%
	2.0%	5.5%	16.7%	25.8%	36.9%	55.1%
	5.0%	5.5%	15.5%	23.4%	33.2%	49.6%
	10.0%	5.5%	13.6%	19.8%	27.4%	40.7%
$x_H = 100\%$	0.0%	0.0%	0.2%	1.8%	10.3%	47.8%
	2.0%	0.0%	0.2%	1.6%	9.1%	44.2%
	5.0%	0.0%	0.1%	1.3%	7.6%	38.9%
	10.0%	0.0%	0.1%	0.9%	5.5%	30.5%

- At any given level of debt-to-equity ratio, the higher the interest rate charged, the lower ROE is (not a surprising conclusion given the cost nature of interest paid), which in turn can be seen in the higher probability of getting negative extreme values of ROE.

Table 2 illustrates the case of the firm where $\mu = 8\%$ and $\sigma = 20\%$. The probability of losing all the equity in one year ($x_L = -100\%$) increases from virtually zero for an ungeared and modestly geared company (D/E ≤ 0.5) to less than 0.5% for an average gearing case (D/E $= 1.0$) and 1.9–4.2% for a company with high debt. Excessive debt, depending on the real interest rate, increases this probability massively to 19.4–34.5%. Similarly, the chances of equity to double in one year is nearly zero for an ungeared company, improbable in the case of average gearing (0.9–1.8% chance) and quite likely for a highly geared company (5.5–10.3%), with excessive leverage increasing the odds to nearly 50%. Similar conclusions can be reached from the analysis of the likelihood of registering ROE $\leq -50\%$ or ROE $\geq 40\%$. What for an all equity firm is a mere theoretical threat (ROE $\leq -50\%$) or wishful

Table 3 Cumulative Probabilities of Getting Extreme Value of Real ROE ($\mu = 4\%, \sigma = 20\%$).

		Debt-to-equity				
		0.0	0.5	1.0	2.0	10.0
	Interest rate					
$x_L = -100\%$	0.0%	0.0%	0.0%	0.3%	3.1%	25.6%
	2.0%	0.0%	0.0%	0.4%	3.6%	28.7%
	5.0%	0.0%	0.0%	0.5%	4.5%	33.5%
	10.0%	0.0%	0.0%	0.7%	6.3%	42.1%
$x_L = -50\%$	0.0%	0.3%	3.1%	7.4%	15.1%	33.5%
	2.0%	0.3%	3.3%	8.1%	16.7%	36.8%
	5.0%	0.3%	3.7%	9.3%	19.3%	42.1%
	10.0%	0.3%	4.5%	11.5%	24.2%	51.1%
$x_L = 0\%$	0.0%	42.1%	42.1%	42.1%	42.1%	42.1%
	2.0%	42.1%	43.4%	44.0%	44.7%	45.7%
	5.0%	42.1%	45.4%	47.0%	48.7%	51.1%
	10.0%	42.1%	48.7%	52.0%	55.3%	60.0%
$x_H = 40\%$	0.0%	3.6%	12.9%	21.2%	32.0%	50.7%
	2.0%	3.6%	12.2%	19.8%	29.7%	47.1%
	5.0%	3.6%	11.2%	17.7%	26.3%	41.7%
	10.0%	3.6%	9.7%	14.7%	21.2%	33.1%
$x_H = 100\%$	0.0%	0.0%	0.1%	1.1%	7.1%	40.0%
	2.0%	0.0%	0.1%	0.9%	6.3%	36.5%
	5.0%	0.0%	0.1%	0.8%	5.1%	31.5%
	10.0%	0.0%	0.0%	0.5%	3.6%	23.9%

thinking (ROE $\geq 40\%$) becomes a realistic or even a likely scenario with leverage (see Table 2). Figure 7 shows the financial leverage risk for $i = 2\%$.

The change of μ from 8% down to 4% with σ kept at 20% changes practically nothing: the high inherent volatility of ROE gets levered by debt to produce meaningful probabilities even at less than excessive levels of debt (see Table 3).

In the cases where $\sigma = 5\%$, the chances of registering ROE of -100% or $+100\%$ are practically zero regardless of whether the company is geared or not (unless the gearing is excessive). However, the probability of making losses may be several times higher for a not excessively geared company (from 5.5% up to 39.5% when $\mu = 8\%$, and from 21% to more than 70% in the case of $\mu = 4\%$). The probability of getting other extreme values also increases (see Tables 4 and 5).

Table 4 Cumulative Probabilities of Getting Extreme Value of Real ROE ($\mu = 8\%, \sigma = 5\%$).

		Debt-to-equity				
		0.0	0.5	1.0	2.0	10.0
	Interest rate					
$x_L = -100\%$	0.0%	0.0%	0.0%	0.0%	0.0%	0.0%
	2.0%	0.0%	0.0%	0.0%	0.0%	0.1%
	5.0%	0.0%	0.0%	0.0%	0.0%	0.6%
	10.0%	0.0%	0.0%	0.0%	0.0%	5.5%
$x_L = -50\%$	0.0%	0.0%	0.0%	0.0%	0.0%	0.6%
	2.0%	0.0%	0.0%	0.0%	0.0%	1.6%
	5.0%	0.0%	0.0%	0.0%	0.0%	5.5%
	10.0%	0.0%	0.0%	0.0%	0.0%	24.5%
$x_L = 0\%$	0.0%	5.5%	5.5%	5.5%	5.5%	5.5%
	2.0%	5.5%	7.1%	8.1%	9.1%	10.8%
	5.0%	5.5%	10.3%	13.6%	17.5%	24.5%
	10.0%	5.5%	17.5%	27.4%	39.5%	58.6%
$x_H = 40\%$	0.0%	0.0%	0.0%	0.8%	14.3%	80.9%
	2.0%	0.0%	0.0%	0.5%	9.1%	69.5%
	5.0%	0.0%	0.0%	0.2%	4.2%	48.5%
	10.0%	0.0%	0.0%	0.0%	0.8%	17.2%
$x_H = 100\%$	0.0%	0.0%	0.0%	0.0%	0.0%	41.4%
	2.0%	0.0%	0.0%	0.0%	0.0%	28.0%
	5.0%	0.0%	0.0%	0.0%	0.0%	13.0%
	10.0%	0.0%	0.0%	0.0%	0.0%	2.1%

Financial Leverage Risk with Inflation

This subsection is devoted to the analysis of financial leverage risk in the context of inflation, of which four levels — 3.0%, 6.0%, 12.0%, and 24.0% — are used in the simulation. Inflation alters financial leverage risk through the change in the distribution of ROE as well as via the change in the level of interest rate charged. The interest rate changes from i_R to i_N as follows: $(1 + i_N) = (1 + \text{inflation}) \times (1 + i_R)$, where the subscripts N and R denote nominal and real variables respectively. The LCDF folds accordingly now at $i_N = i_R \times (1 + \text{inflation}) + \text{inflation}$. However, the impact of inflation on ungeared real ROE is not so easily tractable as it critically depends on the corporate cost structure. It can be shown that

$$\text{ROE}_{UN} = \text{ROE}_{UR} \times (1 + \text{inflation}) + \text{inflation} \times K/\text{IC} \qquad (7)$$

where K is the amount of costs unaffected by inflation (all revenue stream is assumed to follow inflation). Unlike σ_N, which amounts to

Table 5 Cumulative Probabilities of Getting Extreme Value of Real ROE ($\mu = 4\%, \sigma = 5\%$).

		Debt-to-equity				
		0.0	0.5	1.0	2.0	10.0
	Interest rate					
$x_L = -100\%$	0.0%	0.0%	0.0%	0.0%	0.0%	0.4%
	2.0%	0.0%	0.0%	0.0%	0.0%	1.2%
	5.0%	0.0%	0.0%	0.0%	0.0%	4.4%
	10.0%	0.0%	0.0%	0.0%	0.0%	21.2%
$x_L = -50\%$	0.0%	0.0%	0.0%	0.0%	0.0%	4.4%
	2.0%	0.0%	0.0%	0.0%	0.0%	8.9%
	5.0%	0.0%	0.0%	0.0%	0.0%	21.2%
	10.0%	0.0%	0.0%	0.0%	0.3%	54.3%
$x_L = 0\%$	0.0%	21.2%	21.2%	21.2%	21.2%	21.2%
	2.0%	21.2%	25.2%	27.4%	29.7%	33.1%
	5.0%	21.2%	32.0%	38.2%	44.7%	54.3%
	10.0%	21.2%	44.7%	57.9%	70.3%	84.6%
$x_H = 40\%$	0.0%	0.0%	0.0%	0.1%	3.1%	52.9%
	2.0%	0.0%	0.0%	0.0%	1.6%	38.6%
	5.0%	0.0%	0.0%	0.0%	0.6%	20.1%
	10.0%	0.0%	0.0%	0.0%	0.1%	4.0%
$x_H = 100\%$	0.0%	0.0%	0.0%	0.0%	0.0%	15.4%
	2.0%	0.0%	0.0%	0.0%	0.0%	8.4%
	5.0%	0.0%	0.0%	0.0%	0.0%	2.7%
	10.0%	0.0%	0.0%	0.0%	0.0%	0.2%

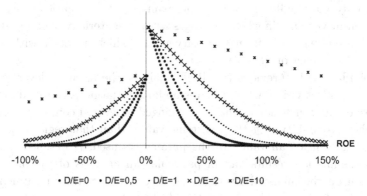

Fig. 7 Leverage Cumulative Distribution Function for Real ROE ($\mu = 8\%, \sigma = 20\%$), $i = 2\%$.

$\sigma_N = (1 + \text{inflation}) \times \sigma_R$, the value of μ_N depends on K. If $K = 0$, i.e. all the costs move with inflation, then $\mu_N = \mu_R \times (1+\text{inflation})$. If $K = \text{IC}$ then $\mu_N = \mu_R \times (1+\text{inflation})+\text{inflation}$. To summarize, the LCDF for ungeared nominal ROE_{UN} is derived from the LCDF for ungeared real ROE_{UR} using the following parameters:

$$i_N = i_R \times (1 + \text{inflation}) + \text{inflation}$$

$$\mu_N = \mu_R \times (1 + \text{inflation})$$

$$\sigma_N = \sigma_R \times (1 + \text{inflation})$$

$$\text{for } K = 0; \text{ and}$$

$$i_N = i_R \times (1 + \text{inflation}) + \text{inflation}$$

$$\mu_N = \mu_R \times (1 + \text{inflation}) + \text{inflation}$$

$$\sigma_N = \sigma_R \times (1 + \text{inflation})$$

$$\text{for } K = \text{IC}.$$

The LCDF for an ungeared company is subsequently transformed into the LCDF for a geared company using a relevant algorithm (see Eqs. (1)–(6)) and one of the four D/E ratios. The two cases, where $K = 0$ and $K = \text{IC}$, are later used in the simulation as two scenarios referred to as "no depreciation," and "full depreciation," respectively. It is worth noting that in the "no depreciation" case, inflation changes the distribution of ROE only marginally. This case approximates also scenarios other than inflation-driven ones in which i changes without materially affecting ROE_U distribution (e.g. a shift in monetary policy which affects i without an immediate impact on ROE_U).

Similar to the previous real ROE analysis, the financial leverage risk effects are most visible when a high standard deviation is assumed but the nature of the conclusions remains unchanged: a levered company registers a higher probability of getting extreme values than that registered by an all-equity firm for all values of the parameters used. A detailed analysis of the simulation results and in particular an analysis of the impact of inflation on the financial leverage risk deserves a separate treatment. In Figs. 8 and 9, financial leverage risk is illustrated for the case corresponding to that in Fig. 7 ($\mu_R = 8\%, \sigma_R = 20\%, i_R = 2.0\%$) with inflation of 6.0% added. Figure 8 describes the "no depreciation" scenario ($\mu_N = 8.48\%, \sigma_N = 21.20\%, i_N = 8.12\%$), Fig. 9 the "full depreciation" scenario

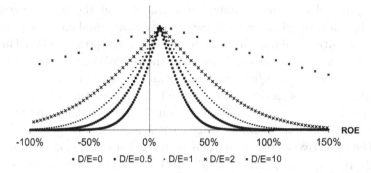

Fig. 8 Leverage Cumulative Distribution Function for "No Depreciation" Case ($\mu_N = 8.48\%, \sigma_N = 21.2\%$ and $i_N = 8.12\%$).

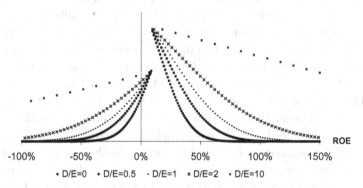

Fig. 9 Leverage Cumulative Distribution Function for "Full Depreciation" Case ($\mu_N = 14.48\%, \sigma_N = 21.2\%$ and $i_N = 8.12\%$).

($\mu_N = 14.48\%, \sigma_N = 21.20\%, i_N = 8.12\%$). In both cases, the effects of financial leverage are clearly visible.

7. CONCLUSION

The risk of each financial product is geared up by leverage either in-built internally in this product or tailor-made by an investor financing it with debt. The portion of risk which corresponds to the leverage is called financial leverage risk here. It is shown that this risk comes from two separate sources: the act of taking debt and the act of paying for it. The failure to distinguish between those two different sources of leverage and subsequently between two different leverage effects, denoted as simple and cost leverage respectively, is arguably responsible for the "terminological confusion" and "conceptual chaos" surrounding the definition and the measurement of financial leverage risk for over 50 years. A new, simple and intuitive proposal for the definition and measurement of financial leverage risk is offered in this chapter. This new definition emphasizes the role of debt in spreading the returns of the company/investor away from the centre of the distribution (defined by the cost of debt) towards the tails of the return distribution. It is this increase in the probability of getting extreme values of return for a geared company that makes leverage what it is.

The objective of the simulation performed was to quantify the scale of this risk and to provide an illustration of the concepts introduced. In order to describe various macro- and microeconomic conditions, the simulation used different inputs: the mean (two levels) and standard deviation (two levels) of real ROE distributions, real interest rates charged against debt (four levels) and inflation (four levels). As inflation may affect the distribution of returns in many ways, the simulation was repeated separately for two cases with two different depreciation policies. In total, 128 different simulations were used, each for five different levels of D/E, of which only a fraction was discussed in detail in this chapter.

The financial leverage risk can be clearly seen in the figures provided. The graphical form of the distribution which shows the utility of the new definition and the size of the risk most effectively is a modified version of the cumulative distribution function "folded" at the cost of debt, called the leverage cumulative distribution function. The thicker tails for levered companies/investors illustrate the size of the risk involved. Detailed calculations of the magnified (levered) probabilities of getting extreme values of returns resulting from leverage are also provided for selected simulations.

REFERENCES

Berent, T. (2010a). "Duality in Financial Leverage: Controversy Surrounding Merton Miller's Argument." *Zeszyty Naukowe Uniwer sytetu Szczecinskiego*, 587:27–38.

Berent, T. (2010b). "Financial Leverage Risk Revisited: Theory, Definitions and Determinants." *Prace Naukowe Uniwersytetu Ekonomicznego Wroclawiu*, 99:66–78.

Dilbeck, H. (1962). "A Proposal for Precise Definitions of 'Trading on the Equity' and 'Leverage': Comment." *Journal of Finance*, 17(1):127–130.

Dudycz, T. (2007). "The Different Faces of Leverage." Available at SSRN, http://ssrn.com/abstract=950554.

Ghandhi, J.K.S. (1966). "On the Measurement of Leverage." *Journal of Finance*, 21(4):715–726.

Hamada, R.S. (1972). "The Effect of the Firm's Capital Structure on the Systematic Risk of Common Stock." *Journal of Finance*, 27(2):435–452.

Hunt, P. (1961). "A Proposal for Precise Definitions of 'Trading on the Equity' and 'Leverage'." *Journal of Finance*, 16(3):377–386.

Keenan, M. and Maldonado, R.M. (1976). "The Redundancy of Earnings Leverage in a Cost of Capital Decision Framework." *Journal of Business Finance and Accounting*, 3(2):43–56.

Martin, D.R. and Sloane, W.R. (1980). "Financial Leverage: A Note on a More Precise Approach." *Journal of Business Finance and Accounting*, 7:585–590.

Miller, M.H. (1991). "Leverage." *Journal of Finance*, 46(2):479–488.

Modigliani, F. and Miller, M.H. (1958). "The Cost of Capital, Corporate Finance and the Theory of Investment." *American Economic Review*, 48(3):261–297.

Rubinstein, M. (1973). "A Mean-Variance Synthesis of Corporate Financial Theory." *Journal of Finance*, 28(1):167–181.

Shalit, S.S. (1975). "The Mathematics of Financial Leverage." *Financial Management*, 4(1):57–66.

Walter, J.E. (1955). "The Use of Borrowed Funds." *Journal of Business*, 55(2):138–147.

Zwirbla, A. (2007). "Dzwignia finansowa — proba krytyki oraz syntezy pogladow." *Zeszyty Teoretyczne Rachunkowosci*, 41:195–221.

Chapter 9

ENABLING TECHNOLOGY FOR MORE PERVASIVE AND RESPONSIVE MARKET RISK MANAGEMENT SYSTEMS

Matthew Dixon, Jike Chong and Kurt Keutzer

1. INTRODUCTION

While the microprocessor industry has recently introduced transformative computing capabilities in the form of C++ programmable graphics processing units (GPUs), its potential for quantitative risk estimation is currently unrealized despite the flaws in risk infrastructure highlighted by the latest financial crisis.

In January 2009, the Bank for International Settlements released a consultative paper on the principles for sound stress-testing practices and supervision (BIS, 2009a). The paper raises fundamental issues including the weaknesses in risk infrastructure that limited the ability of banks to identify and aggregate exposures across each bank and the effectiveness of risk management tools, including stress testing. The paper also calls for further investments in IT infrastructure to enhance the availability and granularity of risk information, needed for timely analysis and assessment of the impact of new stress scenarios designed to address a rapidly changing environment.

Most UK- and Germany-based firms who partook in a recent anonymous survey by a leading database vendor (GARP, 2010) indicate that they have responded to the crisis with plans to invest more in risk systems, improve integration of information systems and, in many cases, move to more frequent updating and valuation of global financial market risk in accordance with the July 2009 revisions to the Basel II market risk framework (BIS, 2009b).

In stepping up to this revised framework, quantitative risk managers in financial institutions are facing a number of technical challenges, both in the short and the longer term. A few key challenges being currently tackled across the industry are

(i) The need for a more extensive set of market risk factors to capture the risks across all markets in which the firm is exposed.

(ii) The estimation of the 99% VaR (the 1-in-100 maximum loss event) on a daily basis with an assumed minimum holding period of ten days. A stressed VaR should also be calculated weekly. Historical datasets, used for VaR estimation, should be updated whenever there is a material change in market prices.

(iii) The use of simulated stress scenarios to test the current portfolio against past periods of significant disturbance and evaluate the sensitivity of the bank's market risk exposure to changes in the assumptions about volatilities and correlations.

As the survey reveals, over a third of these firms indicated that the current risk infrastructure isn't fast enough for the needs of the business and only approximately 5% of the firms currently perform complex risk analysis on portfolios and global positions in real time. Participants point to the gap between IT and business domain expertise as one of the major sources of dislocation in the deployment of risk management systems. This calls for a more comprehensive approach to the design and deployment of complex risk analytics with a stronger emphasis on using financial domain knowledge and expertise to enhance the software optimization process.

2. OVERVIEW

This chapter is primarily intended for risk IT managers in financial institutions responsible for maintaining and developing quantitative market risk infrastructure and are looking to new hardware technology as a way to improve the performance of existing risk infrastructure and pave the way for more comprehensive and responsive quantitative market risk infrastructure across a financial institution.

For completeness, this chapter provides

(i) An introduction to computing with GPUs, identifying the recent breakthroughs that ease its adoption, its current deployment status in the finance industry, and going forward, the key challenges that the deployment of this technology faces.

(ii) An overview of the critical considerations in the optimization of Monte Carlo-based applications on GPUs. Focusing on market Value-at-Risk (VaR) engines, the core of financial institutions' market risk analytics, we show that these considerations guide the management of a team of programmers in realizing the potential of the GPU. The description of this approach in Sections 3 and 4 is the primary contribution of this chapter.

(iii) Sample performance benchmarks to illustrate the potential performance gains from optimization of a VaR engine — a decisive factor in cost-benefit analysis of GPU deployment.

(iv) Example applications where GPUs may improve the responsiveness and pervasiveness of market risk management systems.

3. USE OF MULTICORE AND MANYCORE MICROPROCESSORS IN THE FINANCE INDUSTRY

We review the current status of the microprocessor industry with the caveat that this chapter is not about comparing the GPU against the CPU in order to identify a winning candidate. As we shall explain, the two are quite separate and each has their own merits which the reader should keep in mind.

Modern CPUs are multicore devices, largely designed to run serial code very efficiently. They provide myriad hardware features to improve performance while remaining transparent to the programmer. However, the rate of performance improvements for a CPU core is slowing; instead, multiple cores are being placed onto a single device. Multiple cores can provide better performance when the application can take advantage of the parallel computing resources they provide. A number of software technologies are being developed by CPU hardware manufacturers to facilitate this task, including packages such as OpenMP (Chapman, Jost and Pas, 2007) and Threading Building Blocks (Reinders, 2007). But ultimately, there is no guarantee of scalable application performance on multicore architectures without recompilation or recoding of the code base for existing applications.

GPUs are manycore microprocessors that are fundamentally different from CPUs: rather than provide complex hardware and features to run through a few threads or sequences of instructions as fast as possible, they instead allocate the vast majority of the silicon area to relatively simple processing units to increase total instruction throughput with the assumption that there are going to be hundreds to thousands of threads that can be executed at the same time. As a result GPUs are particularly suited to computationally intensive applications with a high degree of independence between the individual computations, which is referred to as parallelism.

GPUs are ideal for simulation-based risk estimates such as VaR and economic capital (EC) on the global positions of financial institutions. Here, estimation typically requires a small set of parameters to set up the estimation process, involves a large amount of independent computation, and outputs a concise set of risk profiles as the result. Consequently, software architects and developers can expect to significantly reduce execution time and improve the performance for VaR-type estimations, provided that they can rearchitect the code to expose its parallelism and avoid too much data movement between the units of execution.

GPUs are no panacea. While they can be programmed in CUDA (NVIDIA, 2010), a programming environment based on C++ with minor keyword extension, high-performance implementations require detailed knowledge of the vector instruction limitations, memory hierarchy characteristics, and cross-thread synchronization capabilities. GPU programming calls for technical skills outside those held by a typical software architect or programmer working in the finance industry and significant experience is required to architect highly parallel implementations to avoid the many pitfalls in parallel programming.

Whilst the need to improve risk infrastructure remains strong, the prevailing response to GPU technology by the risk IT managers we have interviewed is hesitance. This appears to stem partially from both a reluctance to modify existing VaR engine implementations and an anticipation of rivalling technology breakthroughs to achieve this. This response is partially justified because it is difficult to estimate the true cost of migrating risk engines to GPUs. The wide range of developer expertise makes performance improvements hard to quantify. A further legitimate concern amongst risk IT managers is the dependence on a hardware vendor through the apparent need to use CUDA, the proprietary programming language for GPUs.

On the other hand, few experts would concur that multicore computing technology is undoubtedly here to stay and there is general consensus amongst software experts that legacy serial code won't be compatible with parallel computation platforms without programmer intervention. Moreover, GPU technology has been heavily adopted by many other industrial sectors and there is widespread agreement amongst application developers that GPUs offer transformative computing capability.

The concern over dependence on hardware vendor technology has been addressed through the introduction of the OpenCL programming standard (Munshi, 2010) to enable code to be executed on either GPUs or multicore CPUs. The software infrastructure available to support the development of GPU applications is extensive and numerous technology consultancies have the expertise to support migration projects.

A number of investment banks and financial data vendors have already adopted GPU technology. In some of these cases, the quantitative technology groups had already developed legacy parallel systems and distributed computing clusters, long before the advent of GPUs, and the move to GPUs can therefore be perceived as a "warm start". The purpose of this chapter is to explain and demonstrate how GPUs can be integrated into risk infrastructure when there has been no prior use of parallel computing technology by an in-house team of developers.

We begin by revisiting a widely used model of market VaR on a group-wise portfolio and introduce our GPU-based solution approach in the context of this model.

4. MONTE CARLO-BASED MARKET VaR ESTIMATION

Market VaR estimation uses the Monte Carlo method to simulate the price of a portfolio based on the state of a number of random market risk factors. The Monte Carlo method is a general approach where the solution to some problem is estimated by statistically sampling the problem's parameter space with thousands to millions of experiments using different parameter settings (Chong, Gonina and Keutzer, 2010). The ease and intuitiveness of setting up the experiments makes the Monte Carlo method a popular approach (Glasserman, 2003).

The Monte Carlo method has several properties that make it desirable for implementation on a high-performance GPU accelerator:

(i) *Experiments are independent and parallelizable*: The approach assumes that experiments are independent and identically distributed (i.i.d.), such that the set of experiments provides a statistically valid sampling of the parameter space. This independence between experiments provides significant parallelization opportunities for GPU-based implementations.

(ii) *Execution is computationally expensive*: By the law of large numbers, the statistical error (standard error) in the solution is proportional to the inverse square-root of the experimental size, i.e. to achieve 10x more precision in the result, one needs to run 100x more experiments. The GPU-based implementation can provide the necessary speedup to allow many problems to become computationally feasible.

(iii) *Input specifications and results are concise*: The Monte Carlo method takes a small set of experiment parameter inputs, generates thousands to millions of experiments, executes them, and assimilates the results as a single solution. There is a large amount of computation consumed with little input/output data transferred. This is ideal for GPU-based implementations, as input/output data has to be transferred between the CPU and the GPUs and all computation is performed on the GPU.

Solution Structure

A typical implementation of the Monte Carlo method involves the simple solution structure illustrated in Fig. 1, where experiments are generated, executed, and the experimental output is assimilated to provide a concise estimate. The perspectives and considerations that guide the implementation of the Monte Carlo method are described more fully in Section 3.

Market VaR estimation is computationally expensive when the number of market risk factors required to capture market movements grows large. Major banks model the joint probability distribution of hundreds, or

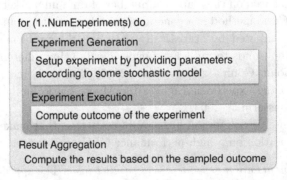

Fig. 1 The solution structure of a VaR implementation (Chong, Gonina and Keutzer, 2010).

even thousands, of market risk factors (Youngman, 2009) across many financial markets in order to estimate their group level VaR. So although a comparatively small set of parameters is required to set up the estimation process, experiment execution requires a large but independent amount of computation.

Software Architecture

Figure 2 outlines the software architecture of a Monte Carlo-based VaR engine which is composed of a uniform random sequence generation, parameter distribution conversion, portfolio loss calculation (including instrument pricing) and finally VaR estimation at a given confidence interval and period of time.

This software architecture is general enough to encompass the pricing of any instrument in the portfolio. In practice this is too computationally intensive and the loss function is approximated to permit the simulation of the underlying market risk factors instead. Monte Carlo-based Δ-Γ-VaR estimation simulates the correlated market risk factor log returns (value changes) over the time horizon and then aggregates the losses to second-order accuracy.

More precisely, each kth experiment, where $k = 1..M$, is set up by first generating uncorrelated Gaussian random variables, X_{ik}, where $i = 1..N$. These are the uncorrelated Gaussian random perturbations away from the current market scenario which is defined by the current value of the risk factors R_i. The input to a Monte Carlo-based VaR estimation includes

(i) *Statistical parameters*: The estimated mean μ_i and Cholesky factor matrix $\hat{Q}$ of the covariance matrix $\Sigma_{ij} = \hat{Q}^T\hat{Q}$ for the

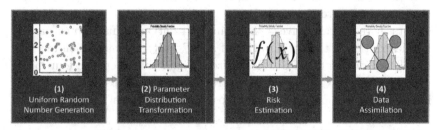

Fig. 2 The key components of the software architecture of a Monte Carlo-based VaR engine with instrument pricing functionality (Chong, Gonina and Keutzer, 2010).

Gaussian-distributed market risk factor log returns $d\ln(R_i)$, where $i = 1..N$, $j = 1..N$, are obtained from historical time series.

(ii) *Delta term:* Δ_i, where $i = 1..N$, is the sensitivity of the portfolio to a change in the log of the R_ith market risk factor.

(iii) *Gamma term:* λ_i and U_{ij}, where $i = 1..N, j = 1..N$ are the eigenvalues and orthogonal matrix of column eigenvectors of the s.p.d. matrix $\hat{Q}_{mi}^T \Gamma_{ij} \hat{Q}_{jn}$, Γ_{ij} is the sensitivity of Δ_i to a change in the log of the R_jth market risk factor. Since the Δs from simple models of instrument prices typically only depend on one or a small number of risk factors, Γ is generally sparse and sometimes even diagonal.

(iv) *Percentile for VaR evaluation:* This is typically either 1% or 5%.

(v) *Time horizon:* The duration of the simulation is typically at least a day and is measured in units of years.

Experiment Execution

The execution of each kth experiment outputs the change of value of the portfolio dP_k using the (rotated) delta-gamma (Δ-Γ) approximation

$$dP_k = \sum_i \Delta_i Y_{ik} + \frac{1}{2}\lambda_i X_{ik}^2, \tag{1}$$

where $Y_{ik} = \mu_i + Q_{ij}X_{jk}$ are the correlated Gaussian random variables obtained from multiplying the (rotated) Cholesky matrix factor $Q = \hat{Q}U$ with the i.i.d. standard Gaussian random variables X_{ik}. Expressing the approximation in rotated random variables simplifies the expression in the gamma term.[1]

Hundreds of thousands of experiments are typically required to reduce statistical error in the estimated distribution of dP to an acceptable precision. The results of these experiments are sorted and a percentile is chosen according to user selection.

It is here that we arrive at the main contribution of this chapter, namely the description of the optimization of a Δ-Γ-VaR implementation required to take advantage of GPUs. Recall from Fig. 2 that there are four major components of a VaR engine which translate to the steps of the Δ-Γ-VaR implementation shown in Fig. 3a. Steps 1 and 2 implement the experimental

---

[1] Readers more familiar with the approximation in original variables should refer to Glasserman (2003) for further details of the coordinate transformation.

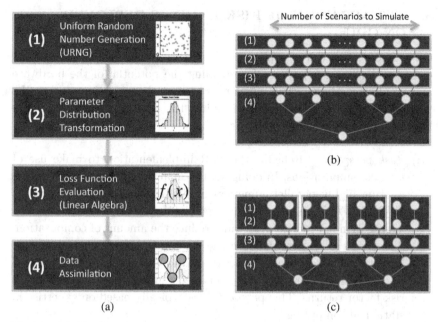

Fig. 3 (a) The four key steps of a Monte Carlo-based Δ-Γ-VaR implementation. (b) A depiction of the computation inherent in these four steps and (c) in a GPU optimized implementation (Chong, Gonina and Keutzer, 2010).

generation, step 3 aggregates the portfolio loss for each scenario, and step 4 assimilates the results over all scenarios.

As shown in Fig. 3, a Δ-Γ-VaR implementation executes one step at a time, with intermediate results written out to memory. Figure 3(c) illustrates the structure of an optimized implementation which involves both merging and blocking the steps to leverage the many levels of memory hierarchy on the GPU platform.

However, the illustration in Fig. 3(c) is by no means representative of a comprehensive software optimization. In order to access a wider set of software optimizations, it is necessary to draw upon a more general approach for software optimization, which will be discussed in the next section. We will see that adopting this approach will lend itself to the project management of software migration and ultimately lead to a more collaborative schedule of team activity.

5. OPTIMIZATION OF RISK ENGINES DEPLOYED ON GPUs

Optimized deployment of applications on GPUs is based on a set of general considerations or perspectives for enabling the potential of the hardware and avoiding common pitfalls which may hamper the migration process. We propose organizing these optimizations into three perspectives that require multi-disciplinary technical expertise:

(i) *Task perspective*: Refactor the VaR implementation to make use of matrix computations. In doing so, the quantitative developer can use existing highly parallel numerical library routines for GPUs such as CUBLAS. A more advanced but powerful step reformulates the loss aggregation in order to drastically reduce the amount of computation.

(ii) *Numerical perspective*: Choose the random number generator which leads to the fastest convergence rate of the VaR estimates as measured by the standard error of the simulated multi-variate distribution of risk factor returns. This perspective is typically based on expertise in statistical computing.

(iii) *Data perspective*: Design performance critical computations to best leverage the capabilities of the underlying platform and scope the data set to reduce memory access delays. This perspective is typically based on expertise in computer science and systems engineering.

Organizing a VaR engine migration project in this way reveals its complex multi-disciplinary nature. The task perspective requires the most in-depth understanding of the VaR model in order for a GPU implementation to be flexible enough to support various modelling assumptions, but only to the extent foreseeable by risk modelling experts. Moreover, modelling assumptions imposed to improve risk engine performance on CPUs may no longer be necessary on GPUs and it may be advantageous to factor this into the migration process.

In the interests of conveying the technicalities and performance implications of various VaR implementation optimizations, these perspectives will be now be described in more detail.

Task Perspective

Optimization should identify known high-performance building blocks in the software architecture and focus on leveraging existing implementation support infrastructure. This is done by refactoring algorithms to take advantage of existing fast library matrix routines.

For market VaR estimation, this involves understanding the relative performance of various linear algebra routines and taking advantage of more efficient types of CUBLAS library components. It also involves looking for opportunities to reformulate the computation in order to reduce the amount of computation.

Because statistical sampling of the parameter space with the Monte Carlo method involves running thousands to millions of independent experiments, the experiment execution step often has the largest amount of parallelism. For this reason, the evaluation of the Δ term in the loss function (Eq. (1)) can be efficiently implemented as a dense matrix computation using existing well-parallelized CUBLAS library routines.

This dense linear algebra formulation is illustrated in Fig. 4 for the delta component of the loss function evaluation (excluding the drift term) with N risk factors and $M \gg N$ experiments. The figure shows how the random $N \times M$ matrix Y is formed by matrix-matrix multiplication of the $N \times N$ Cholesky factor matrix and the uncorrelated Gaussian random $N \times M$ matrix.

Problem Reformulation

Refactoring loss estimates to use random matrices rather than random vectors can also expose bottlenecks in the algorithm which, in special cases, may be removed altogether. We continue with a proof of concept using the form of the loss estimate shown in Eq. (1). Under the dense linear algebra

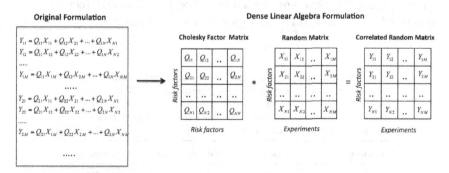

Fig. 4 The correlation of random vectors X_i, X_i is refactored as a dense matrix-matrix multiplication in order to use existing well-parallelized matrix libraries for GPUs (Dixon *et al.*, 2011).

formulation, the Δ component of the portfolio loss function computes in two steps: (i) correlation of random matrices using matrix-matrix multiplication and (ii) estimation of the loss by multiplying the correlated random matrix with the vector of positions.

It is possible to reformulate the computation of the Δ component of the portfolio loss function to avoid the first step. Instead, the Cholesky matrix factor Q and the Δ vector is stored in a vector $q := \Delta^T Q$ using a call to the BLAS level 2 matrix-vector multiply function $Sgemv$. The Δ-Γ approximation of the portfolio loss can then be rewritten as

$$dP_k = dP_k^\Delta + dP_k^\Gamma = \sum_i q_i X_{ik} + \frac{1}{2}\lambda_i X_{ik}^2. \qquad (2)$$

Precomputation of q this way reduces the amount of computation by a factor of the number of risk factors N and removes a computational bottleneck. So this simple refactorization has illustrated the importance of understanding the various steps of the algorithm and avoiding naïve implementations, which although conceptually similar to serial implementations of VaR, significantly hinder the performance.

Table 1 shows the comparative effect of the reformulated Monte Carlo algorithm on the time taken (seconds) to evaluate Δ-Γ-VaR on an Intel Core i7 CPU processor and an NVIDIA GeForce GTX 480 GPU. The numbers in parentheses are the loss-estimating portion of execution times, excluding the time for random number generation.

We've taken 4,000 normally distributed risk factors and generated several blocks of random matrices in order to fit within the memory of the GPU. With a maximum block size of 32,768 for the available memory, 23 blocks ensures that approximately 7.5×10^5 (753,664) scenarios are generated to achieve 0.1% accuracy in the standard error of the loss distribution.

Table 1 The comparative timings (s) of the standard and reformulated Monte Carlo algorithm for evaluating Δ-Γ-VaR on the GPU and CPU using 4,000 risk factors with 7.5×10^5 simulations. The parenthesized values represent the times and speedup factors in just the loss function evaluation step (Dixon et al., 2011).

Timing (s)	Standard	Reformulated	Speedup
CPU	457 (384)	73.9 (1.17)	6.18× (328×)
GPU	58.9 (58.5)	0.951 (0.540)	61.9× (108×)
Speedup	**7.76×(6.56×)**	**77.7×(31.5×)**	**481×(711×)**

With the loss estimated in the form given by Eq. (1), we observe only a 7.76× speedup going from baseline CPU to baseline GPU implementation. With the reformulated loss estimate given by Eq. (2), we observe a 108× speedup for the loss estimation from baseline GPU implementation to reformulated GPU implementation. Overall, reformulation enabled a 61.9× speedup for the Δ-Γ-VaR estimation problem.

Overall, the reformulated algorithm performs 77.7× faster on the GPU than the reformulated algorithm on the CPU.

Numerical Perspective

Optimization should focus on improving the convergence rate of Monte Carlo-based approaches through careful selection of well-known techniques that have desirable numerical properties and existing reference implementations shown to perform well on the GPU platform (Howes and Thomas, 2007). For market VaR estimation, this involves the selection of high-dimensional quasi-random number generators (QRNG) and distribution transformation algorithms, such as the Box–Muller algorithm (Box and Muller, 1958), that preserve Sobol's measure of uniformity — Property A (Bratley and Fox, 1988). Efficient generators should also use a skip-ahead method to efficiently generate sequences on parallel architectures.

As VaR estimation typically requires Gaussian random numbers, a distribution conversion function must also be used to transform the uniform random sequence to a Gaussian random sequence. The best choice of distribution conversion function isn't always obvious, however, and the decision should be approached on a case-by-case basis. We illustrate a method for choosing the best function.

Two of the most widespread functions are the Box–Muller method and the Moro interpolation method (Moro, 1995). The former takes a pair of uncorrelated uniform random numbers on the closed interval (0,1) and uses the polar coordinate transformation to generate a pair of uncorrelated standard Gaussian variables. The Moro interpolation method takes a single uniform random number on the open interval [0,1] and draws a standard Gaussian variables using a polynomial interpolation of the inverse cumulative Gaussian distribution function.

The convergence rate in the standard error of the portfolio loss distribution can be used as a metric for choosing the best distribution method. It is also advisable to compare the Δ-VaR estimate with the analytic estimate. The Δ-Γ-VaR cannot be estimated analytically, of course, but having an understanding of how the standard error compares with the Δ-VaR estimate error can provide some insight into the level of tolerance to choose for the standard error given a target VaR estimate error.

The results of the comparison are presented in Fig. 5. For $4,000$ risk factors, approximately 1.5×10^6 or 7.5×10^5 scenarios are sufficient to estimate the standard error of the loss distribution to within 0.1% when using Moro's interpolation method or the Box–Muller method, respectively. This tolerance corresponds to an error in the Δ-VaR of 0.1%.

> *The primary criteria for choosing the Box–Muller method is that the standard error converges twice as fast in single precision as when using Moro's interpolation method applied to the same sequence of uniform quasi-random numbers.*

Data Perspective

Optimization should focus on improving the memory access patterns between the different stages of an algorithm. For market VaR estimation, this involves identification of key data alignment needs between parameter generation and risk estimation, and the application of flexible data blocking strategies that maximally leverage the shared memory resources (or local scratch-pad memory).

There is a significant amount of intermediate results that must be managed between the four steps of the VaR implementation shown in Fig. 3a. In a basic implementation, as shown in Fig. 3b, the steps are executed one at a time. The amount of intermediate data can be tens of MBytes. Storing them out to off-chip memory after one step and bringing them back in for the next step can be costly, especially when steps such as steps 1 and 2 require very little computation.

The need to maintain large intermediate result working sets is not required by the application. It is usually put in place to achieve function modularity in large projects. To optimize the implementation for execution on GPUs, one must re-evaluate the software architecture trade-offs and work towards minimizing the number of data movements, which can dominate the execution time of an implementation.

In the case of the VaR implementation, merging the uniform random sequence generation and the distribution conversion steps provided a significant performance boost. The distribution conversion step can be

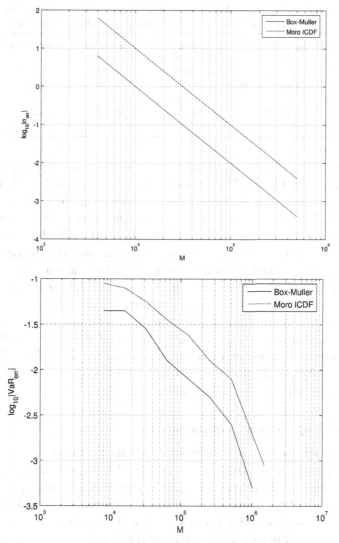

Fig. 5 (top) A comparison of the standard error (%) in the portfolio loss distribution using Moro's interpolation method and the Box–Muller method applied to Sobol' sequences. (bottom) The corresponding error (%) in the simulated 1-day portfolio Δ-VaR ($c = 95\%$) converges to the analytic Δ-VaR (9.87%). Approximately twice the number of scenarios are required to estimate the Δ-VaR to within 0.1% when using Moro's interpolation method compared to the Box–Muller method (Dixon, Chong and Keutzer, 2009).

Table 2 GPU implementation cost in seconds for setting up 7.5×105 experiments each with 4,000 risk factors (Dixon *et al.*, 2011).

Timing (s)	Standard	Optimized	Speedup
	(Separate)	(Merged)	
Box–Muller (step 1)	0.128	0.156	**2.63×**
(step 2)	0.282		
Bailey (step 1)	0.128	0.441	**1.16×**
(step 2)	0.384		

executed in place as soon as the uniform random values are generated, as illustrated in Fig. 3c. This cuts out the execution time associated with writing out the results to device memory and reading them back.

Table 2 illustrates the impact of kernel merging on two functionally similar methods: the Box–Muller and Baileys' methods.[2] The comparative performance impact illustrates another important issue with migrating software to GPUs, namely the sensitivity of the kernel merging optimization. The Box–Muller method was sped up by 2.63× through merging the steps, whereas the Bailey's method sustained only a 1.16× speedup.

On first inspection this appears quite counterintuitive given that the implementation of the Box–Muller method and the Bailey method are almost identical. These extra parameters, however, increase the footprint of the compiled kernels to the extent that they don't fit neatly into on-chip memory and spill off into off-chip memory.

Summary of Software Optimization

By combining these three perspectives, we built up a comprehensive set of considerations for effectively utilizing the GPU implementation support infrastructure in developing financial applications and achieved a 169× speedup in VaR, as shown in Table 3. The columns in the table represent the three steps of execution in the VaR estimation and the content specifies the absolute and proportional timings of the steps.

Our baseline GPU (NVIDIA GeForce GTX 480) implementation of MC-VaR is a straightforward port from the CPU implementation and has a 7.76× speed advantage over an Intel i7 Q920 eight-core CPU-based implementation. By reformulating the VaR estimate to reduce the

---

[2]Bailey's method (Bailey, 1994) also makes use of a polar coordinate transformation of uniform random variables. Unlike the Box–Muller method, however, it produces student-t distributed random variables which give fatter-tailed loss distributions (Jorion, 2007).

Table 3 The overall speedup on the GPU obtained by applying all three optimizations to a Δ-Γ-VaR estimate on a portfolio with 4,000 risk factors, simulated to achieve a standard error in the normal loss distribution within 0.1% (Dixon *et al.*, 2011).

Timing (s)	QRNG	Distribution Conversion	Loss Evaluation
Baseline GPU	0.257	0.564	117
	(0.22%)	(0.48%)	(99.3%)
Problem formulation	—	—	1.08
	(13.5%)	(29.7%)	(56.8%)
Module selection	0.129	0.282	0.540
	(13.6%)	(29.6%)	(56.8%)
Kernel merging		0.156	—
		(22.4%)	(77.6%)
Speedup	5.27×		217×
Total speedup		**169×**	

amount of computation, we achieved a 61.9× speedup. Use of a Box–Muller algorithm to convert the distribution gives an additional 2× speedup over interpolating the inverse of the Gaussian distribution function.

Finally we merged the data-parallel computational kernels to remove redundant memory transfer operations, leading to an additional 2.63× speedup. The overall speedup of 169× against the baseline GPU implementation reduces the time of a VaR estimation with a standard error of 0.1% from minutes to less than one second.

The optimization approach also provides clear interfaces for collaboration within a research and development project and facilitates potentially faster and smoother integration across domains of expertise. This is because quantitative risk developers will tend to have more expertise from the numerical perspective, whereas systems engineers and IT specialists will typically have a sounder understanding from the data perspective. The task perspective facilitates the integration of expertise across both domains as it requires an understanding of the loss aggregation and instrument pricing in addition to software performance analysis and design.

6. RISK INFRASTRUCTURE IMPROVEMENTS

This chapter has so far considered the implementation of Monte Carlo-based financial market VaR estimation on GPUs from three perspectives: the task, the numerical and the data perspectives. The reported level of performance increase achieved in following this approach implies not only a significant reduction in time taken to run daily VaR estimates, but more generally calls for a revision of the existing quantitative risk infrastructure which is currently unable to operate in near real-time.

Going forward, risk managers should be able to access and re-evaluate compute-intensive market risk analysis without delay. This is a highly non-trivial task when the number of risk factors used in the estimate is very large, instrument pricing is comprehensive and VaR estimates are simultaneously required over a hierarchy of business units in a global financial institution.

EC estimation with a larger number of risk factors becomes more computationally intensive because the number of stressed scenarios needed for convergence is typically much higher than for daily VaR. Furthermore, stressed VaR requires the identification of different regimes in time series data — a process which is highly sensitive to statistical assumptions and filtering techniques. In order to reduce model risk, it may therefore be prudent to perform stress tests under various modelling assumptions.

The qualitative impact of GPUs on these specific improvements to the risk infrastructure are briefly outlined in Table 4. By following our approach to expose the parallelism of the application and use high-performance matrix computations, larger numbers of risk factors can be used in existing daily VaR estimates and stress tests. The latest generation of GPUs based on the Fermi architecture also allows for different types of computations to be performed in parallel, thus potentially enabling full Monte Carlo-based VaR rather than just a Δ-Γ approximation.

Table 4 Examples of specific improvements to market risk infrastructure obtainable through using GPUs.

Challenges	Solution Approach	GPU Solution
Increase the pervasiveness of stress tests and risk estimation	Increase the number of market risk factors used and compare a wider set of modelling assumptions	GPUs are ideally suited to large matrix computations
Extend pricing functionality in daily VaR estimates, aggregated at the group level	Increase the accuracy of VaR by accounting for complex features of financial instruments	The new Fermi GPU architecture enables different financial instruments to be fully priced in parallel
On-demand hierarchical VaR estimation	Customize risk aggregation in real-time to sharpen VaR-based risk limits on trading units	GPUs provide near real-time Δ-Γ-VaR estimates on large portfolios

The ability to estimate Δ-Γ-VaR on large portfolios in near real-time opens up the possibility of an interactive tool for reconfiguring risk aggregation at various levels of an institutional hierarchy and refining VaR-based trading limits on business units (Saita, 2007) in response to their intra-day trading activities.

7. SUMMARY AND OUTLOOK

This chapter explains how GPUs can be used to improve quantitative risk infrastructure and identifies some of the key technical challenges and solutions to the effective deployment of a Monte Carlo-based risk engine on GPUs. The core of the chapter presents a general solution approach for performance optimization which lends itself to the management of a multi-disciplinary team of analysts, developers and systems engineers.

For a daily Δ-Γ-VaR estimate on a portfolio of 4,000 risk factors we have demonstrated a 169× increase in performance on a NVIDIA GeForce GTX480, reducing the absolute solution time to under a second. We further showed that this solution approach is not limited to simple modelling assumptions such as normality of risk factor returns by presenting performance results of a GPU implementation of Bailey's algorithm for student-t distributions, known to produce fatter-tailed loss distributions. Finally, we briefly explored the new capabilities that GPU computing can potentially provide, such as on-demand hierarchical VaR estimation and full Monte Carlo-based VaR estimation on group-wise portfolios.

The finance industry does perceive the existence of a GPU adoption barrier, partly because it is borne out of a different computing paradigm, namely parallel computing. The GPU industry has matured to the extent that GPU computing has become more mainstream — quantitative developers can quickly use software building blocks to optimize programs without specialist expertise. GPUs are no panacea of course and shared research expertise in computational finance and risk analysis is vital in targeting the technology to the most challenging applications, quantifying expected performance improvements, and ultimately overcoming technology barriers to on-demand, fully reconfigurable market risk stress testing and analytics.

REFERENCES

Bailey, R. (1994). "Polar Generation of Random Variates with the t-Distribution." *Mathematics of Computation*, 62:779–781.

BIS (2009a). "Principles for Sound Stress Testing Practices and Supervision Consultative Paper." Bank for International Settlements Paper, January.

BIS (2009b). "Revisions to the Basel II Market Risk Framework." Bank for International Settlements Paper, July.

Box, G.E.P. and Muller, M.E. (1958). "A Note on the Generation of Random Normal Deviates." *Ann. Math. Statist.*, 29(2):610–611.

Bratley, P. and Fox, B.L. (1988). "Implementing Sobol's Quasirandom Sequence Generator." *ACM Trans. on Math. Software*, 14(1):88–100.

Chapman, B., Jost, G. and Pas, R. (2007). *Using OpenMP: Portable Shared Memory Parallel Programming (Scientific and Engineering Computation)*. Cambridge, MA: The MIT Press.

Chong, J., Gonina, E., Keutzer, K. (2010). "Monte Carlo Methods: A Computational Pattern for Parallel Programming." *2nd Annual Conference on Parallel Programming Patterns (ParaPLoP'10)*, Carefree, AZ.

Dixon, M.F., Bradley, T., Chong, J. and Keutzer, K. (2011). "Monte Carlo Based Financial Market Value-at-Risk Estimation on GPUs." In Hwu, W. (ed.), *GPU Computing Gems: Vol 2*, Elsevier.

Dixon, M.F., Chong, J. and Keutzer K. (2009). "Acceleration of Market Value-at-Risk Estimation." *WHPCF '09: Proceedings of the 2nd Workshop on High Performance Computational Finance*, 1–8.

GARP (2010). "Risk Management Systems in the Aftermath of the Financial Crisis Flaws, Fixes and Future Plans." GARP report prepared in association with SYBASE.

Glasserman, P. (2003). *Monte Carlo Methods in Financial Engineering*. New York: Springer.

Howes, L. and Thomas, D. (2007). "Efficient Random Number Generation and Application using CUDA." In Nguyen, H. (ed.), *GPU Gems 3*, Boston, MA: Addison-Wesley.

Jorion, P. (2007). *Value-at-Risk: The New Benchmark for Managing Financial Risk*, 3rd ed. New York: McGraw-Hill.

Moro, B. (1995). "The Full Monte." *Risk Magazine*, 8(2):57–58.

Munshi, A. (2010). "The OpenCL 1.1 Specification, rev 33." Khronos OpenCL Working Group, [Online], http://www.khronos.org/registry/cl/specs/opencl-1.1.pdf.

NVIDIA (2010). *NVIDIA CUDA Programming Guide, Version 3.1*, [Online], http://www.nvidia.com/CUDA.

Reinders, J. (2007). *Intel Threading Building Blocks: Outfitting C++ for Multicore Processor Parallelism*. Sebastopol, CA: O'Reilly Media Inc.

Saita, F. (2007). *Value at Risk and Bank Capital Management*. Burlington, MA: Elsevier.

Youngman, P. (2009). "Procyclicality and Value-at-Risk." *Bank of Canada Financial System Review Report*, June, 51–54.

Chapter 10

A NEW METHOD OF STRESS TESTING
INVESTMENT PRODUCTS

Maria Beitz and Matthias Ehrhardt

1. INTRODUCTION

This chapter describes the development of so-called stress tests. These methods relate to the concept of risk-bearing ability and are used frequently in banks to verify how the potential risks of losing money are covered by equity capital.

We propose a modification of an existing stress test from the literature to reduce the data requirements and the computational effort and to improve the approximation quality. Hence our approach makes stress testing faster and more cost-effective for the banks.

The financial crisis of 2007 has shown that the possible risks in extreme situations were not appropriately quantified by existing risk estimation methods. If the losses exceed the height of the equity capital, insolvency can be the result, like the case of Lehman Brothers shows. To respond to this risk, banks are requested to improve their risk management systems continuously. In the past years a change from traditional qualitative technologies to quantitative methods has taken place, but for rarer risky events, existing measurements are still not sufficient.

Stress tests are understood as all analytical methods which differ from the procedures of risk quantification in normal market situations and identify loss potentials in extreme situations. Therefore, stress tests include a wide spectrum of methods.

Section 2 presents a short introduction to the risk management of German banks. Therefore the essential types of risk, the current procedures to measure these risks and their input parameters are discussed. In Section 3 we give an overview of various methods of the realization of stress tests and focus on three of these methods. In Section 4 we introduce macroeconomic methods to estimate failure probabilities of debtors in extreme situations. Section 5 explains how transition matrices, which are important input parameters for risk models, can be adjusted for bad economic years. Finally, in Section 6 it is shown how the tails of probability distribution functions can be modelled appropriately by means of the peaks-over-threshold method (Embrechts, Klüppelberg and Mikosch, 1999; McNeil and Frey, 2000).

2. BASICS OF RISK MANAGEMENT

In the financial world, chances and risks are closely connected with each other and have to be considered jointly. Dealing with calculated risks is a central task of banks. Nevertheless the transactions which promise a big chance of reward are often accompanied by increased risks (Gramlich, 2009, p. 7). The financial crisis has shown once more that an underestimated risk and opportunity profile may have severe consequences. Hence, the establishment of a certified risk management system is of paramount importance. The assignment of risk management is to ensure an adequate risk and opportunity profile (Gramlich, 2009, p. 8). Every new business can unbalance this profile. To respond to these constantly changing risk constellations, banks have to implement a dynamic risk management process. Besides the identification, capture and assessment of risks, active risk control as well as the monitoring of risk measures are central elements of risk management (Gramlich, 2009, p. 62). The identification of essential risk drivers is a major condition for effective risk control. For this purpose the potential risks are divided into different types displayed in Table 1.

The Value at Risk (VaR) is the central measure for the quantification of the loss potential. It is defined as the maximum loss which can occur within a certain observation period, also known as the risk horizon, with a certain likelihood. The planning horizon of banks is usually one year, so the risk horizon is also measured within this time period. Mathematically, the VaR explains a quantile of the loss distribution. The different types of risk are usually measured by means of independent risk models. Afterwards the total loss risk can be calculated by taking the diversification effects between the different risk types into account.

Table 1 Definitions of the Types of Risk According to IBB.

Type of Risk	Definition
Credit risk	The risk that a counter party respectively a debtor is not able to settle its obligation on the contract terms due to deterioration in creditworthiness or the failure of the counter party.
Market price risk	The risk that the value of the portfolio changes on the basis of changes in the market prices or other dimensions observable in the market (e.g. interest rates, spreads, exchange rates).
Operational risk	The risk of losses as a result of inadequacy and failure of internal procedures, persons and systems as well as the dangers of the entry of losses as a result of external events. The definition encloses legal risks but doesn't contains strategical risks or reputation risks.
Liquidity risk	The risk that a financial institution is not able to settle its obligations. The liquidity risk also includes the risk of rising refinancing costs.

Source: Gruber, Martin and Wehn (2010, p. 375).

Counterparty risks can be quantified by means of credit portfolio models. The best-known commercial portfolio models are CreditMetrics^{TM}, CreditRisk+^{TM} and CreditPortfolioView^{TM}. The models CreditMetrics^{TM} and CreditPortfolioView^{TM} developed by JP Morgan and McKinsey, respectively, are simulation models. They determine loss distributions by simulating the creditworthiness classes of the different debtors and considering the interdependency between the debtors. The model CreditRisk+^{TM}, which was developed by Credit Suisse First Boston, is based on an analytic model. It determines the loss distribution of a portfolio analytically with procedures from actuarial mathematics (CreditRisk+, 1997, p. 4). Input parameters of these models include transition matrices, recovery rates in the case of insolvency and market parameters like interest rates and credit spreads of different rest terms, industries and creditworthiness. Transition matrices contain information about the empiric financial loss likelihood of debtors or the likelihood to move into other creditworthiness classes.

Market risks are often measured using historical simulation. The principle of historical simulation is to generate potential portfolio value changes through the utilization of historical changes of the parameters determining market risk, e.g. bond exchange rates, yield curves and interest volatilities.

The quantification of operational risks is often realized with a loss distribution approach (LDA). Within the scope of the LDA, empirically observed damage events are described by distribution functions. A loss frequency distribution models the frequency of the damage events which occur within an certain observation period. The modelling of the amount of damages is realized by damage distribution. By means of a Monte Carlo simulation in the first step a random frequency of damage events is generated with the loss frequency distribution. Then, loss severity of each damage is simulated. The sum of these damages yields the total loss for the intended observation period. Therefore, the modelling of the distribution function is crucial for the quantification of the operational risk.

3. STRESS TESTS: AN OVERVIEW OF TYPICAL METHODS

Stress tests are all analytical methods that deviate from standard risk quantification methods and help to identify the loss potentials. Depending on the number of model parameters and risk factors, one distinguishes between univariate and multivariate stress tests (Fig. 1).

Univariate stress tests, also known as sensitivity analyses, determine the influence of the change of single risk factors on the risk of loss. They can help to identify the essential risk factors of a portfolio and the implementation is simple. On the contrary, sensitivity analyses do not consider any correlations between the risk factors (Klauck and Stegmann, 2008, p. 14). In reality, simultaneous risk factor changes can be observed, e.g. simultaneous increase of failure probabilities and changing market parameters. Thus sensitivity analyses are only inadequate models of real markets. Nevertheless, they are a useful instrument for ad-hoc analyses and to identify model uncertainties. Additionally, univariate stress tests can

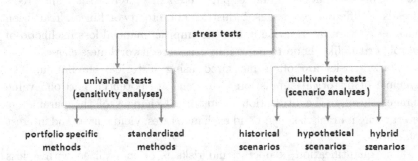

Fig. 1 Overview of Different Groups of Stress Tests.

Source: Klauck and Stegmann (2008, p. 18).

be distinguished in standardized and individual procedures. Standardized analyses are for example the sensitivity analyses suggested from the bank supervision (see Gruber, Martin and Wehn, 2010, p. 71 for further details).

With multivariate stress tests, the effects of several simultaneous risk factor changes can be modelled. These tests permit a clearer picture of the reality, but on the other hand this more complex approach requires additional model acceptances and the interpretation of results is rather complicated. Multivariate stress tests, also known as scenario analyses, are distinguished in historical scenarios, hypothetical scenarios and hybrid scenarios. For further reading we refer the reader to Gruber, Martin and Wehn (2010, p. 67).

4. MACROECONOMIC STRESS TESTS

Besides a huge number of other model parameters, the failure probability of the debtors plays a big role in the quantification of credit risk. Empirical studies, e.g. Bangia, Diebold and Schuermann (2002) and Nickell, Perraudin and Varotto (2000), show that the migration behaviour of the debtors in other creditworthiness ratings and therefore also the financial loss probability of the debtors are strongly determined by the economic development. Hence, it is conceivable to describe the financial loss likelihood by means of a regression as a function of macroeconomic factors. Based on this regression, risk considerations under extreme trading conditions can be carried out. The financial loss probability which can be determined with the regression equation through the utilization of stressed macroeconomic factors can be applied for the calculation of the VaR.

Equation (1) is a linear regression modelling the relation of the dependent variable y_t and one or several independent variables $x_{i,t}$, the macroeconomic factors. The variable ε_t summarizes all influences which cannot be covered by the regression model and t denotes the time:

$$y_t = \beta_0 + \beta_1 x_{1,t} + \cdots + \beta_n x_{n,t} + \varepsilon_t \tag{1}$$

Stress tests can be generated by using extreme values of the macroeconomic variables as input parameters for the already estimated regression equation. It is possible that the results of the stressed financial loss probabilities are beyond the accepted range between zero and one. To fulfil this condition first the financial loss probability p_t is transformed by an logistic function. Afterwards the connection to the macroeconomic factors is given by the transformed variable y_t:

$$y_t = \ln\left(\frac{1 - p_t}{p_t}\right) \tag{2}$$

where y_t is called the *macroeconomic index*. With the inverse of the logistic function, values of the macroeconomic index can be inverse transformed in stressed financial loss probabilities.

While the values of the dependent and independent variables are given, the weights $\beta_0, \ldots, \beta_n$ must be estimated with a suitable procedure, e.g. the least squares method or the maximum likelihood method.

The historical time series of financial loss probabilities and the macroeconomic variables, e.g. the gross domestic product, the rate of unemployment, the commercial climate index, share indices or interest rates can be obtained from statistical offices or financial news and data services, e.g. Bloomberg. If there is no financial loss probability available, these data can also be estimated from ratings. This latter approach is often used in practice (Klement, 2007, p. 110).

To estimate the parameters of the regression, certain assumptions about the stochastic conditions of the error terms have to be met, e.g. an average value of zero, homoscedasticity, no autocorrelation, independence of the independent variables (Poddig, Dichtl and Petersmeier, 2000). These assumptions have to be checked and the quality of the regression equation has to be analysed by means of the coefficient of determination and hypothesis tests (Poddig, Dichtl and Petersmeier, 2000, p. 240).

5. SHIFTING MIGRATION MATRICES

For the calculation of credit risks, usually the so-called transition matrices are necessary. They contain empirically-observed migration probabilities from one level of credit quality to another level of credit quality within a certain observation period.

In practice, average migration matrices are used for the parametrization of credit portfolio models. Average migration matrices contain the average values of (as a rule, one-year-old) migration probabilities which have been observed over a period of several business cycles. They are more stable and more prestigious than one-year-old migration matrices. The migration probabilities are generated just on the basis of the migration behaviour of single calendar years. Nevertheless, they are not suitable to illustrate the actual economic situation of single years. The parametrization with average migration matrices leads to distorted risk indicators (Forest, Belkin and Suchower, 1998, p. 1). In average transition matrices, the probability to migrate to better creditworthiness classes is estimated too pessimistically in times of economic recovery, while this probability is overestimated in times of economic recession.

Below we introduce the one-parameter representation, a method developed by Forest, Belkin and Suchower (1998), that can be used for the generation of more stable, from the economic situation influenced, transition matrices. Then we present our modification of the one-parameter representation method which reduces the costly data requirements.

One-Parameter Representation

In CreditMetrics^{TM} the yield of a debtor is described by means of a standard normal random variable $X \sim \mathcal{N}(0,1)$ (see Gupton, Finger and Bhatia, 1997, p. 92). Forest, Belkin and Suchower (1998) describe this yield as the sum of a systematic component and a debtor's specific component:

$$X = \sqrt{1 - \rho^2}Y + \sqrt{\rho}Z \tag{3}$$

Here, Y describes the debtor's specific component and Z describes the systematic, the economically influenced, part of the yield of the debtor and ρ denotes a weighting factor of both components and a measure for the correlation between the yield X and the systematic component Z. While the specific component of a debtor varies within one year, the economic component Z is a stable quantity within one year.

Subsequently the variable $Z(t)$ describes the value of the systematic component in year t. During an economic recovery $Z(t)$ takes positive values. On the contrary, negative Z values result during times of economic recession. As a standard normal random variable, Z has a mathematical expectation value of zero. Thus the economic situation has on average no influence on the yields of the debtors.

To determine the systematic component $Z(t)$ of a certain year, the observed one-year-old migration probability $\tilde{p}_{i,j}(t)$ in year t will be compared with the average migration probability $p_{i,j}$, which is not influenced by the economic situation. For every combination of an initial rating i and a final rating j, these probabilities can be taken from one-year-old and average transition matrices. Figures 2 and 3 show the transitions matrices published by the rating agency Standard Poor's (S&P) (Vazza, Aurora and Kraemer, 2009).

		endrating							
		AAA	AA	A	BBB	BB	B	CCC/C	default
initial rating	AAA	87,10	6,45	3,23	0,00	0,00	1,08	2,15	0,00
	AA	0,00	80,87	17,94	0,59	0,00	0,00	0,20	0,40
	A	0,00	1,67	92,27	5,18	0,47	0,00	0,00	0,40
	BBB	0,00	0,00	2,74	92,44	3,82	0,29	0,21	0,50
	BB	0,00	0,10	0,00	5,35	83,65	8,95	1,13	0,82
	B	0,00	0,00	0,00	0,16	4,14	82,31	9,09	4,30
	CCC/C	0,00	0,00	0,00	0,00	0,00	14,10	52,57	33,33

Fig. 2 One-Year-Old Transition Matrix of 2008, Data Taken From S&P.
Source: Vazza, Aurora and Kraemer (2009).

		endrating							
		AAA	AA	A	BBB	BB	B	CCC/C	default
initial rating	AAA	91,33	7,88	0,55	0,06	0,08	0,03	0,06	0,00
	AA	0,60	90,51	8,10	0,56	0,06	0,09	0,03	0,03
	A	0,04	2,14	91,50	5,61	0,42	0,17	0,03	0,08
	BBB	0,01	0,16	4,14	90,24	4,28	0,74	0,17	0,26
	BB	0,02	0,06	0,21	5,87	83,87	7,99	0,89	1,10
	B	0,00	0,06	0,17	0,30	6,45	82,97	4,93	5,12
	CCC/C	0,00	0,00	0,27	0,40	1,13	13,77	54,60	29,85

Fig. 3 Averaged One-Year Transition Matrix of 1981–2008, Data Taken From S&P.
Source: Vazza, Aurora and Kraemer (2009).

Following the CreditMetrics^{TM} approach, the density of the standard normal deviation is, for every initial rating, partitioned into transition thresholds $x_{i,j}$ (Fig. 4). These thresholds were estimated by means of the probability of the transition matrices as follows:

$$x_{i,\text{default}} = \phi^{-1}(p_{i,\text{default}})$$

$$x_{i,\text{CCC}} = \phi^{-1}(p_{i,\text{default}} + p_{i,\text{CCC}})$$

$$\vdots$$

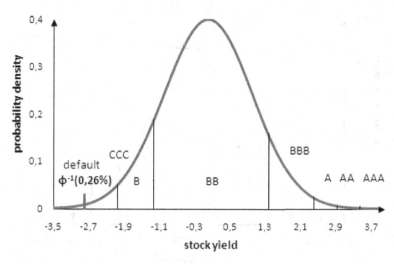

Fig. 4 Transition Thresholds of Standard Normal Distributed Stock Yield.
Source: Gupton, Finger and Bhatia (1997, p. 88).

where ϕ is the standard normal deviation. $Z(t)$ must be chosen such that the cyclical one-year-old migration probabilities $p(t)$ are well approximated by

$$\Delta(x_{i,j}, Z(t)) = \phi\left(\frac{x_{i,j+1} - \sqrt{\rho}Z(t)}{\sqrt{1-\rho}}\right) - \phi\left(\frac{x_{i,j} - \sqrt{\rho}Z(t)}{\sqrt{1-\rho}}\right) \tag{4}$$

See Fig. 5.

Forest, Belkin and Suchower (1998) solve this optimization problem by using a modified least squares method:

$$\min_{Z(t)} \sum_i \sum_j n_i(t) \frac{(\tilde{p}_{i,j}(t) - \Delta(x_{i,j}, Z(t)))^2}{\Delta(x_{i,j}, Z(t))(1 - \Delta(x_{i,j}, Z(t)))} \tag{5}$$

The weighting factor ρ for the calculation of $\Delta(x_{i,j}, Z(t))$ is *a priori* unknown. It will be estimated by means of random values of ρ. For every ρ, all values $Z(t)$ of the observation period will be based estimated. ρ will be based on the value for which the variance of $Z(t)$ has next to a value of one. Based on the assumption that the mathematical expectation value of $Z(t)$ is zero, $Z(t)$ and as a consequence X are standard normal random variables and the model assumption is fulfilled. Transition matrices describing the economic situation of a special year can be generated by means of the transition thresholds $x_{i,j}$, the value of $Z(t)$ and the weighting factor ρ. The transition probability $P(i, j, Z(t))$ of the year t is, for every initial

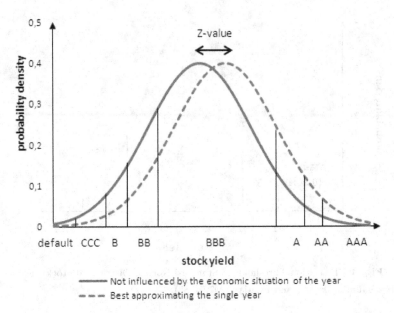

Fig. 5 Approximation of the One-Year-Old Migration Probabilities $p(t)$.
Source: Forest, Belkin and Suchower (1998, p. 49).

rating i and final rating j, given by

$$P(i, j, Z(t)) = \phi\left(\frac{x_{i,j+1} - \sqrt{\rho}Z(t)}{\sqrt{1-\rho}}\right) - \phi\left(\frac{x_{i,j} - \sqrt{\rho}Z(t)}{\sqrt{1-\rho}}\right) \qquad (6)$$

Modification of the One-Parameter Representation

Average transition matrices do not consider any systematic effects and hence the risks are underestimated in extreme situations. Within the scope of stress tests economically adjusted transition matrices should be generated and used for risk quantification.

As described in Gupton, Finger and Bhatia (1997, p. 92), the stock yield X is standard normally distributed in CreditMetrics[TM], i.e. on average, it will not be influenced by the economic situation. Nevertheless, the distribution of the stock yield differs from the standard normal distribution in single years. For the sake of convenience we regard the case where the stock yield X_t of the special year t is normally distributed with a mathematical expectation value of μ_t and a variance of σ_t^2.

During an economic recession the levels of the stock yields are lower than in normal economic periods. Additionally, the insecurity in the capital markets lead to larger fluctuations in stock yields. The mathematical expectation of the share yields during weak economic years should become smaller and the variance should be larger than in positive economic phases. To determine the parameters μ_t and σ_t of the distribution of the stock yields in a certain year t, it is necessary to estimate the threshold values $x_{i,j}$ of the average migration probabilities, cf. *One-Parameter Representation* (Forest, Belkin and Suchower, 1998). Afterwards it is necessary to approximate the one-year-old transition probability $p_{i,j}(t)$ as well as possible by means of the average transition probability, adjusted by μ_t and σ_t^2.

$$\Delta(x_{i,j}, \mu_t, \sigma_t^2) = \phi\left(\frac{x_{i,j+1} - \mu_t}{\sigma_t}\right) - \phi\left(\frac{x_{i,j} - \mu_t}{\sigma_t}\right)$$

The approximation of the one-year-old transition probability by means of the adjusted average transition probability which corresponds to the original method of Forest, Belkin and Suchower (1998) can be interpreted analogously. The calculation of μ_t and σ_t^2 is done with the help of the least squares method:

$$\min_{\mu, \sigma^2} \sum_i \sum_j n_i(t) \frac{(\tilde{p}_{i,j}(t) - \Delta(x_{i,j}, \mu, \sigma^2))^2}{\Delta(x_{i,j}, \mu, \sigma^2)(1 - \Delta(x_{i,j}, \mu, \sigma^2))} \tag{7}$$

In contrast to the original method, the economic influence is not modelled by shifting the parameter Z but rather by shifting the mathematical expectation value and the variance. The migration probability $P(i, j, \mu_t, \sigma_t^2)$ of a year which is influenced by the economic situation can be derived for every combination of initial rating i and final rating j as follows:

$$P(i, j, \mu_t, \sigma_t^2) = \phi\left(\frac{x_{i,j+1} - \mu_t}{\sigma_t}\right) - \phi\left(\frac{x_{i,j} - \mu_t}{\sigma_t}\right) \tag{8}$$

Compared to the original method of Forest, Belkin and Suchower (1998) our new method possess the following advantages:

Lower expenditure for data mining: Instead of a whole history of transition matrices, only an average and a single-year transition matrix is needed to estimate the parameter ρ.

Less computing time: The computing time decreases considerably because only one least squares estimation is needed to estimate the parameters μ_t and σ_t.

Better approximation: An additional degree of freedom decreases the sum of the errors. Hence, a better approximation of the single-year transition matrix is possible.

6. STRESS TESTS BY MEANS OF THE PEAKS-OVER-THRESHOLD METHOD

Operational risk is an essential type of risk along with credit risk and market risk. At the start of 2008, the case of the major French bank Société Générale showed that a single trader can cause damage of over 5 billion euros that can lead, in the worst case, to the insolvency of a bank.

This section shows how to use methods of extreme value theory (EVT) for validating the loss distribution approach in the context of stress testing.

The Loss Distribution Approach

Within the scope of the quantification of operational risk by means of the LDA, empirically observed damage data are described with the help of distribution functions. A damage frequency distribution models the frequency of incoming damages within a certain period. The frequency should correspond to the forecast period (or risk horizon). To represent the extent of the damages, a damage height distribution will be generated. In a Monte Carlo simulation a value from the damage frequency distribution and afterwards, accordingly, values from the damage height distribution are generated. The sum of these damages is the total loss for the forecast period (Fig. 6). Many of such simulations of annual damages generate an empirical distribution function of annual damages. Finally, this procedure allows the calculation of the VaR.

The damage frequency distribution is often modelled with a Poisson distribution which is a discrete distribution and suitable for modelling integers (Steinhoff, 2008, p. 50). On the contrary, the damage height distribution is often modelled with a log-normal distribution. It fits the character of the distribution of operational risks particularly well, e.g. the skewness and leptokurtosis (Steinhoff, 2008, p. 56).

Stress Testing

The observed damages, which are used for the generation of the damage height distribution, represent predominantly the damages of regular scope.

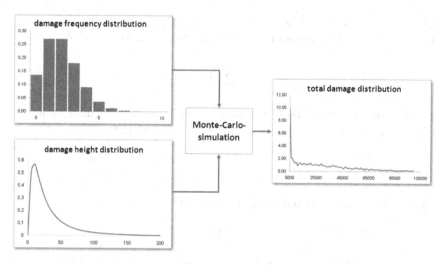

Fig. 6 Loss Distribution Approach.
Source: Steinhoff (2008, p. 68).

Hence, the damage height distribution works especially well around the distribution centre. Because of the insufficient number of observed extreme damages, the tail of the damage height distribution does not describe well the observations. But it is within this scope where most of the existence-threatening damages occur. Hence a stress test should figure out the influence of this weak point. For this purpose a tail distribution should be estimated by means of the peaks-over-threshold method.

The Peaks-Over-Threshold Method

The peaks-over-threshold method is used to model distribution tails in cases where only a few observations are available. Because it is assumed that observations of the distribution centre do not deliver any information about the level and probability of extreme events, only observations above a certain threshold of the distribution will be used to model the tail distribution (Busack and Kaiser, 2006, p. 488). The basic idea is to estimate the left and the right tails by fitting a generalized Pareto distribution (GPD) to the observation lying above a certain threshold marking the beginning of the tail region.

Let $X_1, \ldots, X_n$ denote a series of independent and identically distributed (i.i.d.) random variables with distribution function F. Also, assume that the distribution belongs to the maximum domain of attraction

(MDA): $F \in MDA(H_\xi)$ for $\xi \in \mathbb{R}$. For a threshold value u let $Y_1, \ldots, Y_{N_u}$ be the series of the excesses over the threshold u, where

$$N_u = \sum_{i=1}^{n} 1_{X_i > u}$$

counts the number of these excesses resulting from n random variables $X_1, \ldots, X_n$. Here, $1_{X_i > u}$ denotes an indicator function, i.e.

$$1_{X_i > u} = \begin{cases} 1, & \text{if } X_i > u \\ 0, & \text{else} \end{cases}$$

Hence, the excess distribution of X is given by

$$F_u(y) = \mathbb{P}(Y \le y | X > u) = \mathbb{P}(X - u \le y | X > u)$$

$$= \mathbb{P}(X \le y + u | X > u) = \frac{F(y + u) - F(u)}{1 - F(u)}, \quad y \ge 0$$

The tail of this distribution can be obtained by

$$F(y + u) = (1 - F(u))F_u(y) + F(u) \tag{9}$$

Due to the Pickands–Balkema–de Haan theorem (Dölker, 2006, p. 135) the excess distribution $F_u(y)$ can be approximated for large threshold values of u by a generalized Pareto distribution given by

$$G_{\xi, \beta(u)}(x) = \begin{cases} 1 - \left(1 + \dfrac{\xi}{\beta(u)} x\right)^{-\frac{1}{\xi}}, & \text{if } \xi \ne 0, \\[3mm] 1 - \exp\left(-\dfrac{x}{\beta(u)}\right), & \text{if } \xi = 0, \end{cases}$$

provided the underlying distribution function F_u satisfies the Fisher–Tippett theorem (Dölker, 2006, p. 130) (which is true for all common continuous distributions used in finance).

An estimator for the frequency of these excesses reads

$$1 - F(u) = \frac{1}{n} \sum_{i=1}^{n} 1_{X_i > u} = \frac{N_u}{n}$$

(see Embrechts, Klüppelberg and Mikosch, 1999, p. 354). Thus Eq. (9) can be rewritten as

$$F(y + u) = \frac{N_u}{n} G_{\xi, \beta(u)} + \left(1 - \frac{N_u}{n}\right)$$

Parameter Estimation

To estimate the tail distribution of a given random variable it is necessary to choose a suitable threshold which divides the whole distribution into a distribution body and a distribution tail. Based on this threshold, the excesses can be identified and the parameter of the tail distribution can be estimated. The parameter of the generalized Pareto distribution depends on this threshold u (Embrechts, Klüppelberg and Mikosch, 1999, p. 356). The quality of the chosen threshold influences the results of all following investigations.

In the literature there are different approaches to identify a suitable threshold value. Besides graphical methods, for example the mean excess (ME) plot (McNeil and Frey, 2000; McNeil, 1997) or the Hill method (Bensalah, 2000, Section 3.3), heuristic methods are also used, e.g. an arbitrary threshold level of 90% confidence level (Gavin, 2000) or 1.645 times the unconditional variance of the data (Neftci, 2000) that corresponds to 5% of the extreme observations in the case of normally distributed data. In practice it is usual to take a certain quantile or a constant value of the threshold (Steinhoff, 2008, p. 100). More complex methods, like bias-variance bootstrap, are based on simulations and aim to optimize the bias-variance trade-off (Steinhoff, 2008, p. 100).

After the distribution tail is defined by the choice of a suitable threshold, the parameter of the generalized Pareto distribution can be estimated by means of excesses. Common approaches for the estimation of the generalized Pareto distribution are for example the maximum likelihood method or the weighted moment method (Steinhoff, 2008, p. 356).

7. CONCLUSION

In this chapter we gave an introduction to the stress test method in extreme value theory that is a tool for dealing with probabilities related to extreme and hence rare events. We proposed a modification to the established one-parameter representation method of Forest, Belkin and Suchower (1998) that overcomes several shortcomings. The new method has small data requirements, needs less computational effort, and intensive tests with real market data from the IBB (Beitz, 2010) have shown that the approximation quality is improved significantly.

REFERENCES

Embrechts, P., Klüppelberg, C. and Mikosch, T. (1999). *Modelling Extremal Events for Insurance and Finance*, Berlin: Springer Verlag.

McNeil, A.J. and Frey, R. (2000). Estimation of Tail-Related Risk Measures for Heteroscedastic Financial Time Series: An Extreme Value Approach. *Journal of Empirical Finance*, 7:271–300.

Gramlich, D. (2009). Risikomanagement in der Gesamtbanksteuerung.

Gruber, W., Martin, M.R.W. and Wehn, C.S. (2010). *Szenarioanalysen und Stresstests in der Bank- und Versicherungspraxis*, Stuttgart: Schäffer-Poeschel Verlag.

CreditRisk+ (1997). *Technical Document*, Zürich/London: Credit Suisse Financial Products.

Klauck, K.-O. and Stegmann, C. (2008). *Stresstests in Banken*, Stuttgart: Schäffer-Poeschel Verlag.

Bangia, A., Diebold, F.X. and Schuermann, T. (2002). "Ratings Migration and the Business Cycle, With Application to Credit Portfolio Stress Testing." *Journal of Banking and Finance*, 26:445–474.

Nickell, P., Perraudin, W. and Varotto, S. (2000). Stability of Ratings Transitions. *Journal of Banking and Finance*, 23:203–227.

Klement, J. (2007). *Kreditrisikohandel, Basel II und interne Märkte in Banken*, Wiesbaden: Gabler.

Poddig, T., Dichtl, H. and Petersmeier, K. (2000). *Statistik, Ökonometrie, Optimierung*, Bad Soden: Uhlenbruch Verlag.

Forest, L.R., Belkin, B. and Suchower, S.J. (1998). A One-Parameter Representation of Credit Risk and Transition Matrices. *CreditMetrics Monitor*, Q3:45–56.

Gupton, G.M., Finger, C.C. and Bhatia, M. (1997). *CreditMetrics^{TM}: Technical Document*, New York: J.P. Morgan.

Vazza, D., Aurora, D. and Kraemer, N. (2009). *2008 Annual Global Corporate Default Study and Rating Transitions*, New York: Standard & Poor's. .

Steinhoff, C. (2008). *Quantifizierung Operationeller Risiken in Kreditinstituten*, Göttingen: Cuvillier.

Busack, M. and Kaiser, D.G. (2006). *Handbuch Alternative Investments*, Wiesbaden: Gabler.

Dölker, A. (2006). *Das Operationelle Risiko in Versicherungsunternehmen*, Karlsruhe: Verlag Versicherungswirtschaft.

McNeil, A.J. (1997). "Estimating the Tails of Loss Severity Distributions Using Extreme Value Theory." *ASTIN Bulletin*, 27:117–137.

Bensalah, Y. (2000). "Steps in Applying Extreme Value Theory to Finance: A Review." Technical Report 2000-20, Bank of Canada, Ottawa, Ontario.

Gavin, J. (2000). "Extreme Value Theory: An Empirical Analysis of Equity Risk." Working Paper, UBS Warburg.

Neftci, S.N. (2000). "Value at Risk Calculations, Extreme Events, and Tail Estimations." *The Journal of Derivatives*, 7:23–38,

Beitz, M. (2010). "Konzeption und Implementierung von Stresstests für das Portfolio der Investitionsbank Berlin." Master's thesis, Technische Universität Berlin, Germany.

INDEX